Networks in the Russian Market Economy

Networks in the Russian Market Economy

Markku Lonkila

First published 2011 by
PALGRAVE MACMILLAN

Palgrave Macmillan in the UK is an imprint of Macmillan Publishers Limited, registered in England, company number 785998, of Houndmills, Basingstoke, Hampshire RG21 6XS.

Palgrave Macmillan in the US is a division of St Martin's Press LLC, 175 Fifth Avenue, New York, NY 10010.

Palgrave Macmillan is the global academic imprint of the above companies and has companies and representatives throughout the world.

Palgrave® and Macmillan® are registered trademarks in the United States, the United Kingdom, Europe and other countries.

ISBN 978–0–230–25239–4   hardback

This book is printed on paper suitable for recycling and made from fully managed and sustained forest sources. Logging, pulping and manufacturing processes are expected to conform to the environmental regulations of the country of origin.

A catalogue record for this book is available from the British Library.

A catalog record for this book is available from the Library of Congress.

10 9 8 7 6 5 4 3 2 1
20 19 18 17 16 15 14 13 12 11

Transferred to Digital Printing in 2013

Contents

List of Figures and Tables

Figures

Tables

Note on Transliteration

For transliterating all citations of bibliographical material and words other than names or places, the Library of Congress system (without the diacritical marks) is used. For details, see *The Transliteration of Modern Russian for English-Language Publications* (Shaw, 1967) and the information on the Library of Congress website. All personal and place names in the text are transliterated according to the British Standard (or 'System I'; see Shaw, 1967).

Preface

My research on networks in the Russian economy and society started in the early 1990s as part of a larger European research project on personal networks coordinated by Professor Maurizio Gribaudi at the École des Hautes Études en Sciences Sociales. The Finnish part of the project was led by Professor Risto Alapuro at the University of Helsinki. The interest Risto and I had in Russian society led us first to add the case of Russia to the network data corpus on other European societies and later on to conduct several other research projects on the Russian economy and society. Without Risto's continuous support and encouragement, intellectual interaction and stimulation, this book would not exist.

Anna-Maija Castrén and Anna-Maria Salmi joined our Finnish research group and worked intensively on the network data collected within the frame of our common project. I have always been able to count on Anna-Maija's and Anna-Maria's help, and their serious and uncompromising attitude to the researcher's profession remains exemplary for me.

Russia turned out to be a tenacious research topic. After 1992 all the research projects in which I have participated or which I have led have, in one way or another, had to do with Russia. Within these projects I have, with Risto Alapuro and other colleagues, collected and analyzed data on the personal networks of Russian secondary school teachers, factory workers, young mobile phone users, and IT professionals, often in a comparative perspective.

I am grateful to the many people who assisted in the realization of this book. Aleksi Aaltonen, Svetlana Kirichenko, Eeva Nironen, Sylvi Nikitenkov, and Olga Tarasenko helped in preparing the online survey on the personal networks of IT professionals. Tatyana Kozlova collected the Russian interview data, which was coded by Sylvi Nikitenkov at the Department of Sociology, University of Helsinki. As native Russian speakers, Sylvi Nikitenkov and Viktor Sinelnikov have been constant sources of help at the Department of Sociology, both in practical terms and in helping to make sense of the linguistic details and cultural specificities of the Russian interview data. In addition, Sylvi has diligently and competently worked as my assistant during all phases of the research, gathering and analyzing data from various sources.

My gratitude also extends to the people who helped either in the fieldwork, the data analysis, or the writing period through discussions concerning Russian business practices, the features of Russian culture, or network methods: Zhanna Tsinman, Alexander Etkind, Kapitolina Fedorova, Timo Harmo, Natalya Ganina, Boris Gladarev, Jukka Gronow, Melanie Feakins, Arkady Khotin, Meri Kulmala, Nikolay Likhodedov, Elizabeth Moore, Sanna Määttänen, Tiina Saajasto, Pekka Sutela, Terttu Turunen, and Alexey Yurchak.

Risto Alapuro, Alena Ledeneva, Anna-Maria Salmi, Philipp Torchinsky, Larisa Shpakovskaya, and anonymous reviewers at Palgrave Macmillan have read the earlier versions of the manuscript and made many invaluable comments. In addition, Philipp deserves special thanks for his permanent and valuable help in all phases of the study. Taiba Batool and Gemma Papageorgiou at Palgrave Macmillan were indispensable aids in converting the manuscript into the final book.

The Academy of Finland, the Aleksanteri Institute, Collegium for Advanced Studies and Department of Sociology at the University of Helsinki have supported the research financially and offered peaceful but stimulating research environments. I owe special thanks to Risto Alapuro and Markku Kivinen for arranging for the financing of the study in the interstices of two research projects.

During recent years the research seminar led by Risto Alapuro at the Department of Sociology has been a permanent source of collegial support and constructive criticism. Wise advice from and discussions with Eeva Luhtakallio and Tuomas Ylä-Anttila from the seminar have been especially significant. I have also been fortunate to be able to lean on the substantial knowledge and expertise of the Russian society provided by the staff and the researchers of the Aleksanteri Institute, the effective and quick library and information services of the Institute, and the library of the Faculty of Social Sciences at the University of Helsinki.

The most important of my international connections have been with France and Russia. The French connection has been effectuated through yearly research exchange visits to the École des Hautes Études en Sciences Sociales (EHESS) within the exchange program between EHESS and the University of Helsinki. The advice of Alain Blum, Pascal Cristofoli, Myriam Désert, Gilles Favarel-Garrigues, Maurizio Gribaudi, Anne Le Huérou, Anna Lebedev, Anna Zaytseva, Kathy Rousselet, and Laurent Thévenot has been particularly beneficial. In addition, the conferences of the International Network for Social Network Analysis (INSNA) and the collegial help and discussions effectuated through the

INSNA international e-mail distribution list SOCNET have been irreplaceable resources.

In Russia my main contact has been with the European University at St. Petersburg, the home base of my research visits in Russia. I thank Vladimir Gelman, Oleg Kharkhordin, Anna Temkina, Vadim Volkov, and Elena Zdravomyslova for their intellectual stimulation and practical assistance.

In addition to the European University, another important node in my St. Petersburg network is the Center for Independent Social Research led by Viktor Voronkov. The Center and its researchers, particularly Boris Gladarev, have been invaluable resources for this study. In Moscow the expertise, support, research, and contacts provided by Vadim Radaev at the Higher School of Economics are gratefully acknowledged.

My greatest thanks go to the Russian IT professionals who took time out of their busy schedules in order to be interviewed or to participate in our web survey. Those who were particularly helpful, and with whom I still continue to exchange opinions after the completion of the research project, cannot be singled out here in order to protect their anonymity, but I would like to warmly acknowledge the gift of their time and thoughtful interaction. The responsibility for the conclusions, interpretations, and outright errors in the text is, naturally, mine only.

Ursa Dykstra revised the language of the book with great care and expertise, and also translated parts of the manuscript from Finnish to English. Irina Vesikko assisted in the final phases of the book editing and checked the English transliterations of Russian words.

I am also obliged to the writer Antti Hyry, a legend of Finnish literature, who believes that finishing a book manuscript is, after all, a matter of sheer will and resolution. In an interview after having received a major Finnish literary prize Hyry said: 'If you intend to write a book, you just have to write it'. These words pushed me during moments of doubt to finish this book.

Finally, I want to thank my wife Anu-Katriina Pesonen, my daughter Ruut, and my son Elja for their patience and endurance.

1
Introduction

The software industry as an exemplary case of the functioning of the Russian market economy

If Russia has indeed 'become a market economy' as Anders Åslund claimed already in 1995, what are the roles of the social, cultural and moral aspects of this economy and how does it function at the level of individual actors and their personal relations? In more concrete terms: what kinds of resources are transmitted through the personal networks of Russian business managers and directors, and which mechanisms govern this transmission?

This book searches for answers to these questions by contesting the separation of the economy from the social world and by setting the interactions of real people in their everyday economic activities at the center of inquiry (Swedberg and Granovetter 2001). The investigation will be accomplished through the analysis of interviews and an online survey conducted among specialists, managers, directors and company owners of St. Petersburg software development companies between 2003 and 2006.

The software industry is a particularly indicative test case through which to investigate the Russian market economy and its networking practices.[1] A study of one of the most sophisticated and modern (though still relatively modest in terms of turnover and profit) parts of the Russian economy should better reveal the actual functioning of the markets than, say, a study of the state-controlled energy sector. The Russian software industry is also relatively less influenced by the 'Soviet heritage' than many other branches of the Russian economy: though its roots are in the scientific and technical knowledge already accumulated in the Soviet era and imperial Russia, the first companies emerged only

1

during perestroika and as a rule did not inherit outdated Soviet production facilities or management structures.

This book contributes to the literature on post-Soviet transition, affording a rarely available micro-level view on the new Russian knowledge-based economy. In addition, it has both economic and political importance. From the viewpoint of the development of the Russian *economy*, this book's significance lies in pointing out perspectives on economic diversification in terms of mathematical-technical expertise instead of on energy production and export. A developed software sector is not only essential for the modernization of all fields of the economy; the examples of Ireland and India suggest that it may also function as a major source of revenue in a national economy (Terekhov 2003). Increasing global connections in the field of information technology may also encourage the adoption of international business practices, for example through ISO and CMM quality certification (Feakins 2007).

Finding the Russian economy a way out of the 'resource curse' is all the more necessary since the economic policy based on energy production has had its time in the sun and the growth in output of basic energy commodities is likely to remain low (Sutela 2008a, b). This necessity has not gone unnoticed by the Russian leadership: both Vladimir Putin and Dmitry Medvedev have on several occasions emphasized the need to diversify the Russian economy.[2] The latter, for example, has criticized harshly the backwardness of the Russian economy and its anchorage in the Soviet past, naming information technology as one of the five new priority areas of the economy. When announcing the creation of a presidential commission for the modernization and technological development of Russia's economy in May 2009, Medvedev openly admitted that none of the precedent measures taken to boost innovation-based high-tech economy in the 2000s, such as industrial parks, technology transfer centers, special economic zones or Russian venture companies, had yielded serious results but rather existed 'only on paper' (Butrin and Granik 2009). He returned to the economic modernization theme in his opening address for the commission in June, in his widely debated article 'Go, Russia!' in September, and in his address to the Federal Assembly in December of the same year (Medvedev 2009a, b, c).[3]

From the viewpoint of *politics*, the investments by and collaboration with foreign IT firms in Russia as well as the Russian IT entrepreneurs' activities may open up the Russian economy and create preconditions for a new kind of state–business relationship, currently characterized by the dominance of the state over the economy (Yakovlev 2006). More importantly, modern information and communications technology plays an increasingly important role for the horizontal communication among civil society actors, substituting for the biased coverage of the Russian mainstream media (Lonkila 2008).

The role of social networks in the Soviet and Russian economy and society

Thanks primarily to Alena Ledeneva's (1998) work on *blat* – a Soviet system of using connections to obtain private gain from state resources – there is agreement among researchers on the central role social networks played in Soviet society.[4] In order to get by in daily life, most Soviet citizens had to pull strings, for example, to get decent meat, a car, an apartment or exemption from army service.

However, the use of social networks for purposes other than *blat* in the Soviet Union is a clearly under-researched topic. *Blat* practices certainly did not cover all the instances of mutual favors or helping others out in Soviet daily life. Moreover, even the actual prevalence of *blat* in the Soviet Union is difficult to estimate in retrospect. As noted by Anna-Maria Salmi, it is not known how many Soviet citizens actually obtained, say, their apartment or car by using *blat* (Salmi 2006, 2009).[5]

The critical notes by Salmi also warn against hasty answers to the question 'What happened to the use of connections when the Soviet Union collapsed?' If we lack reliable empirical data on the prevalence of these connections in the Soviet Union, the estimates of the *changes* in post-Soviet Russia in these ties will be educated guesses at best.

Despite the problems, a natural expectation would seem to be that the privatizing of the economy and the spread of market relations would have torn apart old Soviet era practices such as *blat*: most goods which were in short supply in the Soviet Union are now freely available on the market, there are less state property, goods or services to use in private exchanges, and the market costs of these exchanges are clearly visible to all participants (Ledeneva 1998; for a closer look at *blat* and its transformation in post-Soviet Russia see Chapter 4).

However, a growing body of research on the use of social networks in the post-Soviet era suggests that connections still play an important role in Russian society, for example, in health care (Salmi 2003; Rivkin-Fish 1997, 2005), education (Lonkila 1998), civil society and collective action (Alapuro 2001; Alapuro and Lonkila 2000; Gibson 2001) and many other fields of life (Salmi 2006; Ledeneva 2009).[6] Though, because of the fading of the Soviet shortage economy, there is less need to pull strings to get access to goods and services, connections are still needed – often in conjunction with money – to ensure their quality.

The results of these studies are lent further support by an all-Russian survey on the non-market forms of exchanges of help in Russian families' daily life conducted by the Russian Academy of Sciences in 2000 and 2006. The study revealed that the number of Russian families getting various types of help from their personal networks had increased in regard to almost all types of help. The study also found that the types of help obtained from one's social networks varied according both to the local context (help being more prevalent in growth regions such as Moscow and St. Petersburg) and to the socioeconomic level of the families. The poor families used their social ties mainly to survive in daily life, whereas the 'multifunctional' networks of the more well-to-do families also helped them in improving their situation. The results of the study suggest that social networks are not only the result of social stratification but also reproduce this stratification.[7]

Similarly, a face-to-face survey conducted in 313 Moscow families in 2005–6 about their engagement in non-market work found that the vast majority of the households studied participated in non-market economic practices, including the subsistence economy, non-monetized exchange with friends, neighbors and kin and informal monetary exchange (Williams and Round 2007).[8]

Networks are not only used, however, for Russian households' subsistence, but to solve a wide variety of daily life problems in various arenas and fields of life. Expanding the area surveyed outside the household income formation allows us to conclude that the connections still have an important role in post-Soviet Russian society.

In line with the findings regarding the role of networks in Russian society, the studies of networks in the Russian *economy* have confirmed their role across a variety of economic contexts such as labor markets (Clarke and Kabalina 2000; Yakubovich and Kozina 2000; Yakubovich 2005), banking (Guseva and Rona-Tass 2001) and entrepreneurship and firm performance (Aidis et al. 2008; Shmulyar Gréen 2009; Batjargal 2003, 2005a, b, 2007; Rogers 2006).[9]

Because of the wide range of study areas, different theoretical backgrounds, a range of methods mostly not designed for network research and often-metaphorical notions of networks, this literature does not produce coherent or accumulating results. These difficulties notwithstanding, the main conclusion points to the continuing and central importance of social networks in Russian economic life.[10]

The significance of networks in the Russian economy is often related to lacking or incomplete market institutions such as the banking system, the distrust of most societal institutions penetrating Russian society[11] and the patterns of behavior inherited from the Soviet era. In Russian daily life several aspects that are taken for granted in 'Western countries'[12] may turn out to become problematic; and in solving these problems, one is inclined to turn to his/her social ties for help.[13]

Despite the wealth of research on social networks in the Russian economy, there is still a remarkable lack of empirical studies describing in detail *how* these networks function in practice at the grassroots level. How do the network ties emerge and form? What kinds of resources flow through these ties? Which mechanisms govern the transmission of resources? These are the questions this book seeks to answer by paying attention not only to social, but also cultural and moral aspects of the Russian economy.

Incorporating cultural and moral aspects into studies of networks in the Russian economy

Studies of social networks in the Russian economy seem to suffer from a double bias: it is as if any use of social networks in Russia has a somewhat dubious or instrumental character, and the networks of *economic* life are even more contaminated by pervasive instrumentalism and illegal or immoral behavior. Consequently, other aspects of the social networks, such as friendship or non-instrumental mutual help, have received much less attention (but see Kharkhordin 2005: 132–54, 2009).

At least two reasons for this state of affairs can be distinguished. First, due to the vagueness or complete lack of definition of the notion of 'network', the term may be used to refer to anything from formal interorganizational ties to social interaction in general (Salmi 2006). Second, social networks are often confused with *blat* and post-Soviet informal practices despite the fact that not all informal practices are effectuated through social networks, and networks also have other, non-instrumental functions such as sociability.

This book seeks to overcome these problems by taking the notion of *personal network* both as the theoretical point of departure and methodological tool of the study, enabling an analysis of networks as an alternative means to markets for coordinating economic activities. This analysis will reveal the tensions resulting from the sometimes-contradictory requirements of personal ties and markets and illustrate the intertwining of social, cultural and moral aspects in the Russian economy.

This book focuses, instead of on illegal or immoral practices, on more supportive and mundane aspects of favors, ranging from a hint about a good job from a friend to the help of a lawyer acquaintance in writing a contract or the advice of an old schoolmate to locate a key person in a client organization. Without these kinds of favors – mostly invisible in any statistics – neither the Russian nor any other economy would work properly. It is essential to note that these favors are often quicker, cheaper and more effective than alternative, formal ways of action, and they do not *necessarily* have to have either an illegal or immoral character. At the same time, they may have important consequences for the economy and society as a whole, as is the case in job searches, for example.[14]

Thus this study complements previous research on economic networks and informal practices, particularly Alena Ledeneva's important work on the economy and society of the Soviet Union and post-Soviet Russia, including such works as *Russia's Economy of Favours: Blat, Networking and Informal Exchange* (Ledeneva 1998) and *How Russia Really Works: The Informal Practices That Shaped Post-Soviet Politics and Business* (Ledeneva 2006), but differs from Ledeneva's research in several respects.

First, Ledeneva's (1998) examples concern the daily life problems of ordinary people and various fields of business in both the Soviet Union and post-Soviet Russia, whereas this book deals solely with the most modern part of the post-Soviet Russian economy. Second, this study focuses on personal networks instead of informal practices. Third, the material of Ledeneva's latest book (2006) describes the situation mainly in the 1990s, ending with her study of informal practices up to the year 2003. The online survey data of this book were collected in 2004 (describing the situation in 2003), but the interviews cover the years 2003–6, with updates to the present. Fourth, this study deals with 'the economy of favors' in post-Soviet Russia, which differs from *blat* exchanges in two important ways: the mutual favors analyzed in this book do not have to have the dubious character that marked *blat* exchanges, nor is state property or access to it as a rule used as a medium of exchange. Finally, this book shows that the Russian market economy is not only embedded in social networks but also that the actors in the networks justify their economically relevant transactions by referring to *moral* principles.

Structure of the book

The next chapter describes the theoretical idea, methods and data of the study. It introduces the notion of personal network to the reader and analyzes the advantages of the notion in the studies of the Russian economy and society. The chapter also describes in detail the use of the researchers' own personal ties when trying to get interviews from the busy Russian IT professionals. This description is not only of a methodological nature, however, since it simultaneously illustrates the central theme of this book: the importance of personal network ties in solving problems in post-Soviet Russia.

Chapter 3 contextualizes the network data on Russian managers' and directors' networks analyzed in this book. The chapter begins with a case description of the birth and development of the St. Petersburg software company 'Arcadia'. This case is then placed in a larger context by a portrayal of the evolution of the IT field in the Soviet Union and post-Soviet Russia.

Though the IT sector has been less affected by the Soviet past than many other fields of Russian industry, this past is still in many ways present in today's IT sector. Chapter 4 discusses both the constraining *and* enabling aspects of this 'Soviet legacy'. It offers examples of the gradual transformation of informal Soviet practices, such as *blat* (pulling strings), to the transition-era barter and present-day *otkat*, a new and widespread form of corruption.

Social networks do not grow haphazardly; rather, new acquaintances are usually made in social contexts and milieus where people are brought together by some common purpose and are likely to have regular or prolonged interaction. Chapter 5 studies the social milieus and 'interaction foci' important to personal network growth among St. Petersburg IT professionals. They include schools with a special emphasis on mathematics, the several technical universities of St. Petersburg, virtual milieus such as Russian weblogs and social networking web sites, the association of Russian software developers and the special importance and social functions of birthdays in the Russian economy and society.

Chapter 6 describes in detail the contents of the network exchanges, illustrated by quotes from our respondents' interviews. These exchanges transmit various kinds of information and other important economic resources, such as jobs, advice and concrete help.

While the previous chapter dealt with the contents of the Russian managers' informal transactions, Chapter 7 analyzes the social mechanisms governing these exchanges. The chapter focuses on three such mechanisms: reciprocal obligations, the use of brokers in resource transmission and evaluation and the mixing of professional and personal spheres of life. In discussing reciprocal obligations, the chapter shows – drawing from the justification theory developed by Luc Boltanski and Laurent Thévenot ([1991] 2006) – how the economically relevant exchanges between Russian IT professionals are related to and supported by the *moral* resources used to justify these exchanges.

Chapter 8 connects the micro-level analysis of preceding chapters to an assessment of the nature of the emerging new Russian capitalism, building on the results of an online network survey conducted among St. Petersburg IT professionals in 2004. Having established the importance of personal network ties in the Russian economy and society, this chapter examines the extent to which this significance is indicative of the emergence of the 'new spirit of capitalism', which values constant networking, projects and mobility (Boltanski and Chiapello 2005).

The study's conclusions are offered in Chapter 9.

2
Using Networks to Find Out about Networks

The significance of *personal* networks in studies of the Russian economy

The notion of network refers to a system consisting of nodes and the links between them. A *social* network may be distinguished from, say, computer networks by the fact that the nodes of the network are social actors. Often the nodes are individual persons, but in principle they could also be groups of people, cities, states, social organizations, and so on.[1]

In this book, however, a notion of *personal* network consisting of an individual person (*ego*) and the people (network members or *alters*) with whom s/he has relations is used.[2] What constitutes a 'relation' depends on the study question. Typically, though not necessarily, a personal network may contain colleagues, family and kin, friends and acquaintances, neighbors, and so forth.[3]

The central idea of this book is that in the Russian context the notion of personal network is, in addition to being a researcher's tool for collecting and analyzing empirical data, also recognized by the *actors themselves* as a conventional means of coordinating economically relevant transactions. In more concrete terms: turning to one's personal network instead of formal economic institutions is a common way of conducting various transactions and solving problems in the Russian economy.

As will become evident later in this book, this convention of turning to one's personal network has its roots not only in the Soviet period – and probably in Imperial Russia – but also in perestroika and the transition era. On the one hand, and somewhat paradoxically, the introduction of the principle of market competition to the economy forced the new Russian entrepreneurs to turn to their existing networks, but on the other hand, it led to conflicts and tensions between the 'network' and 'market' modes of coordinating transactions.

In studying the Russian economy, the notion of personal network has several advantages. First, in Russia the ties connecting organizations generally and firms in particular are often highly personal in nature. In other words, the interrelations between organizations are based, instead of on formal organizational roles, on the personal relations between particular individuals (Salmi and Bäckman 1999; Brygalina and Temkina 2004; Salmenniemi 2008).

Second, the notion of personal network allows for relating the life history of an individual to the interaction with his personal network members. This makes it possible to combine aspects of both agency and structure in the analysis, but more importantly, to investigate the *formation* of social ties, often neglected in social network research.

Third, and closely related to the previous point, the notion of personal network enables one to illustrate the mixing of 'personal' and 'professional' spheres of life in Russia.[4] A network study focusing only on the ties between colleagues within one organization cannot grasp the overlap and intertwining of social ties at and outside work (Lonkila 1998, 2010).

Fourth, the notion of personal network corresponds closely with the way Russians speak about their social relations. The Russian language contains several expressions referring to personal networks, such as *moi krug* (my circle), *okruzhenie* (surrounding), *blizkii krug* (close circle), *krug obshcheniia* (circle of socializing) and *krug znakomykh* (circle of acquaintances).[5] It is central for the purposes of this book that these expressions depict precisely *personal* networks anchored around focal individuals and containing different types of social relations such as family, kin, friends, and colleagues. The mixing of these relations in the personal networks of Russian IT business is one of the main findings of this study, but seems also to be a more general feature of the Russian society.[6]

Finally, the great amount of time and effort placed on specific social *rituals* related to personal networks, such as birthday parties and celebrations, is indicative of their significance. In Russia, birthdays of the members of the extended family, friends, acquaintances, and colleagues are remembered and celebrated – often on several occasions – both at home and at work to a much greater extent than, say, in the US (Visson 2003, for a closer account on birthdays see Chapter 5).

Our use of personal networks in social research owes much to the works of the Manchester school anthropologists (see, for example,

Mitchell 1969). For them the use of the notion was a conscious theoretical and methodological choice which allowed, for example, the investigation of the *multiplexity* of social ties (Gribaudi 1998).[7] This book follows that lead by paying particular attention to the overlapping spheres of life as detected through personal network data.

The micro-level perspective implied in the use of the notion of personal network is similarly indebted to the recent anthropological research on Russia. This research, which emphasizes the importance of studying Russian society on a grassroots level, has produced some of the most interesting views on the Russian economy and society (e.g. Burawoy and Verdery 1999a; Ashwin 1999; Humphrey 2002; Yurchak 2006).[8]

In all, turning to one's personal network is a conventional way to effectuate transactions and solve various problems in the Russian economy. Understanding the nature of the present-day Russian market economy requires a detailed examination of the functioning of these networks, which is the aim of the empirical analysis of this book.

The qualitative approach in social network analysis

Many of the contributions and achievements of social network analysis have come from the 'structural school' (e.g. Wellman and Berkowitz 1988), which is based on modeling and analyzing the patterns of ties between the members of networks. The critics of the structural school have claimed since the 1990s that this modeling has been carried out at the expense of reflection on the nature and content of the ties (e.g. Emirbayer and Goodwin 1994; Smith-Doerr and Powell 2005).

Stressing network structure at the expense of the nature of social ties runs the risk of universalizing the results mainly based on data collected in Western countries and consequently downplaying cross-country differences. The comparative research on friendship networks suggests, for example, that there is variation in the rights and duties related to friendship (Fischer 1982; Castrén and Lonkila 2004). From this viewpoint, the questions on friendship used in international comparative surveys take as a fixed point of departure a category which itself should be questioned and studied.

This study belongs to the strand of qualitative and mixed-methods approaches to network analysis (Lonkila 1999a; Castrén 2000; Salmi 2006; Fuhse 2009) in which, instead of network structure, the meaning and formation of personal network ties are at the center of attention.[9] It responds to the call by Smith-Doerr and Powell (2005: 394) for 'more process-oriented, case-based approaches' which should offer accounts of 'why ties are created, how they are maintained, what resources flow across these linkages, and with what consequences'.[10]

Because an important part of the respondents were shareholders or owners of St. Petersburg IT firms, this study also contributes to the research literature on entrepreneurship. Following Hoang and Antoncic (2003), this research addresses three essential components of social networks: the content, governance, and structure of the relationships. As for the *content* of the networks, network ties are considered to be the media through which actors gain access to resources held by other actors. The *governance* refers to mechanisms that coordinate network exchanges, and the *structure* denotes the pattern of relationships between actors (Hoang and Antoncic 2003: 166).

In this book, emphasis is laid on the role of personal networks in the transmission of resources. In the classification by Hoang and Antoncic, the focus is thus on the content of the ties (dealt with in Chapter 6), as well as on the mechanisms governing the functioning of the network (dealt with in Chapter 7). The modeling of network structure, which is primary in the structural network analysis tradition, will receive less attention and is included in the analysis mainly while discussing the role of brokerage (Chapter 7).

From the viewpoint of resource transmission, this study thus started as a 'connectionist' variant of social network analysis (Borgatti and Foster 2003: 1002) focusing on the resources that flow through social ties:

> Ties are seen, often quite explicitly, as conduits through which information and aid flow (...) In this conception, an actor is successful because she can draw on the resources controlled by her alters, including information, money, power, and material aid. This perspective is also implicit in the social support literature (...) and in most network research on entrepreneurs.
>
> (Borgatti and Foster 2003: 1002)

However, during the study it became evident that the transmission of economically relevant resources in the networks could not be separated from social, cultural, and moral issues. Both the qualitative and quantitative data suggest that the mechanisms governing the network exchanges were not only based on atomistic individuals' rational calculations, but were also deeply affected by social and moral considerations.

Network data and how to get them

This book is based on the analysis of semi-structured interviews and personal network data collected among St. Petersburg IT professionals during 2003–6 (interviews) and in 2004 (network data).

The qualitative interview data

The interview data consist of semi-structured interviews conducted in St. Petersburg from 2003 to 2006 with 50 top- and mid-level IT directors and managers.[11] Of the 50 respondents, 38 were under 40 years of age and eight were women.[12] Except for two respondents, all had a university degree, and several had either a licentiate[13] or doctoral degree. The majority of the companies where respondents worked were owned by Russians, but the data also include foreign-owned companies and joint ventures. The bulk of the firms were established in the 1990s.[14]

Independently of this study, Melanie Feakins (2007) conducted interviews among St. Petersburg software companies involved in off-shore programming. Feakins' vivid characterization of her respondents applies *mutatis mutandis* to ours – more so since some of our interviewees were probably overlapping:

> A large proportion of the firms interviewed were established by entrepreneurs with PhDs who had left teaching, research, and academic life to establish firms with colleagues, friends, spouses, and as individuals. (...) Many were hesitant, amused, pleased, and sometimes still shocked that they have become entrepreneurs in the post-Soviet world, particularly because it had not been imaginable in the Soviet Union. (...) As a category of people, their deliberate distance from state administration and enterprise life of the Soviet period separates them distinctly from apparatchiks and new elites whose positions and wealth in post-Soviet society are derived largely from conversions of their political status to material wealth and/or participation in privatization schemes of enterprises and natural resources.
>
> (Feakins 2007: 1892)

In line with Feakins' account, one of our respondents, a middle-aged Russian firm owner, described his situation upon the demise of the Soviet system as an unemployed engineer 'who was of no use to anyone'. Starting from nothing, he had built a flourishing software company that employed a considerable number of people and was growing yearly. Despite this success, he lived, behaved, and dressed modestly and, instead of using the profits to improve his lifestyle, he invested most of his money in the development of the firm.[15]

Finding respondents was tricky. As IT professionals are generally busy people, finding time for one to two hour interviews from the daily chores of Russian business required a remarkable amount of work and preparation from our native Russian research assistant. Luckily, the process of locating and persuading potential candidates to be interviewed turned out to be part of the phenomenon we studied in several ways.

First, the respondents were often found through the interviewer's personal networks, and sometimes through the network of the author of this book. This process illustrated the importance of personal ties and brokerage in making things happen in Russia, as becomes evident from the field notes of the research assistant:

> Respondent [project leader, p23] was found thanks to Vadim Grigor'evich [a friend of the author] (...) Generally, the interview went very sympathetically but this was basically due to Vadim Grigor'evich's mediation. After the interview the respondent confessed that without this mediation he would not have agreed to be interviewed.

Another reluctant respondent (system administrator, p32) finally agreed to be interviewed, probably influenced by the fact that he had been the classmate of the son of our interviewer's acquaintance, who, in his turn, was acquainted with the interviewer's mother.

Second, the respondents often seemed to agree to be interviewed thanks to the particular role of the 'ethics of helping out' in Russian culture which will be analyzed in detail in Chapter 7 of this book.

Third, our research assistant's field notes about the atmosphere and communication prior to, during, and after the interview illuminated the mixing of professional and personal spheres of life, one of the main themes of this book, in the interaction between the Russian interviewer and the Russian respondents. On several occasions the interview started out in a professional tone and floated to the areas of common interests and personal life of both parties.

All these aspects will be discussed in detail in later chapters. Here it suffices to say that the very process of data collection already illustrated the main substantial results and theoretical ideas of this book, justifying its detailed examination here as much as a result of the study as a description of its methods.

As a rule, interviews were conducted in a relaxed atmosphere either at the office, café, car, or even home, often accompanied by a cup of coffee or tea. The main disrupting factors were work-related time pressures and occasional interruptions by workmates. Out of 50 interviews, only one turned out to be a truly unpleasant experience:

> I would not want to meet this person another time. He demonstrated benevolence, willingness to help. But his whole tone of speaking, expressions and questions could be experienced as an attempt to show who is who here. I felt like I was interrogated. The only reason I let the respondent treat me this way was that this was for him the most natural way of interacting with people whom he considered inferior to him. Prior to the interview the respondent asked questions about my university and faculty and my understanding of sociology. Then he said that I have exactly one hour for the interview, and put the clock on the table in front of him. When he saw my list of questions, he grabbed it and started reading and answering the questions himself. In the course of the interview I asked complementary questions. When the interview had ended, the respondent boasted about that we managed to finish in one hour.
>
> (interviewer's field notes)

During his reading and answering the questions, the respondent mentioned that his firm was working for 'state structures' (*gosstruktury*) and replied 'confidential', for example, for questions about the number of employees and the location of offices.

Fortunately, this kind of reception was an exception. Generally, our respondents related to the study positively and seriously, trying to explicate the details of their business practices and use of social ties to the best of their understanding.[16]

Though interviews were conducted by a native Russian and the respondents were guaranteed anonymity, it would be naïve to assume that the respondents would have openly shared all aspects of their business activities. Some refused to answer certain questions referring to business secrecy while others expressed right away that they wouldn't reveal all they knew about the topic at hand:

> I won't tell everything about this case. There are simply things I won't tell even if protected by anonymity. Believe me, there are situations where not even close to everything can be written into a

contract. And in this case the guarantee for everything being done right and on time is the word of the person you are dealing with.

(general director, p4)

Therefore, one most likely 'underrepresented' theme of the study is the corrupt and informal practices of Russian business (cf. Chapter 4 of this book). Because of the wealth of studies on this topic and the focus of this study on the 'routinized' and legal ways of acting through networks, this is not a serious shortcoming.

Personal network data

Data on personal networks were collected in spring 2004 through a web-based network questionnaire.[17] Respondents were selected from the catalogue 'The whole computer world, St. Petersburg 2003' (*Ves' kompyuterny mir, St. Petersburg 2003*), which contained data on 1048 firms in the field, and through the research group's own connections. Though the catalogue hardly included all firms active in St. Petersburg at the time, it contained a wide variety of entrepreneurs dealing with software development, hardware, system integration, consulting, service providing, and so forth. (The firms dealing only with computer hardware trade were not included in the survey.)

Selected firms were first approached by phone to find the e-mail address of a person who could and would answer our questionnaire. This person was then sent the weblink of our survey by e-mail. In the survey the respondents were asked to describe a successful project or work task which they had completed in 2003, and to name the three most important people (that is, their personal network members or 'alters') involved in the implementation of the project.

In addition, they were asked to name two more people who had been important for their whole career in ICT. Lastly, the respondents were asked to name one person who lived abroad and had had the most important effect on their whole activity in ICT (for more details, see Lonkila 2006). After having generated the list of names of their network members, the respondents indicated in a network matrix if, to their knowledge, their network members knew each other – that is, had been in mutual contact. In addition, the questionnaire contained free-form fields where the respondents could characterize their network members in their own words. This qualitative data turned out to be very interesting for the purposes of this book.[18]

The complete web survey network data corpus contains information on 72 respondents and 343 network members. The *respondents* were

67 young or middle-aged male and five female ICT professionals from St. Petersburg, almost half of them younger than 36 years. Seventy percent of them had an MA degree, 22 percent were licentiates or doctors, and they were working in mostly small- or medium-sized ICT companies. The respondents were well placed in their own organizations: 28 percent were CEOs, 39 percent top directors, and 29 percent managers. In addition, 43 percent were shareowners in their companies. The 343 *network members* were also mostly young and middle-aged men, the majority of them working either as CEOs (18 percent), directors (20 percent), or managers (20 percent).

The web survey data cannot be considered representative. Neither can we calculate the response rate since the information of our study was also diffused through our own connections who informed their acquaintances and friends of our survey. Nevertheless, combined with the interview data, it gives a vivid picture of the meaning and functions of personal networks in the most modern part of the Russian economy.

Limitations of the study

This book focuses primarily on factors *facilitating* the transmission of resources and *connecting* actors. Network ties can, however, also be used strategically to exclude others, and their use may also have negative consequences both on micro and macro levels (e.g. Ledeneva 2004: 8–9). Ronald Burt's influential theory of structural holes, for example, is based on the *tertius gaudens* (the third who gains) idea borrowed from Georg Simmel. In this perspective, network member A takes advantage of the fact that he is connected to both B and C, who do *not* know each other. This intermediary position allows A the possibility to use it to his own advantage. However, this study follows David Obstfeld's (2005) lead instead. Obstfeld has in his study of brokerage employed the *tertius iungens* (the third who joins) perspective, that is, the active role of network members in creating the connections between other network members (see Chapter 7).

Second, this book does *not* use the concept of social capital. Without denying the achievements of the large research literature on social capital, the notion is problematic for the tasks of this study. In her review on the problems of the notion, Salmi (2006: 51) notes how the leading theorists (Pierre Bourdieu, James Coleman, and Robert Putnam) all stress different aspects of the concept. More importantly, the very essence of the notion remains vague. In the well-known formulation of

Robert Putnam (1993: 167), for example, social capital consists of trust, norms, and networks, each of which remains vaguely defined.

> One problem pointed out by critics is that social capital is often used in a very unfocused manner. Social capital means different things depending on the tradition one draws from and, in the worst case, can mean just about everything, as has been argued by Portes. He claims that Coleman started the proliferation of the concept by including 'a number of different and even contradictory processes' in the term, some of which are the mechanisms that generate social capital and some the consequences of its possession (Portes 1998, 5).
>
> (Salmi 2006: 51)

Third, this book focuses on the role of social ties between human beings involved in economically relevant transactions. Formalized solutions such as standards and certifications are certainly of importance, but the emphasis of this study is rather on the ways of *circumventing* these standardized solutions with the use of social ties.

Problems of generalization

The structure, composition, and functioning of the personal networks is influenced by several factors which have to do with the properties of the respondents (age, sex, place of birth, life course), their position in the organization (programmer vs. manager), and the characteristics of the company (field of industry, size, age, and so forth). For example, the role and meaning of networks is likely to change during the life cycle of a company. When acquiring customers, a small, start-up firm may be more inclined to use personal relations than a bigger company that has already established a stable client base.[19] On the other hand, as will become evident later, even big companies are sometimes forced to turn to their networks, in order to win tenders, for example.

Many respondents also noted that networks function differently in offshore IT companies oriented toward foreign customers and adapted to Western standards of conducting business on the one hand, and in companies operating in domestic markets alongside big state-owned companies on the other hand. Because of the qualitative nature of this study, all of these 'background variables' cannot, however, be systematically investigated.

Finally, the gender aspect merits both methodological and substantial comment. From the methodological viewpoint one has to note that the interview situation consisted of a young Russian female student conducting interviews mostly with middle-aged Russian men. Because of the Russian gender system, this age and gender difference probably helped in obtaining interviews from the busy IT directors and managers. Moreover, in the interview situation some of the interviewees took a 'teaching position', which was often helpful in terms of creating an overall picture of the field. Most important, however, is to acknowledge that the gender difference most likely emphasized some aspects of the phenomenon studied and concealed others.

Substantially, both Russian business and the IT field are male-dominated areas of life. This provoked a lively discussion between one of our female respondents (team leader, p37) and the female interviewer about the role of women in the IT business. The respondent noted that women are treated differently, and those starting from the bottom in the IT business have a harder time than men. This difference is, however, of complex character and contains several contradictory elements. According to her, being a woman has negative consequences until one has gathered enough experience, when the gender factor 'starts to function strongly in your favor.' Moreover, there are both places 'where they don't take you because you are a woman' and places 'where they will take you exactly because you are a woman.' The respondent also related the gender aspect to the nature of the male Russian 'work collective' in IT business:

> Firstly, many [Russian IT professionals] think that women cannot work as programmers. Secondly, many think that it is a crazy idea to take a woman into a company consisting of 20 men, because this spoils the collective and the mood of the men. And then one has to remember that women have a tendency of taking maternity leave. In the firm I worked at earlier, practically all of the women took maternity leave. Well, not all, but those with whom I myself had come to the company.
>
> (team leader, p37)

Another female respondent belonging to top management stated that programming and engineering professions 'are not women's affairs' (*ne zhenskoe eto delo*) – unlike marketing, where women can use 'fine tools' (*tonkimi instrumentami mozhno vladet'*) (director, p41). Still another female respondent (PR manager, p2) considered how 'for women the family will always be first'.

These replies illustrate aspects of the Russian gender system that cannot be dealt with in detail here (for an account of entrepreneurship in gender terms, see Shmulyar Gréen 2009: 93–8). However, considering the examples given above, it is likely that a systematic analysis of the women managers' networks would confirm rather than refute the tendency toward mixing of personal and professional spheres of life observed in this study.

In sum, this book describes mostly owners', directors', and managers' use of networks in small- and medium-sized Russian software companies, though it also includes interviews with employees from some of the biggest software companies in St. Petersburg. For the purposes of this book this bias toward SMEs (small- and medium-sized enterprises) firms is not fatal. First, the flourishing SMEs are considered important to the dynamics of the market economy, and even the biggest companies have started small. Second, the larger and more important the company is, the more it runs the risk of getting involved in deals with state-owned companies or involved in the top-level politico-economic struggles. Thus, for a study of the emerging Russian market economy, SME companies are a good starting point.

3
The Evolution of Russia's IT Sector

This chapter describes the formation of the ICT field in post-Soviet Russia. The first section introduces the reader to the realities of a start-up Russian software firm and the role of personal networks in the company growth through a detailed description of the birth and development of Arcadia, one of the central software companies in St. Petersburg. The second section places this case in a larger historical context by depicting in a necessarily limited form the evolution of computing in the Soviet Union. The third section describes the role of information technology in the collapse of the Soviet Union, drawing on the work of Manuel Castells. The last section focuses on ICT in post-Soviet Russia by describing its role in the Russian national economy, the use of ICT by the Russians, the state's supportive measures in the IT field, and the position of Russian IT in the global economy.

Arcadia: The birth of a St. Petersburg software company

Arcadia's story is told here to illustrate the role of personal networks in the early phase of the emerging Russian software industry. The story relies on the account of Arcadia's founder and CEO Arkady Khotin, and will be reproduced here on the basis of a series of meetings and e-mail exchanges between the author and Khotin, and the article by Cook (2009).[1]

Khotin was one of the thousands of Soviet engineers, computer scientists, and mathematicians whom the collapse of both the economy and governmental support for scientific research forced to find new jobs. Many emigrated, but those who did not had to make a living at a time when the economy and society were floating from one crisis to another, when the institutions of the market economy had not yet been created but the Soviet ones had started to fall apart.

Khotin's recollections describe vividly the background of the first Russian IT entrepreneurs coming from the ranks of research institutes, the difficulties they faced in the early years of the formation of the software industry, and the central role of social relations in overcoming these problems. The story will be presented in chronological order, depicting the most important steps taken and the resources accumulated during Khotin's professional career.

Potatoes and punchcards at a scientific research institute (1972–8)

After graduating from the Leningrad Institute of Aviation Engineering as a radio engineer, Khotin served two years in the Red Army base near Tallinn, the capital of Estonia. After serving in the army Khotin, now a reserve lieutenant, landed a job in 1972 as a hardware developer in a research institute, conducting studies in the field of hydrological technology in his native Leningrad. Khotin's institute was secret, as were many Soviet research institutes – even the researchers in the different departments were not supposed to know what was being studied next door. As Khotin's work was not in any way related to computers and his laboratory did not have one, he was introduced to the world of computing by a lucky coincidence.

In the Soviet era, the employees of the institute were sent once a year to help nearby state farms to harvest potatoes. During these trips, which were called *kartoshka* (potato) by the staff, there was not much to do in the evenings but drink vodka and get to know the researchers from the other laboratories. Bumping into one of these acquaintances at the institute later on proved crucially important for Khotin's future:

> I ran into this guy in the corridor of our institute. He was carrying a huge pile of Hollerith cards [punch cards used for programming]. I did not know what they were because our laboratory did not have any computers and I jokingly swiped the whole pile to the floor. He got very angry and shouted that he'd been working on them for months and I had ruined everything. I apologized, helped him to pick the cards up and sat with him several evenings helping to re-sort them. While doing this I grew interested in programming and computers. 'What is this computer? What do you do with it?'

Khotin started to study programming voluntarily in evening courses. One of his young teachers – today a professor of computer science at a prestigious St. Petersburg university – told the course participants that they needed to start learning programming or they would find themselves on the street in a few years' time.

Computerizing Soviet factories at the state computing firm 'LSMNU' (1979–89)

Khotin took this advice seriously and left the research institute in 1979 for the state firm LSMNU,[2] which specialized in the computerization of Soviet factories under the ministry of industrial instrumentation and engineering (*Minpribor*). The Ministry had given orders to allocate computers to individual factories, many of which did not understand or know how to operate them. It was Khotin and his work brigade who were responsible for helping the factories under the command of the ministry nation-wide to install copies of Western minicomputers. M40, which Khotin was installing and programming, had only one kilobyte of RAM (random access memory) and 16 kilobytes of ROM (read only memory).

Instead of waiting to be ordered to visit the clients, Khotin travelled to the Moscow factory producing M40s. He managed to get the names and phone numbers of the client factories where the computers were to be distributed. His initiative, which earlier could have been subject to disapproval as divergence from the behavior of an average Soviet engineer, was backed up by the introduction of the *khozraschet* ideology in the Soviet Union, which emphasized independent economic accounting for the individual production units.

According to *khozraschet*, each Soviet enterprise should make ends meet on its own, requiring initiative and sales and marketing skills that had not been top priorities for Soviet factory managers. With the allocation list of M40 minicomputers in hand, brigade leader Khotin – worried about the future of his job – started phoning factories, introducing himself, and offering help in M40 installations. This marketing campaign resulted in a long chain of work trips throughout the vast Soviet state. Khotin visited factories that produced anything from shoelaces to gunpowder and rockets, helping their staff unpack, install, connect, and program the new machines. However, with the years he grew tired of continuous traveling. Also, the state of affairs in the Soviet periphery differed drastically from the official rosy picture:

> In the mid 1980s our brigade visited a factory in a Siberian town that was producing shells for Katyusha rockets. When we had finished our job in the evening and were about to return to the hotel, the factory engineer asked us to wait for a moment. He left the room and

returned after a while with a one meter long sharpened metal stick. He insisted on walking us to the hotel, protecting our safety with this metal stick.

For Khotin's future career the time at LMNSU was important, not only in terms of gaining concrete though necessarily limited work experience but also in making new connections with the management of the Soviet factories. It was one of these managers who invited him to take a job as software director in a Russian–American joint venture in Leningrad in 1989, the next important step in Khotin's path toward founding his own software company.

Gaining contacts and competences in the Russian–American joint venture Dialogue (1989–92)

Dialogue was one of the very first Russian–American joint ventures – Russians supplying the programmers and Americans the funding – established in the Soviet Union. It had an office in both Moscow and Leningrad, and it worked as a Russian dealer for several Western IT companies, mostly selling computers and, among other things, conducting localization of MS Word and other Microsoft products.[3] Khotin's role in the Leningrad office was to develop software projects inside and outside Russia. Getting projects outside of Russia was hard, so he focused on getting factory computerization projects in the Leningrad area.

The job at Dialogue was an eye-opening experience, exposing Khotin to a world totally different from his experience in the Soviet economy. It allowed him to, among other things, travel to New York and Boston as early as 1990, when visiting abroad was still impossible for all but a few people in the Soviet Union.

During his time with Dialogue, Khotin established a network of important connections, gained competences vital for conducting business, and got connected to the world outside the Soviet Union. The joint venture functioned as a nexus of contacts and a springboard for many future Russian businessmen such as Khotin's boss, Vitaly Savelev, who is currently the CEO of the Russian airline company Aeroflot. Khotin, who himself was asked to join Dialogue by his former client at LMNSU, continued the chain by inviting another former client of LMNSU to join Dialogue and, years later, to join Khotin's own software company.

The connections made during my years at Dialogue were very important and they still are. If you look at my LinkedIn network [a business-oriented social network site], you will see that many people in my network have had some relationship with this company.

Most importantly, Dialogue allowed Khotin to meet with and learn from many US businessmen. In the early 1990s there was a keen interest in Russian transition, and Dialogue had several high-caliber visitors. Among them was Bill Gates, with whom Khotin shook hands and talked during Gates' Russian trip where he was spreading his vision of getting computers 'on every desk'. Khotin learned both business skills and terms from these encounters and gained experience in speaking English. Every one of these encounters taught a former Soviet radio engineer something important, from the English language to Western business practices, and one of them also forced him to face an existential question:

> I met a 17-year-old American student whose father had sent him to Russia to gain experience. He asked me what I am going to do in five years. That was first time anyone had asked me such a question and the first time I had ever thought about it. The Party was supposed to take care of us, so there had been nothing to think about. I realized that I had been living like a vegetable!

When conducting computerization in a factory located in Vyborg, a small town near the Finnish border, Khotin actively used the programming language Clipper, which was mainly used for database programming. Having gained considerable expertise in this language and being surrounded by Americans 'who believed that users had some rights', he founded the first Russian Clipper users group, which was joined by some two hundred Russian IT specialists. Having close contacts with this professional community later encouraged him in his decision to establish his own business:

> One of the most important factors behind my decision to leave Dialogue and start up my own business was the idea that there were two hundred developers whom I knew and with whom I could work on projects. If I had been a single guy with no support, I probably would not have dared to do it.

Among the important lessons Khotin learned at Dialogue was how to communicate abroad through computers. The company built one of the first Bulletin Board System nodes in Russia and joined FidoNet – a network connecting Russian and foreign personal computers through modem and phone line – in the early 1990s when the Internet was not yet available in Russia.[4] The first connection between the Russian nodes of the network to the West was established through the personal computer of a Finnish user who every night received data in a trunk call from his Russian counterpart for whom it was possible to phone abroad for free.

However, the commercial success of the joint venture did not come about as wished. The enthusiasm of the employees could not replace the lacking business skills and control of funds, only a part of which was used for business development. When Dialogue widened its sphere of activities and started trading 'all kinds of goods', Khotin began to look for other options, already having decided to start up his own company.

Founding and early years of the software company Arcadia (1992–present)

Khotin was invited to a teaching job at an educational institute in St. Petersburg in 1992, again by an acquaintance, also a former employee of Dialogue. The meager salary was compensated by the free use of a computer and free access to the Internet – both rare opportunities in the Soviet Union in the early 1990s. At Dialogue Khotin had already understood the importance of foreign contacts and learned to use the Internet, which knowledge he now put to use:

> At that time one of my friends gave me a small laptop computer. Consequently, in the daytime I was teaching, while in the evening I was using computers and Internet at my office and at night browsed BBS world from that tiny laptop with just small floppy instead of HD.
> (Cook 2009: 4–5)

Though the idea of his own software company had emerged for the first time already during his second or third year at Dialogue, the final decision was made in March 1993 in Khotin's kitchen, together with his wife, a professional programmer, and their daughter – all former graduates of the same technical university. The firm was named Arcadia, mimicking Khotin's first name, 'after 30 seconds of reflection' and the accountant, a key person in a Russian firm, was recruited from among the former students who had gone through summer training by his wife at her office at the university.

Khotin's experiences of Western connections from the Dialogue years and the lack of demand for software development services in domestic markets encouraged him to look for customers outside of Russia. He tried every possible channel to raise the interest of potential foreign clients through active e-mailing to various bulletin boards. Following up on an idea from a friend, he even sent an email in 1993 to the NBC nightly news, which was inviting viewers to send in e-mail messages from all over the world. This mail was read on air by the NBC news anchor, because it differed from the other 3000 messages sent in (Cook 2009):

Subject: From Russia with Love

Dear Americans,

My warmest seasons greetings from St. Petersburg Russia. Please keep up your great work in helping us to dig ourselves out from the deep hole that we got into about 70 years ago. I am sure it will be rewardable for both nations!

Cheers, Arcady Khotin

In addition to e-mails, Khotin started writing articles in *Boardwatch* magazine, one issue of which was read by the Florida-based US citizen Philip Schwartz, who asked Khotin to transmit a message from Schwartz' Russian friend to St. Petersburg. This contact started an intensive communication between the two men, which continues until today, and provided Khotin with an important mentor who advised him how to conduct business:

It turned out that we were same age and had similar interests in many areas. Philip and I began a very heavy e-mail communication over a period of weeks and then months and now even years. I was asking him tons of questions about how to do business. We called that e-mail stream Schwartz University. This was possible for me to accomplish in part because of the time shift. I would take care of my daily affairs and then send him e-mail. He would be up and running in Florida by late afternoon my time and we would exchange three or five or even 10 e-mails in a 24-hours period. He was extremely helpful. He sent me the modem, then a laptop, and then invited me over. He gave me invaluable help in developing my early business.

(Cook 2009: 9)

Finally one of Khotin's e-mails on a bulletin board was read by a US citizen from Long Island, who became his first customer. This first contract helped him to rent a two-room office on the outskirts of St. Petersburg, buy three computers, and hire three programmers from among his old contacts in the Russian Clipper user group.

The first contract, which was based on the fact that a good program-mer's pay was at the time USD 150 a month in Russia, kept Khotin afloat but was not enough. Khotin continued his search for clients by following the Internet, reading articles in *Computerworld* or on BBS message boards and sending innumerable e-mails offering IT services. To overcome the trust gap, he volunteered to do some work for free, hoping that a happy customer would continue to work with him for pay. This was not, however, an easy effort, since he still lacked expertise in basic business practices such as how much to charge the customers, as the following recollection from 1994 shows:

> I had no idea about how to speak at the terms of payment. I had no idea of the concept of things like retainers. My Soviet mentality did not allow me to ask. (...) when someone asked me how much I wanted to be paid for this activity, I had no idea how to arrive at an appropriate figure. I began to ask Philip for help and advice which he began to generously offer me. In trying to price a small project I had no idea how to say it would be about $500 or it would be in the lower hundreds of dollars. Philip had software development experience and he was very good in helping me formulate proper estimates.
>
> (Cook 2009: 9)

In addition to the problems with foreign business practices and cus-toms, the domestic ones proved to be even more difficult. Starting as an entrepreneur in Russia was not easy in the early 1990s, when many basics for the normal running of a company such as computers, print-ing paper, or properly working phone lines were hard to get, unreliable, or expensive, regulations concerning business were constantly chang-ing, and banks were unreliable and often bankrupting.

The domestic markets were riddled with corruption and violence and the cat-and-mouse game with tax inspectors was one of the many prob-lems which had to be solved with the help of trusted social ties:

> [personal contacts were used] to find out how to write a report to tax inspection. This was very important because our state agencies did not know what we were doing, they did not understand it. (...) For us it was enough to send the software to the client through the Internet. But the tax inspector did not understand what the Internet was. They

suggested that we save the software on a diskette and send it by mail so that there would be a tangible product crossing the border. We started sending diskettes like fools but then someone realized that we could send state secrets on them – their contents should be checked at the corresponding state agency which could then authorize the sending. What idiotism! Well, we of course asked each other how you solve this problem, what do you write in the contract?

By 1996 Khotin had grown tired of flying three times a month to meet the US clients and started looking for customers closer to home. A natural choice was neighboring Finland, whose capital Helsinki was located only 300 kilometers west of St. Petersburg. Khotin decided to pay a visit to Finland in order to attend an IT seminar with his best programmer in 1996:

> I had no money to pay for his seminar but I said look if I can make a presentation, will you let me in? He [the Finnish seminar organizer] said sure. (...) We went to the seminar and spent six hours listening to presentations in the Finnish language and then we made our own presentation in English. People were complimentary and I thought 'wow, we will get some projects' but we returned back to St Petersburg and nothing happened. I definitely had raised some interest but I had a zero marketing skills including a lack of understanding of how to follow-up. I even went without business cards. They said we will send you something but they did not even know my e-mail address. I was still a very inexperienced person.
>
> (Cook 2009: 10)

Despite Khotin's inexperience in selling services, this conference led later on to an important contract with the owners of the Finnish antivirus company Data Fellows (currently F-Secure) which remains his customer to this day. Observing and learning from the Finns doing business has been a practical business school whose example Khotin is still in the process of applying to his own firm.

The fall of the Russian ruble in 1998 was a catastrophe for many Russians, but for Khotin and other software exporters whose customers paid in dollars, it meant a sudden and large rise in income. For the first time in his career, Khotin was able to hire staff – in addition to himself, an accountant, and a system administrator – whose hours were not directly billable from customers. The company joined the RUSSOFT association in 1999, and the 2000s have been marked by the growth of the company from the original four-man office to one of the major St. Petersburg software houses. Arcadia has, among other things, started its own recruiting agency, opened a Finnish office, and completed ISO certification. The growth also translates to the continuous need for keeping the hired programmers employed. Here, again, personal relations come in handy:

> I am pulling all my strings. I have almost 600 connections on LinkedIn. To e-mail my contacts about the availability of these people I would search within LinkedIn for data security and throw in a few other appropriate terms to find a subset of my contacts in Scandinavia or in Russia to whom I would send e-mail. If the guys are in my network, I can send e-mail directly to them. If they are in the network of an acquaintance and look especially good, I can ask the acquaintance to help out. I knock on the door and say 'hey I have spare resources. Can you help me to find someone who can put them to work?'
>
> (Cook 2009: 24)

In hindsight, all the phases in Khotin's professional career now seem to have been in some way beneficial for his future entrepreneurship. Work at the research institute introduced him to computers and programming, and the job at the state computing firm gave him practical experience in collaborating with enterprises. Particularly significant was the period at the joint venture Dialogue which connected him to the world outside the Soviet Union and taught him communication and linguistic and business skills. Most importantly during his time at Dialogue, he established a great number of both domestic and foreign contacts, such as the Russian Clipper user group and his US mentor Schwartz.

In all, Khotin's career testifies not only to his personal abilities but also to the power and reach of his personal network ties and the overlapping of the personal and professional spheres of life. Khotin was invited first to work at Dialogue by his former customer at the state computing firm and then to a teaching job by his former colleague at Dialogue. While at Dialogue, he himself recruited his former client from the state computing company to work with him, and founded a professional Clipper community, from which he later recruited his first programmers. Finally, the founders and key persons of Arcadia were selected in and through the trusted ties of family – a natural choice under the conditions in Russia in the early 1990s.

These ties and networks formed the social basis for Arcadia's birth and growth. But the story of Arcadia also illustrates how, in addition to the social aspects, the emergence and success of a post-Soviet Russian firm has to be placed and understood in historical perspective. This is what the next two sections try to do for the Russian IT sector.

Computing in the Soviet Union

The basis for Soviet computing and later post-Soviet Russian IT was already laid by the development of higher education and scientific research in imperial Russia. Though the turmoil of the 1910s and 1920s hampered progress, both mathematics and electronic engineering developed intensively in the 1920s and 1930s, stimulated by Lenin's famous GOELRO program (*Gosudarstvennaia komissiia po elektrifikatsii Rossii*) for building a nation-wide electricity distribution network in the Soviet Union. The strong growth of power engineering had great impacts on the early period of Soviet computing, whereas later on the computing needs of the Soviet military sector came to be of primary importance (Fitzpatrick et al. 2006).

The construction of the first Soviet digital computer MESM (*Malaia Elektronnaia Schetnaia Mashina*, 'small electronic calculation device') during the years 1947–51 under the leadership of S. A. Lebedev, one of the founding fathers of Soviet computing, illustrates well the material, organizational, and ideological constraints under which the pioneers of Soviet computing operated.[5] Researchers of the history of computing even claim that 'no all-electronic computer was ever built under more difficult conditions' (Goodman 2003: 21).

Crowe and Goodman (1994) offer a vivid account of the struggles of Lebedev, who was appointed the director of the Institute of Energy of the Ukrainian Academy of Sciences, located in a former monastery in a suburb of Kiev, in 1946.[6] Lebedev had already started working on electronic triggers and arithmetical research related to computing systems in 1939, but the Second World War interrupted his work. The work by his institute was slowed down by the shortage of materials in the war-torn country, as it was unable to deliver the needed quantity and quality of components. Lebedev also had to fight the administrative, ideological, and science policy barriers, the protagonists of analog computing, and, in the 1950s, with a competing Soviet computer design project, 'Arrow' (*Strela*).[7] When building MESM, Lebedev had to convince the Soviet leadership and scientific community of the importance and future of digital computing, which at the time was evident in neither the Soviet Union nor the US.

Despite the obstacles, MESM solved its first simple problem on November 6, 1950, was exhibited to a commission of scholars from the

Ukrainian Academy of Sciences in January 1951, and was accepted into full operation in January 1952 (Crowe and Goodman 1994).

In the 1950s Lebedev moved to Moscow and continued his work, first with a new high-speed computer, BESM (*Bystrodeistvuiushchaia Elektronnaia Schetnaia Mashina*, 'high-speed electronic calculating machine'), and then from 1954 onwards with M-20, a computer based on germanium diodes, which would replace the unreliable vacuum tubes of the earlier models.[8] M-20 was completed in 1958, about the same time as a project named BESM-2, and its serial production started in Moscow in early 1959 (Crowe and Goodman 1994). The beginning of the production of M-20 computers marked the starting point for the development of the Soviet computer industry, and stimulated the production of a series of M-20 compatible computers. In 1961 the M-20 computers' users association, the first professional association of computer specialists in the Soviet Union, was established (Prokhorov 1999: 5–7).[9]

During the Cold War, military reasoning gained a primary position in the development of Soviet computing. Military computing had special requirements for the components, which also had to be domestically produced. The beginning of commercial production of Soviet transistors in 1956–8 started the production of special computers adapted to military purposes (Khetagurov 2001: 192). The large share of these specialized military computers was a particular feature of Soviet computing, and, according to Susiluoto (2006: 147–8), even the universal computers were mainly used for military purposes.

Three military programs (nuclear weapons, ballistic missiles, and anti-missile defense) dominated not only post-war Soviet computing, but also Soviet science and technology more generally. Their importance is illustrated by a quote from the Soviet cosmonaut Grechko recalling his experiences of working in the mid 1950s at the Academy Computation Centre on the BESM:

> Kurchatov's people [nuclear weapons researchers] used it in the daytime and during the night Korolev's people [designers of ballistics missiles and spacecraft]. And for all the rest of Soviet science: maybe five minutes for the Institute of Theoretical Astronomy, maybe half an hour for the chemical industry.
>
> (Harford 1997: note 54, 220, cited in Gerovitch 2001: 269)

The tremendous investment of resources in the military sector in the Soviet Union produced well-known achievements in the areas of space flight and military technology, among others, at the expense of the consumption and daily life needs of the general population. According to Manuel Castells, between 1940 and 1960 Soviet mainframe computers were not very far behind the achievements of the West,[10] but in 1965 the country's leadership decided to shift from developing its own production to imitating Western computer technology – in the late 1960s and 1970s copying the architecture of the IBM 360 (Crowe and Goodman 1994: 11).[11] As a result of this decision the USSR's information technology sector became dependent on copying chiefly American technology and began to lag more and more behind the development of the West.

Castells' assessment, based on his research both in Soviet and post-Soviet Russia, is in line with that of the US experts from 1988 (*Global Trends in Computer Technology*, 1988). According to this report, in the late 1980s the Soviet Union was lagging years behind the West in most areas of computing, with possible exceptions in the theory of programming languages and information retrieval systems.[12]

Many of the reasons for the backwardness of the Soviet computing industry were the same as for that of the Soviet economy in general. Not only did the individual Soviet factories not necessarily know what to do with computers but they also had little incentive to be more efficient than what was required to fulfill the plan. There was a shortage of high-quality components needed for reliable hardware production, service for hardware and software was poor or lacking, and the ideological control of information did not fit the needs of the new economy, increasingly based on the processing of information (*Global Trends in Computer Technology*, 1988).

The excessive demand and lack of competition allowed the production units to continue their Soviet-era habits of production, and the complex and overlapping organization of the industry led to catastrophic shortages:

> The production of floppy disks has been a disaster. Production was assigned to four different ministries with the brunt of the task falling on *Minpribor*. However, at the lower levels in *Minpribor*, there was a scramble to find productions space, and the full capacity of 50 million diskettes per year will not be reached before 1989. (...) The end result is a great shortage of diskettes.
>
> (*Global Trends in Computer Technology*, 1988: 159)

In addition to problems of organizing production, Soviet computing also had to balance between ideological and pragmatic aspects of the field, which was to have lasting consequences for its development. According to Gerovitch (2001), computing scientists and professionals in the Soviet Union were torn by the contradictory requirements of emulating and surpassing American computing on the one hand and keeping at a distance from cybernetics, which was ideologically discredited in the Soviet Union as reactionary pseudo-science, on the other. This tension was solved through a discursive strategy of distancing computing from cybernetics. This had, however, long-term impacts on Soviet science by limiting computer uses to mathematical physics:

> Soviet specialists in 'machine mathematics' had to walk a fine line between two mortal dangers – falling behind the West in computing, and following Western trends too closely. To avoid unwanted associations with controversial American cybernetics, they chose to 'de-ideologize' Soviet computing and place emphasis on the narrow technical functions of computing and information theory, ignoring any potential conceptual innovations. This strategy severely limited the field of prospective computer applications. The computer was legitimized in this Soviet context as a giant calculator; its capacities as a data processor for economic and sociological analysis, and as a tool for biological research, were downplayed, to avoid ideological complications.
>
> (Gerovitch 2001: 279)

In order to meet the ideological requirements, the Russian translations of Western computer literature were furnished with introductions condemning the ideological errors of these publications and the most dubious parts were just left out. Domestic publication of computer-related works was prevented both by a fear of revealing state secrets as well as helping out rival Soviet computing programs. Only after Khrushchev's rise to power was cybernetics rehabilitated and legitimized (Gerovitch 2001: 270–5).

As a combined result of the problems and weaknesses described above, the Soviet Union missed the explosive growth of personal computing taking place in the West during the 1980s. While in the US interactive and user-friendly personal computers were revolutionizing office work, home entertainment, and computer-mediated communication, this development was absent in the Soviet Union. According to the estimate of a firm negotiating an agreement to sell computers to the USSR, and the information published by the *New York Times*, the USSR had 50,000 personal computers in 1988 – one for every 5600 people – while the US had roughly 30 million PCs – one for every 8 people (*Global Trends in Computer Technology*, 1988).[13] The assessment of the missed chances in the Soviet Union by US experts in 1988 is devastating:

> [T]he phenomenal growth of the PC in the United States depended on the characteristics and availability of the PC and its software, the demand environment, and marketing effectiveness. The PC offers such dramatic gains in simple areas such as maintaining a mailing list, generating form letters, doing word processing, and tracking budgets, to name but a few central applications, that it has become as indispensable to the office as the telephone and the copying machine. None of these conditions has been present in the Soviet Union. The Soviets have been unable to mass produce a reliable personal computer on the order of the IBM-PC, and support service is questionable at best. (...) The software distribution system is convoluted, and good software often never receives distribution because of the lack of copyright protection. Lower-level managers have far less autonomy, have not received any training in computing, and have little desire to start using computers. Generally speaking they are not in a data-rich environment where they could connect PCs to mainframes or networks. The individualistic and entrepreneurial strains are generally missing from the Soviet culture, and the absence of any home computers, for all practical purposes, has precluded the possibility of the emergence of the home computer phenomenon so familiar in the West.
>
> (*Global Trends in Computer Technology*, 1988: 160)

In the spirit of perestroika, many problems of the computing industry could be discussed publicly, and attempts at reorganizing the field of the Soviet computing industry were made by creating two new organizations in 1986: the State Committee for Computing and Informatics was to coordinate and develop Soviet computing and promote the use of computers in the economy; and the Interbranch Scientific Technical Complex for Personal Computers was established to address the problem of continuity in the research and development cycle and the problem of ministerial departmentalism. Both institutions had to struggle with the already existing Soviet organizations and their results were meager (*Global Trends in Computer Technology*, 1988).

The collapse of the Soviet Union finally brought to end these and other experiments to revive the Soviet system from the inside.

According to Manuel Castells (2000), information technology played a notable role in this collapse, and this role will be the subject of the next section.

Information technology and the collapse of the Soviet Union

Castells bases his interpretation both on his own fieldwork in the Soviet Union during the years 1989–96 and on the studies conducted by his wife, Emma Kiselyova (Castells 2000: 5).[14] After Castells and Kiselyova the development of post-Soviet Russia's IT sector has, with a few rare exceptions, been studied chiefly by private companies and market research departments. Exceptions in the area of information technology are, for example, Castells 2000; Gaslikova and Gokhberg 2001; Averin and Dudarev 2003; Hawk and McHenry 2005; Lonkila 2006; Rantanen 2001; and Susiluoto 2006.

In Castell's interpretation a central reason for the Soviet Union's bankruptcy was the inability of the Soviet economy, or, in Castell's terminology, the centrally planned 'industrial statism', to mold itself to the demands of a new economy based on information processing.[15]

Purely from the viewpoint of extensive economic growth, the growth of the Soviet Union's economy after the Second World War was a success story – although it was bought at the expense of human suffering and overuse of natural resources. According to Castells, for the greater part of its history the Soviet Union's economic growth was in fact larger than in Western countries and the speed of the country's industrialization is unequalled in world history.

Comparative growth abated only in 1975 and came to a standstill in 1980. Because of the absence of the price mechanism, the economy's resources were not allocated efficiently, and Soviet citizens became accustomed to life in a shortage economy. Nor was the economy able to develop internationally competitive, non-military products: the role of the Soviet Union in the international market became the massive export of raw materials, especially oil and gas which, coming into the 1980s, comprised 90 percent of the USSR's exports to capitalist countries (Castells 2000: 10–24).

Most catastrophic, however, was the drop-off in the speed of techno-scientific development. The primary reason for this was the hegemony of the military-economic complex as well as an untenably large defense budget, which in the 1980s was about 15 percent of the gross national product – proportionally about twice as much as Reagan's government comparatively spent. The complex siphoned off both the best material and human resources from productive use, but it did not produce a spin-off effect on the side of the civil economy. The Soviet economy's priorities were always the security needs of the Soviet state as defined by the military-economic complex, and the fundamental conservatism of the security ideology would not tolerate the risk-taking necessary for an innovation-based new economy.

In addition to the central role of the military-technological complex, another important reason for the failure of the Soviet economy was the lack of an innovation system. The rigid centrally managed planning system, international differentiation, and lack of competition did not compel innovation and risk-taking, but rather led to the organization of production in the accustomed way. The Soviet Union's science academy was disconnected from the production plants, the research and development of which were based on each ministry's own research institutes. These in turn were not in contact with each other with the exception of an unsuccessful experiment in the Khrushchev era at the end of the 1960s.

Finally, the information-technological revolution did not fit together with the Soviet system's bureaucracy and ideological repression. Only a few Soviet scientists got to participate in international congresses, and the free circulation of information important for innovation was far from the Soviet system, where the use of typewriters and copy machines was tightly supervised. The new networked style of production could not be conciliated with the concentrated, hierarchical command economy (Castells 2000: 5–37).

If information technology had an impact on the demise of the Soviet Union, it also helped to save the fragile Russian democracy during the August putsch in 1991. Based on his interviews with key players, Rafael Rohozinski (1999: 1–2) describes in detail how the programmers of Relcom/Demos, one of Russia's private Internet providers, were among the first to testify to the coup from their offices near the Kremlin, and started transmitting the information to network nodes across the Soviet Union:

> Within hours, they had established a temporary network node at the White House and were e-mailing Yeltsin's defiant declaration, rejecting the legitimacy of the coup committee to Russia's regions and abroad (...) By evening, the Relcom network was acting as a major channel of information between Moscow and the regions, linking the multitude of major and minor actors opposed to the coup. (...) As

local and republican press organs increasingly drew upon Relcom for information about the unfolding drama in Moscow, the information vacuum, a key factor in the coup plotters' game plan, was filled.

(Rohozinski 1999: 1–2)

The whole story of the collapse of the Soviet empire with its ensuing transformation of economic, political, and geographical orders in the 1990s will not be reproduced here. Suffice it to say that the collapse of the economy destroyed the state budget which in its turn shattered the financial base of Russian scientific and research institutions. Some of them, however, managed to find a niche in the post-Soviet Russian ICT field, the description of which is the focus of the final section of this chapter.

The ICT sector in the Post-Soviet Russian economy

The role of the ICT sector in Russia's national economy

When assessing the role of the Russian ICT industry in the economy one has to bear in mind that it has, similar to other private enterprise in Russia, functioned for only under 20 years, and was born in the 1990s under particularly difficult conditions.[16] The emergence of the Russian ICT field coincided with the global shift from mainframe to personal computing. This shift created a need for private companies providing system integration and software development services for the new platforms and contributed to the formation of the industry (Terekhov 2003: 22).

Despite the recent tendency of Russian software companies toward regionalization, the Russian ICT industry is geographically concentrated in relatively few centers, of which St. Petersburg, the location of our data collection, is the most important after Moscow. Though the St. Petersburg ICT market and companies are clearly smaller than in the capital, the city has been at the forefront of information technology, telecommunications and electronic engineering since imperial Russia through the Soviet Union and post-Soviet Russia: Russia's first phone line was erected between St. Petersburg and Gatchina in 1882 (Sokolov 1992: 66) and Alexander Popov presented his radio receiver to the Russian Physical and Chemical Society in St. Petersburg in 1895.

In the Soviet Union, within the frame of the planned economy, a considerable amount of radio engineering, telecommunications, and electronics industry and research was located in northwestern Russia, and at the end of the 1980s more than 50 industrial enterprises and scientific research organizations operated in Leningrad (Averin and Dudarev 2003: 37–8). The St. Petersburg/Leningrad region also played an important role in the recovery of the post-Soviet Russian economy after the collapse of Soviet industrial enterprises and research organizations. Due to its geographical proximity to Western Europe, availability of educated workforce, and long traditions in the field, northwestern Russia was a central player in the development of the Russian IT industry and mobile telecommunications. The first cellphone call in post-Soviet Russia, for example, was made by the St. Petersburg mayor Anatoly Sobchak through the operator Delta Telecom in 1991, and the main optical fiber connecting the Russian Federation to Europe and the rest of the world goes through St. Petersburg and Finland. Several large international companies in the ICT related fields, such as HP, Siemens, LG, Microsoft, Google, Sun, and Intel, operate in the St. Petersburg area (Kärkkäinen 2008: 70–81).

Today the Russian ICT industry is a small but rapidly developing sector of the economy, which until recently has stayed in the shadow of the energy sector. The ICT sector's relatively small proportion of the economy (5 percent of the gross national product in 2005, according to the minister of communications Leonid Reiman)[17] has been compensated by its extremely rapid growth during the 2000s.[18] One of the main engines of this growth – together with the general boost to the Russian economy fueled by rising oil prices – has been the development of the telecommunications field, particularly cellphone use, in Russia.

In the 1990s cellphones were still out of reach of the general population because of both the high prices of phones and the high tariffs, and they were chiefly considered symbols of the nouveaux riches and organized crime. After the economic crisis of 1998 and especially in the 2000s, prices fell as competition was freed, cellphones lost their elite character, and their use exploded (Gladarev and Lonkila 2008). As a result, telecommunications accounted for 70 percent of the ICT sector in 2007 (see Table 3.1).

Within the IT sector, the table shows how hardware's proportion of the total IT markets diminished from 66 percent in 2003 to 56 percent in 2007, while during the same time the proportion of software development grew from 13 percent to 18 percent, and that of services from 21 percent to 26 percent.

As the example of Ireland shows, software exports may function as an important source of foreign currency revenue in a national economy.

Table 3.1 The development of Russian ICT markets 2003–7, bn USD

	2003		2004		2005		2006		2007	
	bn USD	%	bn USD	%	bn USD	%	bn USD	%	bn USD	%
Hardware	4.6	66	5.4	61	6.6	61	8.1	59	9.9	56
Software	0.9	13	1.1	12	1.5	14	2.2	16	3.1	18
Services	1.5	21	2.4	27	2.8	26	3.5	25	4.6	26
IT total	7.0	100	8.9	100	10.9	100	13.7	100	17.6	100
Telecommunications	12.9		18.8		23.3		31.7		40.5	
ICT total	19.9		27.7		34.2		45.4		58.1	
% telecomm of ICT		65		68		68		70		70

Source: Minkomsviaz' (2009)

Table 3.2 Software exports' proportion of the Russian IT sector 2003–7, bn USD

	2003	2004	2005	2006	2007
Russian IT sector *	7.0	8.9	10.9	13.7	17.6
Software export **	0.5	0.8	1.0	1.5	2.2
Software export % of IT sector	7.8	8.5	8.9	10.6	12.5

Sources: Minkomsviaz' (2009); ** RUSSOFT Annual survey, 2007*

Though the value of Russian software exports has been modest, their proportion of the whole IT sector grew steadily during the first decade of the 2000s (see Table 3.2).

The clear majority of the Russian software export income in 2007 came from software development services (58 percent), followed by sales of products and solutions (25 percent) and from international companies' development centers in Russia (18 percent) (*RUSSOFT Annual Survey*, 2007: 12). The export of ready-made products was very concentrated: four companies accounted for over half of Russian software exports including, in addition to ABBYY products, Kaspersky Lab (antivirus programs), CBOSS (billing systems) and Transas (navigation systems, vessel traffic management systems, marine and aviation simulation systems) (*RUSSOFT Annual Survey*, 2008).

On average the Russian IT companies are small in comparison with international firms both in terms of sales and number of employees (see Table 3.3). Notable exceptions are such Moscow-based firms as Luxsoft, EPAM, and Exigen which employ 2000–5000 people each. The software companies based in St. Petersburg were clearly smaller than

Table 3.3 Median number of employees in the 100 biggest Russian IT companies 2003–7

Year	2003	2004	2005	2006	2007
Median no of employees	204	209	300	368	403

Source: CNews Analytics (2010)

their Moscow counterparts; none of them ranked among the 10 biggest Russian IT companies. The largest of the St. Petersburg companies employ only some hundred people and include companies such as Reksoft, DataArt, Digital Design, Arcadia, and Lanit-Tercom.[19] Of the 30 leading IT companies in northwestern Russia, the sales of the biggest one, BCC, amounted to 3,685,500 thousand roubles (roughly 142 million USD) in 2006 and it employed 720 people (CNews Analytics 2007).

These impressions of the comparatively small size of Russian IT companies are supported by a 2008 survey directed at companies who were to some extent involved in exports of software products and services from Russia. Of the 96 companies who responded to the survey, 47 percent employed up to 30 people, 43 percent from 30 to 500, 5 percent from 500 to 1000 and 5 percent more than 1000 people. In terms of turnover, 43 percent of these firms had up to 0.5 million USD, 47 percent from 0.5 to 10 million and only 10 percent over 10 million USD.

ICT use in Russia

Though the figures on ICT use in Russia vary depending on the source and methodology, the general trend has been that of extremely quick growth. Chachin (2008), for example, estimates the growth rate of Internet users in 2006–7, based on the data from Russia's ministry of communications, at 50 percent, the number of PCs at 36 percent, and number of households' broadband access at more than 50 percent.

Figure 3.1 shows the development in the use of Internet, personal computers, and mobile phones in Russia during the 2000s based on data from the Levada Center surveys.[20]

Despite the rapid growth, the general level of ICT use in Russia is still weak according to the international 'network readiness index'. This index – which combines evaluation of the regulatory macroeconomic environment with the readiness and usage of ICT by individuals, business, and government – positioned Russia in 2007–8 at 72, between Vietnam (73) and Kazakhstan (71). In the same list Denmark was

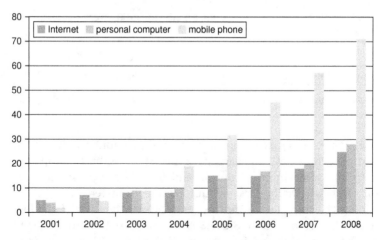

Figure 3.1   The use of Internet, personal computers and mobile phones in Russia, % of population

Table 3.4   The use of Internet in selected European countries in 2008, %

	Germany	Finland	France	UK	Russia
No access at home or work	22	12	22.5	21.1	62.4
Never use	8.8	13.7	10.6	7.5	7.6
Less than once a month	1.6	1.5	1.3	2.6	2.5
Once a month	1.1	1.4	1.4	1.3	1.3
Several times a month	6.1	2.6	2.4	4.2	3.1
Once a week	4.8	6	3.2	4.2	2.3
Several times a week	17.2	16.5	12.8	15.9	8
Every day	38.3	46.3	45.7	43.3	12.7
Total	100	100	100	100	100

Source: European Social Survey (2008)

first, the US fourth, Finland sixth, and the UK twelfth (Dutta and Mia 2009).

This impression is further reinforced by the results of the latest round of the European Social Survey offering comparative data on Internet use in Europe (Table 3.4).

The question was 'how often do you use the Internet, the World Wide Web or e-mail – whether at home or at work – for your personal use?'

The table shows clearly that Internet use in Russia is lagging far behind the level of Western European countries. Internet use is also unequally divided in terms of geography, education, and income, and

Internet access is still hampered by the deficiencies of the old telecommunications infrastructure.

Moreover, the Russian Internet is at least potentially subject to state control: while the original SORM legislation (*Sistema Operativno-Rozysknykh Meropriiatii*, 'System for Operational-Investigative Activities') allowed officials to record all phone discussions, its updated version SORM-2 authorizes FSB to access all Internet Service Providers' computers or other devices in order to monitor Internet traffic (cf. Alexander 2004: 616). In practice the amount of Internet traffic limits the realization of state control (see Alexander 2004 for a closer account of SORM and Russian Internet policy).[21]

State support for the Russian ICT industry

The state can have different kinds of roles in the development of ICT industry. At the center of Finland's information society model, for example, has been a state-mediated relationship between the public and private sectors, in which the state has purposefully supported a politics of innovation both directly and through the universities and research institutes (Castells and Himanen 2001; see also Fligstein 2001).[22]

Throughout the 2000s Russia's government as well has, at least in public speeches, recognized the economic, strategic, and political aspects of the ICT sector, which has manifested in, for example, the Federal Program Electronic Russia covering the years 2002–10. The program was approved by the Russian government in 2002 with a total budget of 2.6 billion USD. It aimed at increasing the effectiveness of government operation, developing the information transparency of the authorities, improving industry legislation and stimulating higher ICT related education. The first results did not, however, meet expectations. The program budget was cut twice in 2003 and its actual outcomes remain unclear (Averin and Dudarev 2003: 109; Susiluoto 2006: 305–6).

During the 2000s there have been further state initiatives to boost non-energy-related areas of the Russian economy, such as the creation of 'special economic zones', 'technology parks', and venture investment funds and plans of reduced tax burdens on export-oriented Russian IT companies (Wilson 2007; Stewart 2008).[23] Assessing these efforts, Gianella and Thompson (2007: 25–6) estimate, however, that without coordination between various state bodies, close monitoring of the budgetary funds, and evaluation of the effectiveness of the projects, there is a risk of duplication of effort, waste, and rent-seeking.

This assessment is in line with the opinion of the authors of the Russian Software Developers Association's report from 2008, based on the annual survey of 96 Russian software-exporting companies. The general views of the companies on the business environment are devastating: a high number of companies gave 'poor' marks for most of the aspects inquired about, such as human resources availability and education system (52 percent), taxation system (45 percent), impact of bureaucratic and administrative barriers on business (63 percent), availability of up-to-date infrastructure (52 percent), financial support to start-ups (67 percent), and state support of international marketing activity (75 percent). These numbers clearly reveal the failure of the Russian state to markedly support working conditions for the software industry. Even in the cases where measures have been taken, as the examples of the e-Russia program and technology parks above show, they have failed to produce substantial results:

> Still there is no significant progress in implementation of projects on technology parks construction specifically for IT companies (including software developers) with state financial support. Design and construction of technology parks in some cities is already in progress. But it goes slowly and the terms for property construction are constantly shifted. Besides, initiators of these projects have little understanding of the final results. There are reasons to assume that within the framework of technology parks ordinary business would be constructed (not only for IT companies).
>
> (*RUSSOFT Annual Survey*, 2008: 22)

This is also the case with taxation, where the law on reduction of the Unified Social Tax for software exporters from 26 percent to 16 percent turned out to be inconsistent with Russian pension legislation. Neither has an amendment in the Russian Federation Tax Code exempting value-added tax on sales of licensed software worked in practice (*RUSSOFT Annual Survey*, 2008: 20).

The authors of the report estimated the situation of the creation of special economic zones, where residents and high-tech companies are granted special privileges, in somewhat brighter terms, but saw no significant progress in the development of 'science cities' in which research centers were supposed to receive additional funding from local and federal budgets (*RUSSOFT Annual Survey*, 2008: 22).

According to the survey, Russian ICT firms consider bureaucratic and administrative barriers to be one of the most important business problems. As noted, 63 percent of firms in the survey described the level of solving bureaucratic and administrative barriers as 'poor', and particularly the St. Petersburg-based firms were among those affected by the Russian bureaucracy. One example, given by the survey authors, was the difficulty in recruiting foreigners:

> The existence of barriers for recruitment of foreign staff in Russian companies looks absolutely illogical. Sometimes the inviting Russian party has to spend up to six months to formalize all required documents to make it possible for such specialist to work for one year in Russia. Some companies are ready to attract experienced foreigner or former Russian citizens to use their expertise and knowledge to arrange sales of ready-made solutions and products on the world markets. But they do not dare to undertake these steps precisely due to complicated bureaucratic formalities.
>
> (*RUSSOFT Annual Survey*, 2008: 21–2)

Though a third of the firms in the RUSSOFT 2008 survey did note an improvement in state support of IT in the last two years,[24] the authors of the report consider this number to be based on hopes of the industry being finally taken seriously and supported by the state. According to the authors, however, no substantial results have been reached:

> The situation was seriously aggravated by the fact that the new Government did not include a ministry responsible for information technologies. The former Ministry of Information Technologies, and Communications was transformed into the ministry of Mass Communications losing IT in its official name.
>
> (*RUSSOFT Annual Survey*, 2008: 25)

In addition to the bleak estimates of the situation in 2008, most parameters of the business environment for software development companies had slightly worsened or remained the same in comparison with 2007 – with the lone exception of property rights. However, the report also concludes that the difficulties hit the medium-sized companies hardest whereas a group of large companies – also facing a lot of problems – had 'more opportunities to overcome them', as the authors ambiguously remark (*RUSSOFT Annual Survey*, 2008).

To summarize, and in line with the crushing statement of President Medvedev cited in the introduction of this book, the available evidence suggests that the Russian state has so far failed to notably support the development of the IT field.

Russia's position in the global ICT market

The Russian share in the global IT market is estimated at between 1 percent and 3 percent (*Russian ICT market overview*, 2007). Russia does not have significant, globally competitive hardware production nor – with some exceptions, such as the document conversion, data capture, and linguistic software produced by the company ABBYY – break-through software applications competitive in the global mass market. Instead it is likely that many software products marketed as Western contain the work of Russian offshore programmers.

Michael A. Cusumano (2006) considers Russia's position in the distribution of labor in the global software industry in comparison with the situations of Europe, India, and Ireland:

> Where does Russia fit into the global software business? Will companies there go the way of many other European firms and emphasize the science more than the business, and on expertly meeting the needs of local industry, but encounter limited success in global product markets? Will Russia go the way of India and emphasize service companies that will do anything the client wants at highly competitive prices but fail to build a products-based business? Will Russia become a lower-cost Ireland, with many small companies and lots of technical expertise, but too much emphasis on leisurely lifestyles and independence from venture capital and the stock markets?
>
> (Cusumano 2006: 33)

He concludes that Russia's competitive advantage lies in the ability to perform very sophisticated technical work at relatively low cost.

In line with Cusumano's conclusion, the high quality of Russian information technology professionals' mathematical competence is commonly recognized. One indication of this competence is the position of Russian students in the International Collegiate Programming Contest. The contest was won in 2009, 2008, and 2004 by the St. Petersburg State University of Information Technology, Mechanics and Optics, in 2006 by Saratov State University, and in 2001 and 2000 by St. Petersburg State University, with other Russian universities commonly occupying other top positions in the contest.[25] Considering the results of the contest, it is evident that top-level programmers are trained in Russia in Saratov, Perm, Izhevsk, Stavropol, Yekaterinburg, Novosibirsk, Ufa, Barnaul, Orel and Petrozavodsk, and about ten other Russian cities as well as Moscow and St. Petersburg (*RUSSOFT Annual Survey*, 2008: 33–4).

The competitive advantage created by a high quality workforce is reduced by deficiencies in the project management and English language skills of university graduates. On the macro level the obstacles to the development of Russia's ICT sector are, among others, the prevalence of pirating,[26] poor infrastructure, underdeveloped legislation, the corruption of the public sector, and the bad image of the Russian state abroad along with its intrusion into the economy.[27]

Moreover, the quick growth of the ICT sector, the concentration of activity in a few centers, particularly Moscow, St. Petersburg, and Novosibirsk, and the arrival and establishment of foreign companies (such as Sun, Microsoft, Alcatel, Motorola, Intel, and HP) in Russia have led to intensifying competition for skilled programmers. The rapid growth of demand together with a limited supply pool has led to a quick rise in salary levels in the early 2000s.[28] Competition for competent workers also forces employers to organize their business activities better. For example, in order to get a bank loan, an employee needs a steady job and an officially paid 'white' salary. In addition to the salary, workers have begun to value social security and health care benefits paid by their employers.

The rise in wages has led to a reduction in the relative cost advantage of offshore programming done in Russia. This has forced companies, especially those concentrating on cheap outsourcing of programming, to develop new business models, such as orientation to the domestic market, establishment of branches outside of the Russian metropolises in places with cheaper labor (other Russian cities and former USSR countries, but also in Scandinavia and Western Europe), attempts to develop their own products and applications, and attempts to reach closer partnerships with customer companies. However, closer cooperation with customers also demands substantial domain knowledge from different fields. The ability of Russian offshore firms to acquire such knowledge and integrate themselves deeper into the business processes of the end customers may turn out to be decisive for the industry's future.

In all, the Russian ICT industry is, despite its small size, a strong and fast-growing field of the economy, with the telecommunications sector having a leading role. In terms of human resources, it also seems to have the potential to capitalize on Russian scientific and mathematical competences for the uses of economic diversification. But as the short review of the history of the field showed, the roots of the industry in many ways date back to the Soviet era. This rooting has commonly been referred to as the Soviet legacy or heritage. The next chapter turns to the analysis of the nature of this legacy, drawing both on the existing research and our own empirical data.

4
The Soviet Legacy and its Transformation in the Russian IT Field

Unlike many other fields of contemporary Russian industry, the IT sector was not built on the relics of Soviet enterprises but on the significant scientific, human, and social resources of the new Russian entrepreneurs. Despite this relative independence of the IT field from the traditional Soviet economy, our respondents live and work in a society that is still influenced by the socialist past in several ways.

In this chapter, this influence is considered in terms of the 'Soviet legacy' and the transformation of this legacy in post-Soviet Russia is discussed. The beginning of the chapter reflects upon both the constraining and the enabling aspects of the Soviet heritage, and searches for the roots of Russian entrepreneurship in the Soviet era. The remaining parts of the chapter describe the transformation of informal practices ranging from the Soviet way of using connections to the barter exchanges of the transition era and the role of 'kickbacks' in the present-day Russian IT sector.

Constraining and enabling aspects of the Soviet legacy

At first glance, our respondents seemed to have little to do with the Soviet legacy. With only a few exceptions, they had clear identities as capitalist entrepreneurs, directors, and managers. Many had indeed started their businesses practically from scratch and built modern IT enterprises through persistence and hard work. Upon detailed inspection, however, the continuing presence of the Soviet heritage in the present could be detected in relation to social structures, individual actors, and their personal networks.[1]

This presence of the Soviet past has often been called the 'Soviet legacy', and it is still used in various contexts to explain post-Soviet

Russian life, most often as a shorthand way of referring to mainly negative phenomena.[2] Under closer scrutiny, this legacy turns out to be a complex phenomenon.

Alexei Yurchak's view on Soviet legacy in his study *Everything Was Forever, Until It Was No More: The Last Soviet Generation* (2006) helps both to make sense of this complex legacy and to solve the enigma of how the seemingly eternal Soviet system could actually fall apart so easily and quickly. According to Yurchak this was possible because the Soviet system – despite its undeniable flaws and atrocities – also contained spaces for creativity and positive experience. Following John Austin's language theory, he differentiates between the 'connotative' and 'performative' functions of the language used in the 'late socialism' of Brezhnev's years. While the connotative function describes reality (an enouncement can be true or false), its performative function achieves actions in the world through use of language (e.g. taking an oath).

According to Yurchak, in late socialism there was a 'performative shift' in language use from connotative to perfomative dimensions. In other words, people participating in May demonstrations, voting or giving speeches in Komsomol meetings did not pay attention to the connotative dimensions since at issue was not the truthfulness of their speech but rather a performing of a ritual. This kind of participation in the common rituals of 'hypernormalized' language use at public meetings enabled citizens to continue functioning within the Soviet system, to which, in actuality, they had attitudes varying from hostility and indifference to full support of communist ideals. In other words, the performative use of language in official contexts allowed them to create alternative spaces for action and interests and to develop their own cultural activities (including Western rock music) in and outside the Soviet system.

On a general level Yurchak's approach adds an *enabling* dimension to the depictions of the Soviet system and deconstructs the binary views consisting of, for example, true believers in communist ideals and pretenders, official and unofficial, or public and private. Seeing the Soviet Union through these binaries prevents us from understanding the complexity of daily life in late socialism, and, by extension, paradoxes such as the communist system as a platform for the emerging new Russian entrepreneurs.

In the following sections the Soviet legacy will be discussed in terms of structures, actors, and networks, keeping in mind both the constraining and enabling aspects of this legacy.

Soviet organizations as platforms for the emerging economy

Komsomol

The constraining *structural* aspects of the Soviet system on the economy have already been addressed in the previous chapter. In line with Yurchak's general idea, however, the Soviet era could also be considered to have contributed to the emergence of the IT field in several important ways. These enabling structural aspects of the Soviet legacy include the high level of mathematic-technical education, mass education of engineers, and the strong tradition in computer-related sciences which provided highly trained employees for the emerging IT sector. In addition, Soviet era organizational structures, such as Komsomol and particularly the high-level research institutions and universities in St. Petersburg, formed important contexts for the emerging Russian entrepreneurship.

According to Yurchak, the new Russian entrepreneurs had come from backgrounds in industry, science, the black market and Komsomol. In his view, many new Russian entrepreneurs had already acquired skills, knowledge, and competence under the structures of the late socialist Soviet system where no official private entrepreneurship existed (Yurchak 2002, 2006: 296–8).[3] He notes how the success of many of the richest Russian businessmen could be traced back to their high-ranking Komsomol positions and describes how the Youth Centers of Komsomol allowed the emerging businessmen an aegis under which to put up the starting capital, find contacts, and transform non-cash funds into cash:

> In the late 1980s, when the reforms of perestroika reached the sphere of economics and the Komsomol was allowed to experiment with private business activity, the knowledge, skills, and forms of rationality that consituted the late socialist entrepreneurial governmentality proved to be of crucial importance in this experimentation. At that time many active Komsomol secretaries started thinking of themselves as private entrepreneurs and businessmen, originally without necessarily giving up their identities as Komsomol secretaries. Eventually their work in 'youth centers' and 'cooperatives' under the auspices of the Komsomol organization turned many Komsomol committees into private firms and banks.
>
> (Yurchak 2006: 297–8)

Yurchak's account is lent credence by the descriptions of some of our respondents who told of having trained in entrepreneurial activities in the late 1980s and early 1990s at the 'Youth Center for Scientific and Technical Creativity' (*Nauchno-Tekhnicheskoe Tvorchestvo Molodezhi*, NTTM) functioning under the auspices of Komsomol:

> At that time the business life started to develop. I organized on the basis of my dissertation topic a brigade which at the time was called temporary working brigade (*vremennaia trudovaia brigada*) (...) it was organized through NTTM. It was possible to work behind the back of the institute [where the respondent was officially employed] and arrange the payment through NTTM.
>
> (technical director, p38)

Another of our respondents (director, p39) had similarly already organized his first, 'quite complex' commercial programming project at the end of the 1980s, through a Komsomol organization headed by his close relative. For the respondent it was evident that at that time this organization did not conduct youth-related activities anymore but closed different kinds of commercial deals.

Universities and research institutes

Because of the nature of the IT field and the concentration of several technical universities and research institutes in Leningrad, for many of our respondents their scientific and academic backgrounds and organizations were more important than their Komsomol connections.

Many respondents also noted their inclination toward and success in mathematics and/or computer science in school. All but two had graduated from university, and several had a licentiate or doctorate degree in computing-related sciences. For many, post-graduate studies in university or a job at a scientific research institute facilitated the acquisition of the human and social capital needed to start a private business.

Company director Egor (p42), for example, started his programming career in a British–Russian joint venture established at a scientific research institute in the early 1990s. Similarly, a well-known St. Petersburg software development company was founded in the early 1990s by young graduates from the university who wanted to earn a living with their skills in software design. In less than 20 years the firm has grown into an important player in the St. Petersburg IT field.

Another director (p22), with a background in the academic world, describes in a vivid manner his scientific activities at the research institute where he was writing his dissertation, and his gradual orienting toward entrepreneurship:

> We made some new discoveries at the institute and everything was very interesting and fun. We sat there all night, worked around the clock. But then the excitement started to wear off. There were no more new discoveries. We ran out of adrenaline and started thinking how to live further. At the same time the first personal computers appeared and we started to do programming. (...) I already had a family and kids whom I should provide for somehow. (...) How could a graduate from *matmekh* [mathematical-technical faculty] make a living, one who has studied mathematics, programming and other subjects related to exact sciences? (...) Automatically one starts thinking of information technology.
>
> (director, p22)

Though at face value this account resembles the starting phases of US firms established by study mates from major universities, the analogy is only superficial. For a US graduate careers in both the academy or in business were normal and customary options – though in both one had to face fierce competition. This was not the case in the Russia of the 1990s where academic careers seemed to have no future: one could not get by, let alone raise a family, based on the meager salaries in the academy. For one wishing to start a business, there were no models, business schools, institutions, or markets. One had to sink or swim.

A well-known example of the symbiosis between academic and business life in Russia is Lanit-Terkom,[4] one of the biggest software firms in St. Petersburg, which was established and is functioning in close connection with the St. Petersburg state university. Averin and Dudarev (2003: 55) describe the nature of this symbiosis:

> The company grew out of the System Programming Department (Mathematics and Mechanics Faculty) of the St. Petersburg State University, headed by the chief of department, Professor Andrey Terekhov. The utilization of the resources of the Mathematics and Mechanical Department gave the company an opportunity to use the knowledge and scientific background accumulated in the department during the decades of the Faculty's history. Moreover, the company has acquired a virtual monopoly over the highly qualified and talented staff – the teaching and research staff, as

well as the best graduates of the department. At the moment, there is no clear boundary between the educational organization and the private company. Almost all teaching staff of the System Programming Department work for the company. The most talented students of the department are engaged in the company's projects within the framework of practical research (included in the curriculum) starting from 2nd–3rd years of education. Such a symbiosis is gainful both for the company and the department. The latter receives financial support and the opportunity to place its students in a job. Lanit Tercom is able, in turn, to prepare qualified personnel and to use the renowned name of the department in its marketing policy.

This is just one example of the survival strategies based on a symbiosis between the academic and business worlds in the early years of Russian transformation. However, as will become evident in Chapter 6, in addition to academic or Komsomol background rooted in the Soviet era structures, a wide variety of other development paths for new software companies came to light in our data. One of them was illustrated by the 37-year-old CEO of a software company employing 80 people:

> There was a factory which had problems and invited me to consult them. I looked around and saw that they had both problems and money. We suggested that they would give up their old software and we would write them a new one. They agreed. We gathered a group of people and started a project. In the course of this project we understood that the project would grow bigger than our temporary group of people and we founded a company.
>
> (general director, p3)

Entrepreneurship and Soviet legacy

As for the *actors*, the term Soviet legacy is often evoked in connection with the continuing role of the 'Soviet mentality' in present-day Russia. The connotations of the Soviet legacy are mainly negative, such as lack of enterprise, sticking to old routines, strict hierarchies, and so forth.

Although in general the IT sector in post-Soviet Russia is thought to be the least affected by the Soviet legacy, one respondent remarked that the legacy indeed still had an impact on domestic markets because of the 'red directors' working with the Soviet mindset and methods of management in customer companies:

> When placing an order or making a deal there comes the moment of decision: to buy or not. Who buys, how and what. And then you will run straight into all these red directors.
>
> (general director, p3)

According to another respondent, the question of the Soviet mentality was connected to generations and was only relevant to those educated in the Soviet era, whereas the new post-socialist generation had new values and new problems:

> P4: Today there has grown a completely new generation which is already in business life. Currently I deal with people who are not solely working in IT firms. They have managers of my age, that is, around thirty. We all went to school in the Soviet era.
> Q: Do you have different values or do you work differently?
> P4: I don't know, it is difficult to talk about the others. I can only say that in my mind those around thirty–thirty-five still remember school well. Those who finished school in the beginning of the 1990s already have completely new values and they look at life in a completely different way. In my head, the Soviet legacy still remains.
>
> (general director, p4)

An example of the problems of transformation for the Soviet generation was learning how to behave in business. This knowledge consists of, for example, working routines and habits and is accumulated over time in organizations but is rarely put into writing (cf. Podolny and Baron 1997). These habitual ways of acting are thus usually not learned from books but typically by imitating or interacting with colleagues or a mentor, or simply by doing.

One of our respondents, who had worked for most of his career in the Soviet Union, emphasized – in addition to learning new habits – the *unlearning* of the Soviet routines and ways of acting when comparing himself with the 20-year-old CEO of a well-known software company:

> Q: There are things which are difficult to learn from books, which you can only learn through your own experience or by observing the experience of your older colleagues. For example, how to think in a new, innovative way, how to relate to people, how to conduct business. Have you had these kinds of cases?

P1: Continuously.

Q: Can you tell examples?

P1: You have to understand that I was born in 1951 [year of birth has been changed]. At that time you had not even been planned yet, probably not even your parents, but I was already crawling, and then grew up in the Soviet Union. My whole mentality is Soviet. Imagine how hard it was for me to change, how hard it was to transform whereas my colleagues, e.g. my colleague in the company NewComp [name of firm changed] is now around 30. Have you yet been to NewComp?

Q: No.

P1: Well, look. This guy is older than you, about thirty. He started his business right after having finished at the institute. For him this is completely different. Of course I keep an eye on him and my other competitors. They are my teachers. I watch how they conduct business, how they regard their colleagues, how they organize everything. And I try to apply this (...) For them it all came naturally, but I had to get rid of the birthmarks of socialism.

(general director, p1)

The same respondent illustrated the moral tension between socialist and capitalist mindsets with the dilemma caused by the installation of a new computerized system in his company to monitor workers:

For me it was very difficult to start [in the company] a computerized access control system, which records the time of arriving and leaving the workplace. Now I know who came later, who has not worked 40 hours a week. It was incredible, how difficult the implementation was for me. I felt as if I was being torn into pieces. What would the people think?

(general director, p1)

Various techniques of controlling and monitoring workers were certainly also used both in the Soviet Union and other industrialized countries. The quote above thus rather illustrates the difficulties in the transition from the position of 'scientific rank-and-file worker' to that of a capitalist company owner and CEO, and the problems and tensions in balancing between the moral requirements of two conflicting sociopolitical orders.

There is, however, also another way of looking at the Soviet mentality. The studies of daily life survival strategies (e.g. Lonkila 1997), *blat* networks (Ledeneva 1998), and the abovementioned research by Yurchak (2002, 2006) suggest that the allegedly passive *homo sovieticus* could in the interstices of the system find spaces and possibilities for complex and innovative maneuvers. In fact, navigating in the opportunity structures of the late socialist and perestroika era allows us 'to speak about entrepreneurship in a context in which there was no market based private business per se' (Yurchak 2002; see also Shmulyar Gréen 2009).

In a similar vein Alf Rehn and Saara Taalas (2004) claim that the students of entrepreneurship have a lesson to learn about Soviet society, where, due to an ideological bias in research, entrepreneurship was not considered to exist at all. The authors even go as far as to claim that 'The Union of Soviet Socialist Republics might be seen as the most entrepreneurial society ever' and maintain that the Soviet system basically forced all citizens to become 'micro-entrepreneurs' in everyday life. They detect entrepreneurship and risk taking in unexpected settings also outside the business and market contexts and consider the *blat* networks to have been the main arena for entrepreneurial activity in the Soviet Union (Rehn and Taalas 2004).[5] *Blat* networks in the Soviet Union and their transformation in post-Soviet Russia will be the focus of the next two sections.

Blat: Transformation of the Soviet-era networking practice

Blat denotes the Soviet habit of using personal relations to direct public resources to private uses.[6] There are no exact English translations, but expressions such as 'using connections', 'pulling strings', and so forth give a rough understanding of the contents of the term. In this section the *blat* system and its transformation in post-Soviet Russia are described both according to Ilja Srubar's comparative investigation as well as Alena Ledeneva's studies of *blat* (1998, 2008, 2009).

In his article on the actual nature of the socialist system, *War der reale Sozialismus moderne?* (Was the Real Socialism Modern?), Ilja Srubar (1991) presents an accurate theoretical description of the role of social networks in a socialist system. Though Srubar's analysis is based on comparison of studies of countries which made up the former Soviet bloc (not including the Soviet Union itself), the comparative aspect of the study strengthens the power of his argument. Srubar manages to show a similar kind of relationship between the socialist system and social networks in historically and culturally varied national contexts.

According to Srubar, the power monopoly of the Communist Party combined with the socialist shortage economy created a mechanism of social integration which was based on social networks and was specific to real socialist countries. In the shortage economy in addition to money the citizens also needed information about how and where to find goods in short supply. These goods and information were obtained through networks which developed into an alternative distribution system. Within the networks, an atmosphere of mutual solidarity emerged out of the reciprocal exchange relations, but it was limited to those who had something to barter, such as access to socialist property. These networks functioned parallel to the official system and were tolerated by the party since they compensated for the flaws of the shortage economy by diverting people's interests from politics to consumption. In addition, they functioned as a means of control since the party's tolerance for them could always be withdrawn.

While the shortage economy forced citizens to turn to their personal relations in order to get by, the party power monopoly produced a non-transparent state bureaucracy, the decisions of which could not be predicted by citizens. A position in this bureaucracy represented capital which could be traded through personal networks. This mechanism of social integration had a profound influence on the individual's social identity. Citizens in real socialism divided the world into the trustworthy 'us' – that is, one's personal network – and potentially hostile 'others.' Instead of general social solidarity, this integration mechanism produced fragmented solidarity within 'an archipelago of networks' and a worldview where moral norms applied to one's own circle were different from those applied to outsiders, for whom there was no moral way to success. A neighbor's wealth, for example, was attributed either to his political privileges or illegal activities in redistribution networks (Srubar 1991).

Parallel to Srubar, but independently of his research, Alena Ledeneva (1998, 2008, 2009, see also Lomnitz 1988) has studied *blat* in detail in the Soviet Union. Ledeneva bases her work on extensive field research and interviews filled with rich descriptions of the content, functioning, and practices of the *blat* ties.

Importantly for the themes of this book, Ledeneva defines *blat* precisely with the help of the notion of personal networks, as 'the use of personal networks for obtaining goods and services in short supply and for circumventing formal procedures. *Blat* networks channeled an alternative currency – an informal exchange of favors – that introduced elements of the market into the planned economy and loosened up the rigid constraints of the political regime' (Ledeneva 2009, 257–8).

However, though *blat* practices were conducted through personal networks, they were not identical, since the latter also had other functions, such as sociability. These functions were difficult to separate because '*blat* merged with patterns of sociability to such an extent that people were unable to distinguish between friendship and the use of friendship. The boundaries became particularly blurred as the exchanged favors were favors of a particular kind – "favors of access"' (Ledeneva 2009: 258).

Blat had an ambivalent character since on the one hand it was necessary for the functioning of the system, but on the other hand it undermined the system and corrupted common morals through its very existence. Though *blat* practices made use of state resources, the state was dependent on the informal ways of distributing the scarce resources. The informal ways could not be discussed publicly, which created a double morality in Soviet society:

> Thus *blat* became an open secret of Soviet socialism, well known but banned from political or academic discourse. The *blat* system of exchange was founded in the possibility of extending favors at the expense of state property. The dubious nature of state property and the repressive nature of the Soviet state contributed to pervasive practices of cheating and outwitting the state: *blat* and other forms of diverting state property, smuggling out (*vynos*), false reporting (*pripiski*), stealing, or absenteeism. These practices indicate not only the popular view of the Soviet state as parasitic, due to its highly exploitative nature, but also the mutual tolerance between the state and the citizens, especially in the Brezhnev era.
>
> (Ledeneva 2008: 123–4)

Ledeneva shows how the inability of the Soviet economy to produce enough goods and services of decent quality, such as food products, medicine, cars, apartments, and so forth, led to resorting to obtaining them 'by *blat*' (*po blatu*). The examples of *blat* practices abound: an acquaintance working at a warehouse could arrange access to goods in short supply 'under the counter', a contact in the army ranks could arrange for avoiding the two to three years of military service, a doctor acquaintance in the hospital could arrange jumping the queue for better treatment or an operation, and so on.

Blat contacts penetrated the whole Soviet society: their amount was large and scale wide, but the common denominator was the use of social ties in order to gain access to state property or services and to use them for the private purposes of one's own circle. Ledeneva (1998: 39–58) distinguished *blat* from its 'extended family', including bribery, corruption, second economy, and patronage. For example, the difference between *blat* and bribery or corruption was that the latter were based on straightforward deals involving buying services with money. Characteristic of the *blat* services, on the other hand, were the long-term cultivation of relationships, a special vocabulary, and a refined etiquette of behavior where the straightforward offering of money could be considered insulting. This meant, among other things, that *blat* practices could penetrate areas where use of money could not.

Ledeneva also discusses the differences between *blat* and the various notions of 'informal' (unofficial, second, hidden, parallel, shadow, etc.) economy. She concludes that *blat* cannot be adequately analyzed in terms of informal economic practices since it implies relations of reciprocity within personal networks, rather than market-type exchanges and activities oriented toward profit, on which informal economic practices are often based. In her mind, the study of *blat* requires a socio-cultural analysis of personal ties and their impact on *blat* exchanges.

Blat exchanges were based on reciprocal obligations. Ledeneva employs an idea borrowed from Pierre Bourdieu, according to whom the partners in a gift exchange take part in a collective 'misrecognition game.' In this game, the exchange of gifts can be perceived as altruistic only because of the time gap between the original gift and the countergift (see Chapter 7 for a closer account of reciprocal obligations).

Though Ledeneva's observations are in many ways extremely relevant to this study, the differences between *blat* exchanges and the exchanges dealt with in this book should be made clear. First, despite the misrecognition game, the *blat* system had in general a negative reputation: no Soviet citizen could have publicly admitted to having engaged in it. Partly because of this nature, asking a *blat* favor was often psychologically difficult (Ledeneva 1998: 156). This was not the case for our respondents with everyday exchanges of small favors, advice, helping out and so forth, most of which did not include a morally doubtful aspect. Second, and related to the previous point, *blat* transactions were about granting favor of access to state services or property, which were redirected to private use, whereas the majority of the favors and services dealt with in this book do not have that character.

Blat in post-Soviet Russia

In her later work, Ledeneva (2008) notes three major changes in *blat* practices. The first change concerns the expansion of the money economy, which has diminished the need for *blat* in personal consumption.

Second, the privatization of the economy has changed the nature of 'favors of access' granted by officials. Instead of exchanging favors of access to socialist property for access to another distribution system, in the 1990s these favors came to be about privatizing state resources and converting them into private capital through various licenses and permissions. These exchanges between the state and business sector often turned into outright corruption. Third, the scale of *blat* exchanges has started to predominantly serve business instead of personal consumption (Ledeneva 2008: 132–3).

However, Ledeneva admits that informal contacts still remained a priority where money was not accepted as a means of exchange (1998: 180), and notes that *blat* was still used in state education and employment (1998: 206). Anna-Maria Salmi (2006: 38–9) adds to this list health services and job searches, which still offer much space for *blat*-type activities.

Ledeneva's (2009) recent assessment of the role of *blat* in post-Soviet Russia in 2009 is in line with these results. With the progress of monetary relations, *blat* has lost its relevance in everyday consumption but is still significant in, for example, the labor market, health care, and education. In her national representative survey conducted by the Levada Center in 2007, she asked respondents to define *blat* by choosing as many prompts as necessary:

> 18 percent of respondents indicated that the term is out of use and five percent noted that the word *blatnoi* means criminal – that is, has returned to its original pre-revolutionary meaning. At least a quarter of respondents associated *blat* with an exchange of favors (22 percent) or best described by a proverb 'I scratch your back, you scratch mine' (*ty-mne, ia-tebe*) (15 percent). With regard to formal constraints, the responses were: 'circumvention of formal rules and procedures' (17 percent), 'problem solving' (12 percent), '*blat* is the necessity in order to give a bribe' (six percent) or gain access to administrative resources (four percent). Tellingly, only seven percent of respondents found it difficult to answer this question and there were respondents who offered their own definitions (including '*blat* is higher than under Stalin' and '*blat* is a leftover of socialism' (*izderzhki sotsializma*) as well as '*blat* is the corrupt system, the whole industry' and '*blat* is life'.
>
> (Ledeneva 2009: 262)

Whatever the exact definition, *blat* still seems to have a central place in post-Soviet society since 66 percent of Ledeneva's respondents considered it either widespread (28 percent) or rather widespread (38 percent) in their own city or region.

In the following text the post-Soviet *blat* is illustrated by our interviews. Due to the nature of our data and methods, these illustrations are not claimed to be generalizable. At the end of this chapter their relevance will be evaluated through comparison with other studies of the topic.

The description by a St. Petersburg IT manager of the vanishing of *blat* practices seems to lend support to Ledeneva's conclusions. According to the respondent, the pressure of efficiency in capitalist enterprise does not leave room for *blat* in present-day Russia:

P1: In socialism, a person working as a butcher can get a carcass of an animal. Another person drives a taxi. A third one is a doctor and can obtain medical services. The butcher cuts the best pieces off the carcass and sells them at a normal state regulated price to the taxi driver or doctor. (...) And the bones he brings to the shop and sells to us engineers (...) Now, if the butcher needs to go someplace by car, he phones the taxi driver who drives him from one place to another. And the doctor will take care of him.

Q: And how does this work today?

P1: Today you go to the shop and buy. Anything is for sale.

Q: So where is there *blat* today?

P1: I told you an example of Soviet *blat*. Today it works on the level of old relations. But I believe it will soon disappear. Slowly *blat* will disappear.

Q: For example, in IT, in outsourcing there is almost no *blat*?

P1: In practice not. IT functions as other sectors. I can for example, appoint my brother as a manager in my firm. And he will turn out to be a good for nothing, he can do nothing. What will my colleagues say? We are trying to make money, what will they say?

(general director, p1)

Parts of this quote were questioned by other respondents, however. Though IT companies working with foreign customers were generally considered *blat* free, they too had to deal with *blat*-type phenomena if also operating on domestic markets. Moreover, in certain cases *blat*-type arrangements may be used either as an alternative to or in combination with bribing.

The interpretation of the term *blat* seemed to be connected to the age of the respondents. While elderly respondents, such as the one describing the *blat* relations among the butcher, taxi driver and doctor, considered *blat* in line with Ledeneva's account, marketing manager Valentina (p15), who was under 30 years of age, regarded *blat* as a synonym for the informal use of social relations in general. According to development manager Viktor (p17, 33 years) '*blat* is not so relevant for young people. Many of them do not know, cannot imagine what *blat* means.' The hesitation of still another of our respondents, a director under 30 years of age, lends support to this:

> *Blat* – it is a tough word. If you define it formally ... how would you define it formally?
>
> (director, p10)

Varied opinions were expressed about the existence, nature, and specificity of post-Soviet *blat*. A director-owner of his own company, aged 50 (CEO, p16) – who thus had his own experiences of Soviet *blat* – compared *blat* to 'protection.' A technical director under 30 (p11) saw *blat* as a Russian version of a universal way of acting that is not inherently immoral.

Despite these variations, a common view was that *blat* still exists in the public sector and big state-owned companies. In particular tenders organized by the state-related actors were considered to be impossible to win without *blat*, bribes, or both. The founder of a young and small company expressed this explicitly:

> We [respondent's firm] probably have not yet reached the level where you participate in tenders, but I know that they are indeed won by those who have acquaintances. If, for example, the five leading firms of my field try as hard as they can, the tender will be won by those with connections anyway.
>
> (technical director, p20)

Another respondent doing business with state structures refused to answer this question ('confidential'), but the third respondent, working in system integration, confirms the quote above:

> In fact, in some market segments it [*blat*] definitely exists. This was particularly visible in system integration which is closely related to the state purchases. It is practically impossible to win a tender without corresponding connections, friends, acquaintances, kinfolk. But this is actually no secret. I am not revealing any secret.
>
> (marketing manager, p18)

When asked about concrete examples of present-day *blat*, in addition to state structures, employment by *blat* was mentioned. Marketing director Svetlana (p6) also referred to the arranging of study places by *blat* – a phenomenon about which there are a lot of rumors and anecdotal evidence from both the Soviet Union and post-Soviet Russia:

> Q: In the Soviet era *blat* relations were still used. Do they still function, does *blat* exist nowadays?
> P4: In state structures it stays as it was. In my opinion there is no doubt about this. But in business – this is a complex question. It is clear that parents try to push their children forward through all means. This is a normal parental instinct, and here *blat* functions. Another matter is that it functions precisely as an exchange of favors. I have an example in mind, where a big boss arranged for his children to work in different companies. With this it happens often that the child does not correspond to the requirements presented by the companies. But the child was employed precisely because dad had given in one way or another a favor to this company. And so this happened in full scale. As for business, I think that in big companies this also functions, but not in small ones. Here I doubt it.
> Q: Why?
> P4: In small companies people are visible (*na vidu*), everything is counted and the budget is small. If a small company has to employ someone to win a state organized tender, this causes a financial calculation: How much do we lose by employing this kid and how much do we win by getting this order.
>
> (general director, p4)

In all, despite the significant changes compared to Soviet-era *blat*, the present-day Russian society and economy still seem to leave room for informal practices more or less reminiscent of *blat*. Even though these practices may be neither as pervasive nor culturally specific as in the Soviet Union, they still continue to exist, particularly in the public sector and state-controlled parts of the economy.

Barter: A transitory phenomenon of exchange

Where *blat* was mainly a phenomenon of the Soviet system, barter (non-monetary exchange between companies) peaked in the late 1990s (see Figure 4.1).[7] Barter will be briefly described here as an example of informal socioeconomic practices of the transition era based on personal connections. According to Caroline Humphrey (2000a), post-Soviet barter was a unique phenomenon on the global scale, since never before had an economy as big as Russia's operated to a large extent through barter.

Though barter exchanges took place in the Soviet Union as well, according to David Woodruff (1999), the 'barter of the bankrupt' of the transition era was a qualitatively different phenomenon with new causes and new consequences. In his mind the new barter was not only an anomaly threatening the implementation of the market reforms, but also a sign of how the reformers had neglected the central role of monetary consolidation in state building.

According to Ivanenko and Mikheyev (2002; see also Clarke 2000: 178–9), in the background of barter there were the structural weaknesses and bottlenecks of the socialist system. The Soviet economy had built a massive industrial production system which was connected to an inflexible and one-sided distribution, trade, and banking network. Big production plants, for example, were planned to serve certain customers and get raw material from certain producers. When one part of the logistic chain saw trouble, this was reflected in the whole chain:

> For example, as steel producers in the Ural region found the demand for their products falling, they became unable to pay suppliers in cash and offered metal products for coal. The coal mines, being unable to find alternative customers along the existing transport lines, had to agree.

(Ivanenko and Mihkeyev 2002: 411)

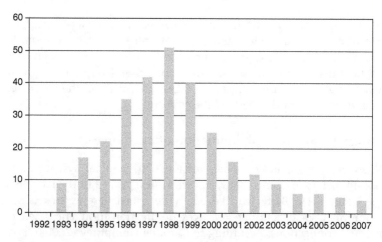

Figure 4.1 The share of *barter* in Russian industrial sales, 1992–2007, %

In addition to leading to barter between companies, the demonetization of the post-Soviet Russian economy in the 1990s also affected households, since some salaries were paid in non-monetary forms (see Clarke 2000: 189–94). Because the retail trade and provision of consumer services were, however, mainly monetary, individual households had to react to the new situations either by lowering their standard of living (Clarke 2000) or by selling the goods received at the workplace on streets and highways or in marketplaces.

It is not our intention to review the large research literature on barter here (see for example Seabright 2000a; Ivanenko and Mikheyev 2002; Woodruff 2000). It suffices to say that barter was not only an economic but also a *social* phenomenon operating through social relations (Seabright 2000b: 8). Consequently, the studies most relevant for this book are those analyzing the dynamics of barter on the micro level (Humphrey 2000a, b; Ledeneva 2000, 2006; Clarke 2000).

Though barter took place between companies and organizations, the practical deals were handled by individuals, and the barter arrangements and exchange chains were often built upon complex chains of exchanging parties (Ledeneva 2000: 298–317, 2006: 115–41). These arrangements were partly founded upon already existing networks, and partly they created new relationships balancing between trust and coercion (Humphrey 2000a, b). Most importantly, the majority of the barter deals were not conducted directly between the exchanging firms but through middlemen (Ledeneva 2006: 125).

In actual fact this means that the Russian economy in the 1990s formed an immense network consisting of the companies (and their workers who were paid in kind) and the middlemen mediating the exchanges. These networks, on the base of which Russia's current form of capitalism was partly built, relied on personal contacts:

> [G]ood personal contacts are vital for making the offsets agreed upon between the parties, for designing schemes, and for making these schemes work. Negotiation skills may help to acquire weak links for the schemes – partners engaged on a rather short-term basis – but it is personal contacts that provide strong links in these schemes, those characterized by absolute trust or long-term technological partnership.
>
> (Ledeneva 2006: 138–9)

In their criticism of the presuppositions of the transition debate, Michael Burawoy and Katherine Verdery (1999b) have stated that in spite of a linear transition from socialism to a market economy, development in Russia will most probably be an uneven development of different sectors of society with occasional 'backlashes'. Though barter will hardly reach the prevalence of the 1990s again, there have been some signs of the return of barter practices on a smaller scale after the beginning of the economic crisis in 2008. Belchenko (2008), for example, describes how certain companies in the Krasnoyarsk region in the beginning of December 2008 paid their workers' salaries in the company's products instead of money.[8]

Otkat: The role of 'kickbacks' in the Russian economy

While *blat* was mainly a Soviet era phenomenon, barter peaked at the end of the 1990s, after which it slowly disappeared. Instead of *blat* and barter, many of our respondents mentioned the rise of *otkat*, an expression for a post-Soviet form of corruption. It roughly corresponds to the English word 'kickback' and, as the Russian discussants are eager to note, is not a particularity of the Russian economy: the first 'Anti-Kickback Act' was passed in the US already in 1946 and was amended in 1960, 1986, and 1994 (Denisov 2005).[9]

Otkat is a noun from the verb *otkatit'* (roll away, roll back). In actual terms it means that a company participating in a public tender promises to 'roll back' a certain amount of the contract sum to the organizers of the tender. *Otkat* is therefore a form of corruption that is not specific only to Russia, and there is no reason to believe that foreign firms operating in Russia would not use *otkat*. What seems to be particular however – concluding from our interviews, the views of Russian observers (e.g. Denisov 2005; Gorbachev 2007) and other information about corrupted practices in Russia – is the prevalence of *otkat* in Russian business.

This prevalence is in line with the general information on corrupted practices in the Russian economy and society, and its actual practices are spiritedly debated both in Russian journals and on Internet forums. Giving *otkat* is often euphemized as 'personal bonus' or 'discount', and the negotiations concerning the deal may be conducted using language which at every point in time could be interpreted as referring either to a completely transparent and legal deal or a kickback agreement:

> In the beginning of the discussion it is very good to test the waters with the potential recipient of *otkat* with the phrases with double meaning: 'For you it will be very profitable (*vygodno*) to deal with

our company', 'we are ready to make concessions (*poiti navstrechu*) so that you would choose our company', 'a reduction may be arranged in any form convenient (*udobno*) for you'.

(Gorbachev 2007)

During such conversation the rich Russian language gives plenty of opportunities to interpret the word 'you' as 'you personally' instead of 'your company', and the well-reflected pauses of speech, change of intonation or tone give an impression of the hidden message behind what is meant to be a transparent deal between the representatives of the two parties, and give the opponent chances to express understanding of this message (Gorbachev 2007).

Though *otkat* is not a big problem in the IT companies operating mainly in foreign markets, many respondents mentioned it in discussions about the transformation of *blat* in post-Soviet Russia and Russian domestic markets:

Q: Sometimes in the Soviet era *blat* relations were used. Does this still function?
P9: It only turned into corruption. Of course it functions.
Q: Have you run into some examples?
P9: Not personally, because I work with foreign business and there this does not exist in general. But in Russia – of course. I don't think you will find a line of business which functions without *otkat* and all this.

(director, p9)

Otkat was taken up by several respondents in connection with tenders which, according to the respondents, were won either through relations or *otkat*, or both. According to another respondent (director, p29) who had worked with Russian companies on domestic markets for a long time, tenders are rarely won based on 'objective' criteria, but with connections and, lacking connections, by *otkat*. At the moment his firm did not participate in tender, considering it a waste of time and resources because the result was predestined:

The firm will do a huge amount of preparation, but the tender will be won by a crazy proposal only because of connections.

(director, p29)

Another respondent, a technical director working with big companies, told openly of the various forms of *otkat*, claiming that in practice all state officials (*chinovniki*) take bribes, and still another admitted that his firm had been involved in *otkat.*

Obtaining reliable information about the prevalence of *otkat* (or *blat* or barter) is understandably hampered by the several problems related to data and methods. One necessarily simplistic and limited way of approaching the subject is to examine the prevalence of these terms in the Russian media. Figure 4.2 is based on a scrutiny of selected Russian newspapers and magazines published in 1992–2007 and stored in the Integrum database. It shows how in the texts of central Russian newspapers and magazines the term *otkat* has become more common during the 2000s while the use of barter and *blat* has diminished (see Figure 4.2).[10]

Though the frequency of these terms in the media is not in direct correspondence with the occurrence of the phenomena in Russian society, it is noteworthy that the estimate of the peak of barter in Figure 4.1 is quite similar to the frequency of the term in printed media in Figure 4.2.

The pervasiveness of corruption in Russia has also been addressed by Russian presidents – up to now without results. The latest data by Transparency International's Corruption Perceptions Index[11] indicate a fall in Russia's ranking from 121 in 2006 to 143 in 2007, and to 147 in 2008, while in 2008 the US was eighteenth, the UK sixteenth and Finland fifth (see Figure 4.3).

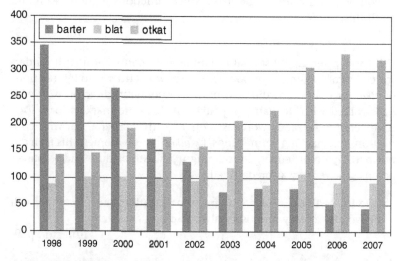

Figure 4.2 The frequency of use of the terms *blat, barter* and *otkat* in selected Russian newspapers 1998–2007

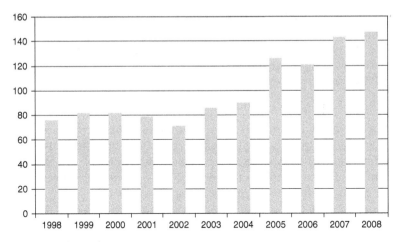

Figure 4.3 Ranking of Russia in Transparency International's Corruption Perception Index

Figure 4.3 shows the deterioration of Russia's ranking during the 2000s despite the anticorruption speeches and campaigns. Russia's closest neighbors in the index in 1997 were Pakistan and Columbia and in 2008 Indonesia and Togo.

The aim of this study is not the analysis of corruption in Russia. Therefore the processes and structures at the base of the corruption index rankings will not be investigated in detail (see, e.g. Lovell et al. 2001). However, even without a detailed analysis one may draw the conclusion that Yeltsin, Putin, and Medvedev have not succeeded in weeding out wide-scale corruption, which seems to be a systemic characteristic of the society and economy, from Russia.

The referrals to corruption and illegal or ambiguous practices in the interviews were mostly related to dealing with state structures. Understandably, most respondents did not clarify these things to the interviewer either because of unwillingness or because they were not responsible for communicating with these structures within their companies. The following interview quote shows how a question not originally meant to refer only to state structures was interpreted as such by the respondent and how the native Russian interviewer read between the lines of the respondent's reply:

Q: Have you sometime been in situations in business, where you could not solve the problem in a formal way and you had to lean on some informal relations, contacts?

P20: Again here it is a question related to state structures. I do not know how this all goes, I do not deal with these things.

Q: Do you mean bribes? OK, it is not a secret to anyone, what there ... Is this related to accounting?

P20: No, not to accounting. I will not answer this question.

(technical director, p20)

One of the few respondents who overtly told of illegal practices such as tax evasion was working in a small company employing only a few people and in a field representing a small fraction of the ICT sector.[12] In his field one did not, in the early 2000s, work on written contracts but on the basis of 'gentlemen's agreements', because 'practically all money goes over the taxman's head'. According to the respondent probably one ruble out of 20 was reported to the taxman in falsified official contracts, the monitoring of which was based on social control and the reputations of actors within the small and specialized markets. Another respondent lent support to this view, stressing the similarity of the business environment for all Russian companies:

[I]n general, companies work in a similar manner, which is defined by the legal environment. The legislation of the Russian federation contains directly both the juridical and financial aspects: taxes, banks and so forth. And I know that up to this day all firms work by and large according to the same model. There are very few firms that pay full taxes.

(general director, p4)

According to still another respondent (general director, p48) working in telecommunications it is not a secret that most of the telecommunications technology sold in St. Petersburg is 'gray', that is, not imported according to legal customs regulations.

Because of the particular nature of the software design sector (relatively small turnover, large share of human and educational capital, orientation abroad), extortion and other forms of organized crime did not emerge as important issues in the interviews. A programming company is less vulnerable to extortion or takeover by criminal groups than, say, a distribution chain of food products. However, particularly in the 1990s, keeping a low profile was considered to be a precaution against these practices, and probably also against the taxman:

Until 1999 our company was not visible anywhere (...) But the level of criminality was at that time much higher than today – thank

God. And we did not want to be seen, to be known of or heard of here.

(general director, p1)

Things were different in the hardware business. Technical director Kirill (p38) remembered a meeting among Russian ICT companies at the beginning of the 2000s. A merry group of software designers was approached by an entrepreneur in the hardware business, who smiling sadly told the entrepreneurs 'How well things are with you, nobody beats up or kills anyone'. (*Nu, kak u vas khorosho, nikto nikogo ne izbivaet, nikto nikogo ne ubivaet.*)

Other informal practices in the post-Soviet Russian economy

In her book *How Russia Really Works. The Informal Practices That Shaped Post-Soviet Politics and Business* (2006) Alena Ledeneva extends her studies of *blat* to other forms of informal practices in post-Soviet Russia which have gained ground parallel to *blat* losing its central role. She defines informal practices 'as people's regular strategies to manipulate or exploit formal rules by enforcing informal norms and personal obligation in formal contexts. Such strategies involve bending both formal rules and informal norms, or navigating between these constraints, by following some and breaking others' (Ledeneva 2008: 119, 2006).

The informal practices include, in addition to the barter dealt with earlier in this book, the use of 'black PR' and *kompromat* (gathering and fabricating blackmail files for political or business purposes), the principle of *krugovaia poruka* (joint responsibility and mutual obligations of a closed social circle), double accountancy, financial scheming, and alternative law enforcement. As with *blat*, the nature of these practices is considered ambivalent, both reproducing *and* undermining the post-Soviet society and economy:

> I argue that informal practices were an integral part of the post-socialist transformation. Informal practices adjusted to and were shaped by formal and informal constraints: they supported formal rules and informal norms but also subverted them; they rapidly accommodated legal changes but also created an obstacle to further change; they were beneficial for certain individuals but also made them hostages of the system. These practices were not simply illegal but integrated the law into political, media, and business

technologies, often manipulatively. Similarly, they did not simply follow or contradict informal norms but relied on some of them and played one set of norms against the other.

(Ledeneva 2006: 190)

Ledeneva's illuminative case studies describe, among other things, different types of sanctions as part of the informal practices:

> The first area encompasses a set of administrative sanctions, that can be organized through well-placed links to official structures such as regional administrations, the tax inspectorate, tax police, the fire department, and the departments of sanitation and public health. It is possible to arrange for a firm's access to water, gas, electricity, and sewers to be cut off by the regional authorities on the pretext of arrears. These techniques have been practiced widely and remain one of the most common ways of neutralizing opponents.
>
> (Ledeneva 2006: 172–3)

Another example of informal practices presented by Ledeneva is the possibility of influencing official investigations and judicial proceedings in Russia. Law cases and investigations can be opened or closed by influencing judges, prosecutors, or police, and if unfavorable judgments are passed, their enforcement can be prevented (Ledeneva 2006: 174).

Informal practices are conducted both in politics and business – and at the intersection of the two spheres. Ledeneva cites a case published in *Kommersant* in 2001 where as part of an anti-black PR action a St. Petersburg agency offered money for 21 press outlets to publish commercial disinformation (a nonexistent company opening a nonexistent shop at a nonexistent address) as an editorial form rather than as a paid advertisement. As a result, 13 outlets agreed to publish this information as an article for prepayment, three recommended to publish it as advertising, four wanted additional information and one published it for free (Ledeneva 2006: 35, citing Kadik and Pyanykh 2001).

Ledeneva's examples of *kompromat* contain, among others, cases of Russian businessmen's and politicians' suspicious political activities (abuse of office and power); shady and often illegal economic activities (e.g. misuse of budget funds, capital flight, giving or accepting of bribes); criminal activities (contract killings), and compromising details of private life (spending habits, sexual orientation) (Ledeneva 2006: 58–90).

Krugovaia poruka refers to 'a pattern in behavior or relationship according to which a person is part of a bigger social unit (a group, network, family, or clan) rather than an isolated human being driven by self-interest. Such a social unit is "tied up" by joint responsibility and mutual obligations' (Ledeneva 2006: 90). The genealogy of *krugovaia poruka* has long roots in both prerevolutionary Russian and Soviet history and its forms have been continuously changing and adapting to the new circumstances. In post-Soviet Russia the principle of *krugovaia poruka* can be found both in politics and business, often connecting the two spheres as with the 'Mabetex case' against Pavel Borodin, the Kremlin property chief, whose bailing out of Swiss prison was considered to be due to his inside knowledge of Kremlin affairs reaching up to Yeltsin and his inner circle (Ledeneva 2006: 107).

Similar to *blat*, *krugovaia poruka* overlaps with the use of personal networks, but is not identical to it. It underlines that in Russian political culture:

–The individual is viewed as a part of a bigger system (such as a circle of *svoi liudi* [one's own people] or a network of interests) rather than isolated and working for oneself
– Individuals are encouraged to seek protection and to repay favors.
– Long-term relationships are kept and nurtured, thus creating mutual dependency rather than operating on the basis of short-term individual gain.
– Governance is by flexible ethical standards rather than by the strict rule of law.

(Ledeneva 2006: 113)

Ledeneva also offers a detailed account of a variety of financial scheming related to double invoicing, capital flight, tax evasion, or tax avoidance which the participants see as necessary survival strategies for protecting themselves against turbulent and changing institutional environments, corrupted authorities, and the arbitrariness of the tax inspection. On the systemic level the financial schemes, however, create a vicious cycle, undermining formal institutions and decreasing their effectiveness (Ledeneva 2006: 161).

Prevalence of criminal practices in the Russian economy

Does the long list of informal practices referred to in this chapter imply that the Russian economy is completely dominated by illegal practices or run by dubious, half-criminal groups? Due to its qualitative nature, this study cannot answer the question of the prevalence of illegal and informal practices in the Russian economy. However, the interviews suggest that most prone to corruption, *otkat* and other informal practices are the IT firms dealing with the hardware trade and those doing business with state-owned or state-controlled sectors.

These conclusions are supported by Chachin (2008), who cites a report by the Commission of Telecommunications and Information Technology of the Russian Union of Industrialists and Entrepreneurs. According to the Commission, the state has not been able to monitor the observation of customs and tax regulations. Therefore the majority of Russian IT imports are effectuated by 'gray schemes':

> [A]voiding value-added taxes and customs (...) leads to the offering of 'gray' IT products to markets 30–35 percent cheaper than is possible for entrepreneurs who pay full taxes and customs. As a consequence all Russian and foreign firms working in Russia are forced to play by the rules, with which many disagree, but which they have to follow.
>
> (Chachin 2008)

Moreover, the commission notes how the equal level of social security payments in all fields of industry particularly hampers the competitiveness of the labor-intensive IT sector, forcing Russian IT firms to use 'gray' schemes of payment. This distorts the accounting and makes Russian firms 'untransparent' to foreign investors.

The role of illegal and criminal aspects of the Russian economy have been also analyzed by Vadim Volkov (2002) who has proposed an interpretation stressing the civilizing effect of capitalism on organized crime in post-Soviet Russia. Volkov does not deal with organized crime as a deviant phenomenon, but sees it instead from a neoinstitutionalist perspective as a response to the requirements of the emerging Russian markets. For him, organized Russian crime was not a rampage of bloodthirsty killers, but the organization and commodification of violence by the 'violent entrepreneurs' – often called 'Russian mafia' by other writers.

According to Volkov's theory, the Russian state in the 1990s was fragmented and weak. It had lost both the fiscal monopoly and the monopoly of force, and could not secure the property rights or other needs of the emerging Russian economy. The splitting of the KGB into five separate agencies by Yeltsin's government in order to diminish the power of Soviet structures led unintentionally to the birth of protection markets in Russia. A great number of unemployed state security officers from the power structures (*silovye struktury*, e.g. security services, interior, and defense ministry) moved to the newly established private security agencies.

These 'violence-managing agencies' such as criminal groups, private protection companies, and police and security forces acting as private entrepreneurs took over many of the functions of the unstable Russian state and, therefore, were an inherent part of post-Soviet Russian state-building. For a beginner businessman, they were a more effective option for settling disputes than turning to the state.

The tightening of competition in the protection business created new informal rules in the turmoil. Some criminal groups were pushed out of the markets, but many were integrated into the local economies and politics. Former criminal leaders became managing directors, who employed public relations consultants to polish their public image. Stabilization of the environment made resorting to violence unprofitable and offered the Russian state a chance to regain the monopoly of force that it had lost under Yeltsin's rule. Ultimately, the violent entrepreneurs paved the way for Putin's government and the strengthening of the Russian state in the 2000s.

In short, according to Volkov, organized crime did not capture the Russian state but participated – without being conscious of it – in the creation of an order within chaos. Thereby the violent entrepreneurs were actors in the state-building process of post-Soviet Russia, during which they were transformed from thugs into economic actors.

All in all, while Volkov's (2002) work stresses the civilizing effect of the markets, Ledeneva (2006) paints a darker picture of contemporary Russian business life. According to her, 'every legal firm or structure is forced (in order to preserve itself) to engage in underground financial scheming, usually having to do with its ownership structure, concealed profits, and multiple accounting systems' (Ledeneva 2006: 160).

A mediating view between Volkov and Ledeneva, though closer to the latter, was offered by a St. Petersburg businessman from whom I asked at the end of 2006 if it is possible to conduct business strictly according to the laws and other official regulations. The reply was 'it is complex, but possible' (*slozhno, no mozhno*).

Both Ledeneva's (2006) and Volkov's (2002) studies deal mainly with the 1990s, and the development during the Putin–Medvedev era requires new empirical research. For the purposes of this book it is important to note that neither *blat*, nor barter, nor corruption debates are the whole truth about the role of social networks in the Soviet Union or today's Russia. The various ways of networking find themselves rather on a continuum ranging from illegal or immoral to completely legal and moral ways of action. It is the latter that the remaining chapters of this book will discuss.

5
Social Milieus and Personal Network Growth in the St. Petersburg IT Industry

Sociologist Michael Eve (1998) has remarked that personal networks do not extend haphazardly, but follow socially probable routes. New acquaintances are less likely to be made with previously unknown people on the street, but rather by spending time with people in the same social milieus frequently or for longer periods.[1] These social milieus include, among others, family and kin, neighborhood, school, university, workplace, and hobbies and leisure. A common milieu allows not only for making acquaintances but also for monitoring the character of a new acquaintance, which in the long run may help to create trust and develop the relationship into a more intimate one.[2]

Scott Feld (1981) refers to these milieus as 'foci of interaction', and defines a focus 'as a social, psychological, legal, or physical entity around which joint activities are organized (e.g. workplaces, voluntary organizations, hangouts, families, etc.)'. According to him, without contextual information concerning foci, conclusions about networks tend to be misleading (Feld 1981: 1016; see also Castrén 2000).

Schools and universities

In addition to the workplace, two of the central milieus for forming networks for St. Petersburg IT professionals were schools and universities. The school system of the Soviet Union/Russia and Leningrad/ St. Petersburg contained special schools whose curriculum had a strong emphasis on mathematics or physics. These special schools which carry numbers (instead of names, for example, schools no. 30, 45, and 239) are commonly known and enjoy high reputations within the city. Among the graduates from these schools are internationally well-known mathematicians, such as Grigory Perelman, a graduate from school no. 239, who won the gold medal in the International Mathematical Olympiad at the age of 16 in 1982. In 2006 Perelman was granted the Fields Medal, which is considered to be the Nobel Prize of mathematics.[3]

At the special schools, the pupils were united not only because of their mathematical talents but also due to the feeling of belonging to a group of the selected and special. Moreover, the teacher–pupil relationships which even in a common Russian school have a tendency to become closer and stronger than in the West (Lonkila 1998) could be maintained even after graduation. One of the respondents remembered his own teacher at school no. 30:

> Everyone loved very much our math teacher, who had worked at several math schools. A circle of former graduates gathered around him, went to congratulate him on his birthday, and got to know each other.
>
> (technical director, p38)

The peer pressure of the mathematically talented pupils led to a competitive study environment, where some of the pupils would voluntarily spend part of their summer holidays at a training camp studying mathematics while their counterparts in common schools were spending the summer at the beach or *dacha*. This kind of environment also nourished the formation of networks, which were later utilized in working life and maintained through annual meetings and/or through social networking sites and Internet forums created for keeping in touch with one's classmates.[4]

One of our respondents moved from a common school near her home to a special school which increased her daily commute to one-and-a-half hours. However, in retrospect she does not regret this move, since it not only gave her a brilliant study environment with other talented pupils, but also extended her networks geographically.

> If I had stayed studying at the local school (*v raionnoi shkole*), it would have been quite a small world (...). [Because of the studies in a special school] I know the whole city and I have friends all over the country. Many kinds of people gather in these elite schools.
>
> (programmer, p36)

For the graduates from the special schools, the natural path of studies led to some of the technical universities in Leningrad/St. Petersburg. The abovementioned respondent – who due to having received the highest possible grade in all subjects was awarded the gold medal of her school – describes the intertwining of the school and university networks in the following manner:

> P36: On Saturday I will go to the meeting of the graduates to socialize (*poobshchat'sia*). We keep in touch very closely (*my obshchaemsia ochen' tesno*). My classmate [from school] used to work with me in the firm but now she has left. (…) I keep in touch closely (*ya ochen' tesno obshchaius'*) with guys from other [university] faculties, some of them are my classmates [from school], some of them I know from common trips, some just appeared I don't know where from. But there are four–five people from the University with whom I keep in touch continuously.
> Q: Did many of your classmates enter the same university? Almost all of them?
> P36: My classmates entered the university but in a different faculty. One of my classmates entered the same university faculty with me. But ten guys went to *matmekh* [mathematical-mechanical faculty]. Of my parallel class (…) only two went elsewhere, but the other twelve came to our faculty.
>
> (programmer, p36)

As a Soviet legacy and because of the needs of the military-industrial complex, St. Petersburg hosts a great number of mathematical and technical universities which not only prepare employees for IT companies but also serve as platforms for forming networks both among the students and between students and teachers.[5] Several software programming firms originated from these milieus, and some were even established within the university infrastructure, keeping in close touch with their *alma mater* (e.g. company director, p31).

The special St. Petersburg mathematical schools, as similar elite schools in the West, created dense and lasting peer networks based on the sense of being chosen ones, in addition to giving a competitive education. One middle-aged IT manager told of having landed a job in several projects because the recruiting persons happened to be graduates of the same special school he had attended.

The graduates of one of the most prestigious special schools in St. Petersburg, the physical-mathematical lyceum no. 30, for example, have organized websites, groups, and communities for keeping in touch with study mates through the Internet. In addition to several individual pages programmed and maintained by individuals, the graduates of the school have founded a group in the virtual community LiveJournal, and another group on one of the most popular Russian social network sites, *VKontakte* ('In Contact') meant for 'all who have studied, study or will study' at this lyceum. The group had 2661 members in August 2009, and in its news column it turned to a fund supported by graduates living abroad to organize, for the ninth time in a row, a collection of gifts for the lyceum teachers.[6] The graduates of the year 2008 (and most likely of the other years) have similarly organized their own *VKontakte* group which is closed to outsiders.

One respondent, speaking of the special role of the networks, referred to the Leningrad academic elite as a 'caste' (*kasta*). There were several researchers and professors among the parents, grandparents, and other relatives of this respondent, whose encouragement led the mathematically gifted son first to a well-known special school and then to the technical university. The networks of family and kin were of great benefit in his university studies:

> When the department of computer sciences [name of the department has been changed], where I wanted to get in, was opened, one of the employees was our family friend (...) These kinds of acquaintances certainly played a role in my entrance and made studies easier.
>
> (director, p22)[7]

Likewise, Kirill (technical director, p38) commented that his career in the academic and research world was much easier because of the help from his kin, despite the fact that he had already shown special giftedness in mathematics at school.

The importance of special schools and universities as the platforms of network growth and start-up companies is a well-known phenomenon in other countries. However, the case of Leningrad/St. Petersburg is different from similar kinds of network dynamics in, for example, the US, due to the specific Russian constraints on geographical mobility which are likely to result in the formation of more locally anchored networks.

The historical background for the specificity of geographical mobility was the Soviet passport system, which tried to regulate internal migration in the country for the purposes of the planned economy. To settle in Leningrad a migrant needed a *propiska*, residence registration, without which one could not get a permanent job. In Soviet times, both the vivid cultural milieu and the better availability of consumer goods in Leningrad were extremely appealing to those living in the countryside or smaller villages. For them, a Leningrad *propiska* was an attractive but hard-to-get document, and different legal and illegal ways to get it, such as false marriages, were used (cf. Lonkila and Salmi 2005).

Being a Leningrader was a sign of special status in Soviet times, and the unique history and character of the city of Leningrad/St. Petersburg is also a classic theme in Russian and Soviet literature. Today, the appeal of St. Petersburg and Moscow is still likely to influence the migration decisions of Russians: whereas a Russian IT professional living in Moscow or St. Petersburg is unlikely to move to the provincial Russian towns, those from the smaller cities often head for the two Russian metropolises striving for employment as well as entertainment and cultural opportunities. One of the migrant respondents explained his decision to move to St. Petersburg from his provincial Siberian town with one million inhabitants:

> To found a company there would have been much more difficult than here. In addition, there is a time difference of plus four hours which would have been a problem. (...) We [Russians] basically only have two important cities, Moscow and Piter [nickname for St. Petersburg]. Then there are of course smaller cities like Nizhny Novgorod, Novosibirsk, naturally, Omsk, well, centres with decent education. But the advantage of Piter is that in addition to education, there are companies in which a programmer can become a professional. If in the city you'd have only one professional software developing firm, where would a programmer gain experience?
>
> (director, p35)

In his comparison of Moscow and St. Petersburg, another director of a small company in the telecommunications sector – himself a native of St. Petersburg – even invoked the tension and competition between the two cities that has long roots in Russian history and culture:

> In relation to Moscow, there is less money [in St. Petersburg] and everything is simpler. But on the other hand, I cannot say that the Moscow companies that will come to our market will get the cream of the crop. This is not the case and it has to do with the Peterburgians' dislike of Moscovians. If you have two [identical] offers on the table, one from a St. Petersburg company and another from Moscow, there is an inner negative attitude towards Moscovians. It exists and often you can use it, it works.
>
> (company director, p47)

The relatively little willingness to leave St. Petersburg (except to go abroad or to Moscow) combined with the great mobility of employees *within* the city led to the network formation where the central actors of the IT field, at least within the same specialized sector, are likely to know each other at least by reputation:

> Piter is a small city. IT specialists do not form that big of a stratum. If someone changes a job two–three times, he already knows about half of all the specialists by name.

(director, p39)

Many of the networks of the special schools and top university graduates have foreign extensions due to the 'brain drain' after the fall of the Soviet Union. In the early 1990s, an academic career in Russia was seen as a dead end. With the crash of the Soviet economy, a great number of research institutes formerly dependent on military orders fell apart. The academic world suffered from the crisis of the public sector, and the nominal salaries of teachers and researchers – if they were paid at all – did not provide a decent living. Consequently, emigration came to be a realistic and tempting option for the best graduates of the Russian top universities. Particularly appealing were the best US universities, which provided study grants for the selected students. One of our respondents (programmer, p40), a graduate of a highly esteemed technical university in Leningrad, recalls how 24 of his 25 classmates emigrated. According to him, an additional factor in the decision was to avoid serving two years in the Russian army, notorious for its practices of hazing and bullying (see Lonkila 2008).

These observations of the brain drain of the brightest Russian students are reinforced by investigation of a list of the graduates of the famed mathematical-physics school no. 239 in St. Petersburg published on the Internet. According to the list 44 percent of the reported graduates of 1985–95 had given an address abroad, mostly in the US (26 percent), Israel (7 percent), or Germany (6 percent).[8] Still, the new information and communication technologies also allow for the emigrated classmates of special schools to be in touch both with each other and their old teachers.

The university networks were not equally important for everyone. One of the older generation CEOs who graduated from a prestigious technical university and started his firm in the turmoil of the early 1990s stressed the generational difference:

> In my case those two cases [school and university milieus] are not important. Sad to say, but in my age group not many people made it to the level to be of professional interest to me. We all are 'survivors

of perestroika.' My school or University buddies are either drunkards or struggle to make it from salary to salary doing something very low level or – most of them – in the grave.

(general director, p1)

Internet milieus

For IT professionals, computer-mediated and mobile communication constitute one central channel for making acquaintances and maintaining relations. Parallel to the explosion of the Russian mobile phone markets in the 2000s (Gladarev and Lonkila 2008), communicating through cell phone calls, SMS, e-mail, and social network sites has replaced fixed phones, letters, and fax:

Q: Are you often in touch with your friends [in the IT business]?
P18: Today the Internet gives a wide range of possibilities for communication (*dlia obshcheniia*).
Q: You communicate with them through the Internet.
P18: Also in person. Practically every day on the Internet. And roughly once a month we also meet. They are of great help, particularly in cases of technical problems.

(marketing manager, p18)

The Internet is an especially important medium for communication, and many respondents used its various applications (email, discussion forums, instant messaging, etc.) actively to search for clients, orders, technical information, or just for socializing.[9]

Contradictory to the general idea of the Internet as a homogeneous global space where connections may be formed regardless of geographic or other limitations, the Russian language segment of the Internet is often referred to as 'Runet'. This practice dates back to the birth of the Russian Internet which was born among the researchers at the institute for nuclear research in Moscow (see Cooper 2006; Lonkila 2008; Schmidt et al. 2006).

One of the particular features of the Runet is the popularity of the virtual community LiveJournal www.livejournal.ru, in Russian *Zhivoi Zhurnal*, often abbreviated *ZhZh*). LiveJournal was originally developed as a blog publishing channel for American teenagers, but the networking functions added to it, such as the possibility of creating links between personal blogs as well as between personal blogs and thematic discussion groups or 'communities' led to the global spread of the system.

Quite unexpectedly, the well-educated Russian urban intelligentsia adopted *Zhivoi Zhurnal* in early 2000 as its avenue of socio-political expression to the extent that, until recently, *Zhivoi Zhurnal* was considered to be a general synonym for the word 'weblog' instead of one particular blogging platform. Though competitors have appeared (see below in this section), it is still a significant channel of expression for Russian urban professionals, as well as an arena for organizing protest actions. For example, the demonstrations of the opposition movement 'The Other Russia' were partly organized through the discussion communities of *Zhivoi Zhurnal*.

The personal blogs and conversations in *ZhZh* deal with personal, political, social and professional matters, often mixing all of these. Our respondent Valentina (marketing manager, p15), for example, told of finding a valuable document from a competing company published by the Ministry of Economic Development (*Ministerstvo Ekonomicheskogo Razvitiia*, MERT) through a link published on *Zhivoi Zhurnal*:

> You could simply read it [the document] at the website of the Ministry. I remember that I found this link through *ZhZh*, LiveJournal, where there have now appeared many kinds of IT communities, in which people are communicating about IT. In general, *ZhZh* is such a virus, it is spreading quickly. (...) there are also people who are in high positions in IT and they are communicating quite informally (*obshchaiutsia sovershenno neformalno*). Somewhere I found this link o MERT.
>
> (marketing manager, p15)

At the time of writing, *Zhivoi Zhurnal* is still a significant part of Russian virtual culture, but several new social network sites are challenging its position particularly among the younger generation of Russian ICT professionals. The two most popular ones are a Russian-made Facebook clone, *VKontakte* ('In Contact' – www.vkontakte.ru) and *Odnoklassniki* ('Classmates' – www.odnoklassniki.ru) whose origins are found in St. Petersburg and Moscow respectively, whereas the popularity of the original Facebook has been modest in Russia.

The opening page of *VKontakte* seems to be a close copy of Facebook design, and the counter on the page indicating registered users is growing continuously, exceeding 36 million users in June 2009 but already 86 million in July 2010. *VKontakte* was founded in 2006 by St. Petersburg brothers Pavel and Nikolai Durov, the former of whom graduated from St. Petersburg state university in spring 2006. While Pavel is the winner of the 'Olympiad in linguistics, information science (*informatika*) and design', Nikolai was a school-time champion of the all-Russian Olympiad in mathematics and information science.[10]

Odnoklassniki ('Classmates') was also founded in 2006 by the Moscow-born Albert Popkov and claimed to have 37 million users on June 17, 2009. The opening page of *Odnoklassniki* differs from *VKontakte*, since it is, as its name implies, designed to find one's classmates. Thus the page contains a long list of Russian regions, asking the user to pick the region s/he went to school in, and further to find the specific school, in, say, St. Petersburg.

Because of great commercial interest, it is difficult to find reliable user statistics corroborating the claims made by the two competing sites. According to the ROMIR survey in summer 2008, for example, *Odnoklassniki* was the clear leader (see Table 5.1).

However, TNS Web Index estimated that *VKontakte* reaches 13.4 million people monthly whereas the corresponding figure for *Odnoklassniki* was 12.9 million.[11] The history of the two sites was still visible in the background of the users: 56 percent of the *VKontakte* users were from St. Petersburg while the same figure for *Odnoklassniki* was 24 percent.[12]

These virtual milieus and others such as *Moi Mir* ('My World')[13] and more instrumental and business-oriented networks (US born LinkedIn, www.linkedin.com, and Russian *Moi Krug* – 'My Circle', www.moikrug.ru) are important arenas for the network building of the new generation of Russian IT professionals. At the same time, characteristic of the distrust permeating Russian society, rumors spread among users of the monitoring of these systems by Russian intelligence and security services.

For professional development, however, there seems to be a difference between LinkedIn and *VKontakte*. In the former, the professional and

Table 5.1 Popularity of the Russian social network sites in summer 2008. Percentage of the respondents registered on the site

Odnoklassniki.ru	72
VKontakte.ru	44
Mail.ru (moi mir)	38
LiveJournal.com	20
Moikrug.ru	20
MySpace.ru	2
Facebook.org	2
None	12

Source: ROMIR (2008)

instrumental aspect of network use is considered to be the 'default' of the relationship – even though friends can also extend their networks through it – whereas the latter is more oriented toward socializing, relaxing, and having fun than building professionally useful contacts. Nevertheless, as will become evident, forming ties based on socializing also extends one's network reach and may in the future provide bridges to economically relevant resources.

Finally, for the younger generation, social milieus provided by various hobbies offer important opportunities to simultaneously have fun and expand one's contact networks, as formulated by a younger generation IT specialist:

> Many IT professionals like mountain skiing, snowboarding, football, dancing (tango, latina), tennis, ping-pong, paintball. Sometimes we have tournaments organized by a company or several companies, with some customers and contractors invited. In more rare case we have tournaments like 'IT football league against St. Petersburg government', when IT guys are playing football with government officials. I believe that such tournaments or relationships started in fitness clubs/ski resorts can be a good start for new professional relationships.

Thus, St. Petersburg IT specialists have a wide variety of options for communicating both face-to-face and through the Internet. These options, particularly the increasingly popular social networking sites, build on the expansion of personal networks and may further contribute to the dissolving of boundaries between professional and personal spheres of life.

The Russian Software Developers Association (RUSSOFT)

The association of Russian software development companies was established in 1999 under the name Fort-Ross. In 2003 it joined the National Computer and IT Industry Association (APKIT), which was accepted the same year as a member of the international 'World IT and Services Association'. In 2004 Fort-Ross merged with the Russian National Software Development Association. The interest and PR activities were continued under the name of RUSSOFT whereas direct marketing events were organized under the aegis of Fort-Ross.

While the original idea of RUSSOFT was to promote Russian software development skills to the Western markets, lobbying the Russian government for the interests of the domestic ICT companies and recruiting new members to strengthen the voice of the association have recently grown more important.

The activities of Fort-Ross/RUSSOFT have thus included reporting and marketing the activities of the members, including organizing the Russian stand in international exhibitions, arranging the annual 'Russian Outsourcing and Software Summit', and lobbying the Russian government in the issues (e.g. legislation) central to the field. RUSSOFT also publishes an annual review of the evolution of the Russian software development field. The number of RUSSOFT members has grown from the original 10 to over 80 companies from Russia, Belorussia, and Ukraine.

One of the important functions of the association is to lobby the interests of the field vis-à-vis the state apparatus. In this the relations of the president and one of the initiators of RUSSOFT, Valentin Makarov, come in handy. Makarov, born in Leningrad in 1955, worked as an electronics engineer in the defense industry from 1978 until 1985 when he started an administrative career, first as the manager of international relations at the Leningrad Polytechnic Institute, where he was then nominated the deputy-vice prorector. During 1996–2000 he worked as the deputy chairman of the foreign relations committee in the administration of St. Petersburg.[14]

In addition Makarov's career also includes business consulting and a diplomatic appointment in the Russian UNESCO delegation in France. This impressive career implies that the IT industry is connected to St. Petersburg and Russian power elites through Makarov, since he most likely also has close ties with the Russian intelligence services.[15]

Among the benefits for software companies joining RUSSOFT, the association lists marketing opportunities (e.g. the possibility to place company information on the RUSSOFT website), discounts on buying licensed software, participating in conferences and other events, and access to nonpublic information of the Association. In addition, the Association has a networking function:

> You will have a right to take part in the Board of Directors monthly meetings. At the meetings not only dealing with current issues is important but also informal relationships between colleagues. The meetings take place in the central office of RUSSOFT in St. Petersburg or in Moscow. The Association also organizes parties for its member on occasions of high-days and holidays.[16]

The Association thus also functions as a milieu for forming connections between the main players of the field. In its meetings and events the representatives of member companies can exchange information about markets, new technologies, government plans, and other significant issues.

These kinds of exchanges also took place outside of the association, since the managers of the most important software companies knew their competitors, and met once in a while to exchange opinions:

> P3: once in a while we'll meet, for example, with Boris Vladimirovich [a well-known St. Petersburg IT entrepreneur]. 'Boris Vladimirovich, how are you? What do you think about this topic?' (...) And then there are these events organized by FortRoss [RUSSOFT]. The leaders of NewComp [one of the biggest St. Petersburg software companies] were my study mates at the institute, and we meet at times over lunch or dinner to find common interests (...) To exchange some fresh gossip from the industry.
> Q: What kinds of gossip?
> P3: All kinds. Gossip about employees' moving between firms, clients' behavior, strategic plans on St. Petersburg markets of some well-known Moscow companies, about serious setbacks or problems of companies. Or whether it is time to start hunting for employees. Well, the kind of news that you don't find in the internet media just because they have a dubious character, but which are good to know to understand the hidden meaning of many ongoing official events.
>
> (general director, p3)

In addition to RUSSOFT activities, IT people participate in seminars, trading and training events, and other meetings organized by, say, foreign companies, trade associations, or chambers of commerce. One example is the gatherings of MobileMonday, a community of mobile professionals which fosters cooperation and cross-border business development through virtual and live networking events.

Birthdays as foci of interaction

In Russian business practices, as in Russian culture more generally, birthday congratulations and birthday parties have a particular role as 'foci of interaction' (Feld 1981) anchored around a single individual. They are considered in this section as *rituals* indicative of the central role of personal networks in Russia. These rituals illustrate several central aspects of these networks such as the embeddedness of the economically relevant ties in social and cultural contexts, mixing of personal and public spheres of life, and the importance of togetherness and communication (*obshchenie*) in coupling the networks of individual people (see also Chapter 7 on *obshchenie*). Therefore they deserve to be discussed here at more length.

One of our respondents, a 35-year-old IT consultant, referred in the interview to her recent birthday, when she had received 40 phone calls as well as the congratulating messages sent to her via other media, and another middle-aged Russian IT manager – probably exceptionally active in terms of social interaction – estimated himself to have received 80–100 congratulations on his birthday. Still another respondent, a middle-aged general director and company owner, describes his birthday in the following way:

> On November 22 [date changed] all kinds of people start phoning. Close ones, acquaintances. Young people trying to impress you. It is a pleasure (...) people that you never thought would remember or know you, start phoning. It is twice as pleasant that even distant people remember you. It is fantastic.
>
> (general director, p3)

Birthdays have a central place in Russian culture, in and outside the workplace. They may be celebrated several times, both at work and home and with friends and other network members. Though birthday celebrations at work have likely become less prevalent compared to the Soviet era, one may encounter birthday congratulations for the bosses on the official websites of Russian organizations. The St. Petersburg weekly analytical newspaper *Delo* (Affair) had until the recent closure of the paper a special column devoted to 'VIP birthdays' of people in more or less important positions in the private or public sector. These columns were devoted to congratulations not only on round year birthdays (i.e. fiftieth birthday) however, but also contained subtly formulated congratulations by colleagues on, say, the sixty-fourth birthday of the person in question.[17]

Similarly, the well-known Russian daily *Kommersant* has a special column devoted to birthday congratulations for significant people in public office, culture, or business. An example is a congratulation by the president of the company 'Komstar-OTS' Sergey Pridantsev to Evgeny Yurchenko, the general director of *Sviaz'invest*, on his forty-second birthday:

> Dear Evgeny Valer'evich, let me congratulate you from the bottom of my heart on your birthday! You are not just the most talented

manager I have ever known, but also a person who loves life and is able to light up the people around him with his energy. This quality enables you to succeed in any walk of life, and I hope that you will just go ahead and be a guiding star for all – for colleagues and for friends!

Pridantsev was joined in these wishes by Boris Belenky, the founder of the theater prize 'Crystal Turandot'. His congratulation was written on a first-name basis, indicating a particularly close relationship with Evgeny Valer'evich:

Dear Evgeny Valer'evich! Forty two years ago the Creator sent you to the earth, and gave you a wise heart, a kind soul and a courageous intellect. During all these years, in spite of difficulties, you not only did not lose, but increased this richness. Precisely because of this you are a great manager. Thank you for tirelessly saving beauty rather than waiting for beauty to save the world.[18]

The ritualized importance of birthdays permeates the whole society up to the highest political and economic power elite. June 16, 1998, the day when a group of Russian oligarchs elected Anatoly Chubais as the representative of the country's urgent loan negotiations with the World Bank and the International Monetary Fund, happened to be Chubais' forty-third birthday. It was celebrated with the oligarchs singing 'Happy birthday to you' for Chubais, with Mikhail Fridman, the main owner of Alpha Bank, on piano (Kolesnikov 2009: 168).

In one of the few existing studies in English of Russian birthdays, Anna-Maria Salmi (2000) depicts the role of birthdays in Russian culture. She draws from the teacher network data corpus described in previous chapters, but her results also extend beyond the particularities of the teaching profession. Salmi shows how aspects of sociability and mutual help get intertwined in Russian birthday celebrations, illuminating the fit of the researcher's notion of *personal* network with the Russian actors' own views on their social life.

Probably the most detailed study of Russian birthdays in the Soviet and post-Soviet period is, however, written by Olga Kalacheva, according to whom the birthday is one of the most important and popular celebrations in Russian urban culture today (Kalacheva 2003: 9–10, 29). Kalacheva describes in detail the socio-historical roots of the Russian birthday, the organization of birthday practices, and their meaning for the formation of individual and collective identity. Especially relevant to the current study and the argument for the significant role of personal networks in Russia are her observations about the practices of solidarity formation during birthday celebrations, such as the gathering of guests around the common birthday table to share food, drink, and discussion. Kalacheva also cites the work by Lynn Visson, a translator well acquainted with Russian culture, which demonstrates well the significance of Russian birthday celebrations vis-à-vis their American counterparts:

> Adult Americans mostly pay much less attention to their birthdays than Russians. As a rule birthday parties are organized, guests invited and so forth only around round numbers of years. Other birthdays are noticed only by close friends. Besides, Americans do not have a need to use birthday as a good excuse to meet their kin and friends, to have a party.
>
> (Visson 2003: 103, cited in Kalacheva 2003: 8)

The birthday celebrations render visible the significance of the role of the personal network but also the proximity of its members. With the closest ones face-to-face celebrations are a must – forgetting the birthday of one's family member or close friend is likely to cause a breach in the relationship – but commemorating the birthdays of close acquaintances and business partners is also important. E-mail, mobile phone SMS, and social networking sites offer new technological possibilities both to maintain the connections and regulate the proximities: the inside circle must be encountered personally, for others one may phone and for still more distant acquaintances an SMS or an e-mail is sent. *VKontakte* provides, for example, a reminder of the birthday dates of one's network members, though an online message may nevertheless be considered a less intimate way of congratulating than a phone call.

In all, birthday celebrations exemplify well the central role of personal networks in Russia. During these ritualized celebrations, personal network ties are maintained and formed, mixing both the public and personal spheres of life as well as economic and social aspects and motivations.

6

The Types of Economic Resources Transmitted through the Networks of St. Petersburg IT Professionals

> Practically everything where the price is not the only meaningful issue it is more effective to do through acquaintances.
>
> (COO, director, p8)

This chapter describes what kinds of economically relevant resources are transmitted within the personal networks of St. Petersburg IT managers. The resources can be both material (transmitting goods, loaning money) and immaterial (passing on various kinds of information, giving advice) or rendering services (fixing a computer problem, helping to write a legal document).

The transmission of resources may be considered to comprise two successive phases or steps. In the first phase the problem is to find or *locate* the wanted resource, for example, an interesting job opening. In the next phase one has to *secure* the transmission of this resource, that is, get the job. Both steps can be conducted either through formal mechanisms or institutions or informally through social ties, or combining both approaches. In the first phase a job seeker could, for example, formally register at an employment agency or search for a job through personal connections. Once a suitable job opening is found, the candidate may rely on formal processing (CV, tests) or try to get someone to recommend him informally to the employer to get the job (Akhlaq 2005; for a classic account on job searches, see Granovetter ([1974] 1995).

This chapter focuses mostly on the first phase of locating the resources, while the second phase of securing the resources with the help of a third person is discussed in Chapter 7 in connection with brokerage.

Unlike in many other fields of Russian industry, the beginning IT entrepreneur did not need a great amount of starting capital, employees, or a factory hall: the most important resources, that is, skill in problem-solving and the mathematical and programming abilities to go with it, were in his head. In the first phase of starting a company, these personal competences of the founder along with owning a personal computer and finding even one foreign *customer* could get the firm going: the projects implemented were small-scale or pilot projects and the founder's home could serve as a temporary office.

With the growth of the project or company, one also had to find a reliable business *partner* or partners and recruit more *staff*, for whom additional *office space* was needed. With increasing business activity, the self-taught entrepreneur had to obtain a wide variety of *information* and *services* concerning taxation, legislation, bookkeeping, financing, marketing, and so forth. Personal network ties were used both in locating and securing the transmission of these resources.

Business ideas and partners

In the 1980s and early 1990s, Western research on entrepreneurship shifted its emphasis from the heroic, individual entrepreneur to one embedded in social networks and started to address the role played by personal and business networks in the start-up phases of firms (Elfring and Hulsink 2003: 409).

Later research has confirmed the importance of network contacts during all stages of company formation starting from the initial idea of founding the firm (Hoang and Antoncic 2003). Researchers have investigated, for example, the optimal mix and functions of the 'strong' ties of family and friends on the one hand and 'weak' ties of acquaintances on the other (Uzzi 1996; Elfring and Hulsink 2003).

For the new Russian entrepreneurs, personal ties played an even more important role than in Western countries, since several tasks, which in developed capitalism could be conducted through market institutions, required help from one's personal network in the early 1990s in Russia. The picture emerging from our interviews concerning the start-up phase of the Russian IT field is in many ways similar to that reported by Ledeneva based on data from 1991–2 (1998: 184–5).[1]

As the launching of private businesses had not been attempted before, advice and help – for example, in presenting registration documents – was essential. Most 'pioneers' of Russian business acknowledged that their registration documents were prepared by friends or contacts. Even when a paid service for drawing up documents became available, informal channels were reported to be an essential factor in starting a business. The advice or information obtained through friends and acquaintances was the advice and information considered reliable. Business was bound to depend on informal contacts, for 'the contract system was not yet developed. There were no efficient mechanisms for managing conflict situations or inflicting sanctions on unreliable partners'.

(Ledeneva 1998: 184–5)

Ledeneva concludes that the informal relations of trust formed in *blat* networks were 'the only guarantee one could rely on'.

While *blat* was an important factor for many of our respondents at some point of their careers (see Chapter 4), mutual help not related to *blat* was also crucial, as will become evident below.

Besides Ledeneva's, other studies lend credence to the importance of personal contacts for Russian start-up firms (e.g. Radaev 2003; Rogers 2006; Batjargal 2006). The 1993 survey of 277 Moscow entrepreneurs conducted by Vadim Radaev's group showed, for example, that 42 percent of them started their companies with personal acquaintances, 23 percent with friends and their kin, 17 percent with the entrepreneurs' own kin, and only 11 percent with unknown people (Radaev 2003).

Our data lend further credence to these findings. Many IT firms in St. Petersburg were born during the transition period when several institutions vital for a market economy, such as financial institutions, independent courts, effective law enforcement and so forth, were – and in many ways still are – either absent, functioning badly, or just about to emerge, and the whole society was penetrated by distrust. Thus, several of our respondents had turned to the help of their study mates, friends, relatives, or acquaintances to start their companies.

Dmitry's career (general director, p4), for example, began thanks to the suggestion of an emigrated friend of his parents who was running a firm abroad. The suggestion led Dmitry to establish a branch office of this firm with the spouse of his good acquaintance in St. Petersburg. The first employees were recruited from among his partner's circle of acquaintances.

In like manner, Nikita (technical director, p20) started a firm in 2004 together with his two friends and study mates from the university.[2] Nikita's friends and acquaintances helped with registration of the firm and obtaining the working space, as well as solving problems with tax officials. In the beginning all orders were received 'either from acquaintances or friends', who still continue to assist in finding orders in addition to the orders found through other, more formal channels. Acquaintances were called for help also in cases of technical problems that could not be solved by the staff. Bookkeeping – often considered the most central function of a Russian firm – had also been entrusted to acquaintances, to whom the company also turned when encountering juridical problems.

Nikita's case was not an anomaly. Kirill (technical director, p38) and Stanislav (general director, p48) had started their firms with their wives, and Oleg's (project director, p26) wife worked for the same company as her husband. Andrey (general director, p1) established his firm together with his family members and Anton (p13) worked as a general director of the company founded by his study mate from the university. The central role of strong ties was similarly evident for Petr (PR-manager, p19), who had established a software company in the early 1990s on the basis of a circle of friends and acquaintances. In the beginning the staff was mainly recruited through connections who also helped to solve technical, juridical, and financial problems.

This kind of developmental path led early on to the mixing of personal and professional spheres of life in the personal networks of St. Petersburg IT professionals – a theme to which we will return in the next chapter.

Clients

Finding clients and orders is the first and most crucial task for a fledgling IT company, and for our respondents personal ties were one of the main channels to find them. In the 1990s foreign customers were particularly valuable, since only one foreign client would provide enough income to pay a couple of Russian programmers, rent office space and start working on the first project:

> Again we run into social networks. A father of one of the founders of the company used to work in Germany [name of the country has been changed]. The son had an opportunity to work there, and he made the acquaintance of the first customer of the firm, a German, who ran his own company. The German found out that the son was a programmer, and asked if he could write him a specific type of program. (…) After having heard the price of programming in Russia he wanted

more. And the son was writing programs though the firm had not yet been founded. This was roughly the way the company was started.

(PR-manager, p2)

If the nascent company managed to assure the client of the quality of its work, another project followed, based on the relatively cheap and competent labor of the Russian programmers. After having established a successful business relationship, the company could get permission from the client to publish a reference on the company's website, thereby attracting other customers.

With the growth and professionalization of the company, personal relations continue to be important in finding clients, but are complemented by all possible means such as participating in software fairs, exhibitions and seminars, opening offices in other Russian cities or abroad, searching for customers through the Internet, and contacting potential customers directly:

> My partner has over ten years' experience in the IT field, including quite big companies. On the one hand he has a collection of personal relations through which he can try to find potential clients (...) On the other hand he already has a certain reputation. In addition our company has customers who are very happy with our work and at times recommend us to others on their own initiative and thereby increase the clientele.

(director, p10)

Starting capital

After the first steps a growing business required more programmers, office space, computers, and other expenditures. Particularly for those interviewees who had started their commercial activity in the 1990s, finding starting capital to cover these costs was complicated because of the underdevelopment of the banking sector and the lack of alternative sources of financing.[3] One of the interviewees who a started one-man small-scale programming business recalls:

> At that time [early 1990s] the banking system functioned very badly. I do not mean the unreliability. Even under these uncertain circumstances people put money in the bank. I mean that everyone was pissed off that banks simply did not know how to work with money (...) in those years there were cases when money was paid [to an IT firm]

but it was impossible to know by whom. One had to ask the client, 'have you by any chance sent me this sum?' Some also charged from one client 200 roubles and 50 copecks and from another one 200 roubles and 52 copecks in order to distinguish between the clients.

(programmer, p40).

Distrust of the banking system, the high level of interest rates, and the constant changes in the business environment made beginning entrepreneurs turn to their kin, family, and friends to obtain starting capital. In the early 1990s this was one of the few legal ways to get financing, but the following description from early 2007 shows how turning to banks was till recently an expensive choice for a St. Petersburg entrepreneur:

> [A new IT company] can only get very small loans from banks. They are rarely tailored to the needs of companies, but rather for travel, leisure, health services or buying cars or apartments. The loans have extremely high interest rates, 18 percent is not unusual (...) It is difficult to start a business with a slightly over 10 000 dollar loan with a high interest rate. For bigger loans one has to have collateral such as a new car or better a luxury apartment. Not many people have them. A big part of the new IT companies nowadays is searching for money from kin or friends or knocking at the doors of existing firms.
>
> (general director, p1)

The importance of social networks from the viewpoint of *banks* at the end of the 1990s has been described in the studies by Dinello (1999) and Guseva and Rona-Tas (2001, see also Uzzi 1999). Natalia Dinello interviewed Russian bankers during the banking boom of 1994 and at the onset of the crises in the summer of 1998. Her conclusion is that 'the F-connection' – that is, the relationships among financial outlets, firms, friends, families, and favorites – 'is pervasive and continuous and will likely outlast the market economy' (Dinello 1999: 24). Her interviewees rejected the possibility that Russian banking could be identity-blind, only based on impersonal economic calculations, and supported the idea that it rather served primarily the inner circle of friends.

Though Guseva's and Rona-Tas's (2001) comparative study of Russian and American credit card markets – based on fieldwork conducted in summer 1998 and fall 1999 in Moscow – did not draw quite as drastic conclusions, the authors also stress the central role of social networks in banking. According to them, due to the inability of Russian banks to calculate risks, they relied on trust created by the social networks both of their own employees and their clients in issuing credit cards:

> Reliance on existing networks of trust allows Russian banks to issue cards to families and friends of top bank executives (...) Here the borrower–creditor relationship is intermingled with close social bonds that serve as an additional guarantee and a channel of information. For instance, one interviewee was granted an American Express card by his friend, a high-ranking employee of AmEx in Moscow. Relying exclusively on personal relations necessarily limits the number of potential cardholders, however. The credit card market turns into an elite membership club, hardly a desirable market for a product whose profitability (and calculability) resides in its numbers.
>
> (Guseva and Rona-Tas 2001: 638)

When assessing the studies of Dinello and Guseva and Rona-Tas, one must take into account the exceptional context of the 1990s and particularly the crisis of 1998. Presently, the Russian banking sector is extremely fragmented, consisting of a few large, Moscow-based and state-controlled banks, which form the backbone of the sector, and a great number of small banks.[4] Though the total number of banks has decreased from 2084 in 2000 to 1243 in 2007, 'the great majority of the banks are still tiny and can hardly be called banks' (Fungáčová and Solanko 2008: 7–11).

The recovery of the banking sector after the 1998 crisis is due to many factors, among them the annual economic growth of more than 6 percent during the 2000s and institutional reforms. These reforms include the laws on private credit bureau operations, mortgage lending, and the deposit insurance system, covering in full private deposits of up to RUB 400,000 in March 2007 (Fungáčová and Solanko 2008: 7–11).

Despite the reforms, the distrust penetrating Russian society extends to banking. According to an interview in early 2007 with a Finnish banker with more than 20 years of experience in Russia, 'the Russians still prefer to draw their salary all at once from the ATM and put it in a safer place.' Though the ruble is the official currency, the amount of US dollars in cash in Russia is second only to that in the US (Kupila 2007). This distrust and the importance of connections in getting a loan were clearly expressed by one of our respondents:

> The credit is given to industrial enterprises. But we are in the IT business. To get a loan, you need such an amount on paper ... fuck them.

It is better to use your own money (...) It takes from two weeks to three months to get a loan, but you would need money tomorrow (...) The loans are given to acquaintances, on the basis of personal relations. This is how things are here.

(CEO, p12)

At the time of writing, the worldwide financial crisis had just hit Russia, and it was too early to assess its ultimate effects on either the world economy or Russia. Exceptional periods are, however, likely to increase the importance of personal contacts.

Office space

In addition to clients, business partners, and starting capital, office space was another central resource necessary for business activities that was located and secured through networks in the early 1990s. Growing turnover necessitated recruitment of additional employees who in turn needed working space furnished with a reliable telecommunications infrastructure:

We are sitting in this office because I know a person who knows the bankruptcy trustee of this factory. He phoned me and said, 'do you need office space?' I said 'of course.' When all others paid 12 dollars, I paid four. When all others pay 25, I pay 12.

(general director, p3)

Another respondent (COO, p8) similarly noted the role of his personal network ties in finding a new office for the company:

P8: One of our directors found out that her husband works in a holding company which was planning to open here a business center with another company. So we moved in here and this happened through acquaintances (*po znakomstvu*).

After the fall of the Soviet Union many Soviet organizations continued a 'shadow life' in their offices and buildings even though their Soviet functions had ceased to exist. It was possible to turn existing ties with the leaders of these organizations into important resources for a start-up IT firm:

[During the Soviet era] my acquaintance knew the leader of the organization who administered this building. The leader was a high-ranking state official who had several offices in the city and he worked in the regional committee of the Communist party. He was the kind of old man (*diaden'ka*) with whom it was in general impossible to get an appointment. (...) My acquaintance phoned him, based on this old connection, and said that my good acquaintances will come to see you, probably you could rent this office to them (...) At that time, as you remember, there was no business and nobody had money. And many state departments and institutes simply rented out offices.

(general director, p1)

Ledeneva (1998: 189) describes abuses and prosecutions that emerged in the Committee for the Management of City Property in St. Petersburg (*Komitet po Upravleniiu Gorodskim Imushchestvom*) after the appointment of a new director in 1991. With the economic growth in the 2000s several business centers have been established in the city and office space is now freely available on the market. For a small start-up firm, however, social relations still come in handy in acquiring office space.

Jobs

The significance of networks in obtaining a job is one of the basic findings of social network research since the classic study *Getting a Job* by Mark Granovetter ([1974] 1995). The main point of Granovetter's study was not only the observation that jobs were found through personal relations instead of through anonymous labor markets. Rather, his interesting and much disputed argument claimed that particularly the 'weak ties' of acquaintances (vis-à-vis the 'strong ties' of family and friends) were especially valuable in finding jobs.

Granovetter claims that a weak tie, such as a former classmate encountered by chance on the street, is more likely to provide new information from outside the job seeker's habitual social milieu. Even though strong ties are more motivated to help the job seeker to get the job, the information they have is more likely to already be familiar to the job seeker and thus redundant.

Our respondents' descriptions of the development of their own careers confirmed the significance of personal networks, including both strong and weak ties, in locating and securing a job in the Soviet Union and Russia (cf. Yakubovich 2005; Clarke and Kabalina 2000). But more importantly, personal networks were still an important channel for recruiting employees in St. Petersburg IT companies, a topic which emerged in several interviews.

According to the respondents, finding qualified staff had become one of the main problems in the IT industry: economic growth along with a limited number of university graduates and the entrance of international IT companies into the local labor markets had led to a shortage of labor and fierce competition for personnel.[5]

Under the conditions of the labor shortage, staff was recruited by all possible means, including ads, internet forums, recruiting agencies, and personal networks. Compared to anonymous recruiting, through ads for example, recruiting someone through personal relations was both quicker and cheaper. Especially in the beginning stages of start-up firms, recruiting through family, friends, or acquaintances could also guarantee the reliability of the employee.

On the other hand, several respondents brought up the disadvantage of using personal networks as a recruitment method: in the case of problems, friends and acquaintances are more difficult to fire. Similarly, with the growth and professionalization of the firm, the stakes, time, and costs related to recruiting grew, which made turning to a professional head-hunting firm a tempting option.

Many firms kept in touch with universities, whose graduates or advanced students were prime targets for recruiting. Since almost all respondents held a university degree, they already had previous ties to the university milieu.

Some firms had combined formal and informal methods of recruiting: one company paid a bonus to its staff members for bringing in a new employee; another asked job applicants to name their possible acquaintances among the company's employees, who were then inquired about the qualifications of the applicant (see next chapter).

Advice and information

Due to rapid technological development and a constantly changing business environment, networks could transmit information crucial to a company's competitiveness. A concrete example of this, in addition to getting orders or recruiting staff, was transmission of information concerning new technologies, markets, or legislation:

My brother, for example, has a close friend, who works in an organization that supplies companies with juridical information. We had to decide from whom to buy this information (...). He helped us to get an overall image and to understand, who, what and how, which organizations are offering what kind of services and how we could make a better choice. This, too, was done through acquaintances.

(general director, p1)

According to another respondent (development manager, p17), information about employees' salary level was also exchanged with competing firms, which helped to 'keep an eye on things' and 'to understand if our salaries were lagging behind others'.

Information is an especially precious resource in the IT field, which is mainly based on information processing and where the share of material production is minor. In some cases social networks are the *only* way to obtain important information, since sensitive and valuable information about, say, tenders or actual projects is usually not made public:

In our business nobody shares information about concrete projects, because our business is about information. And the key to success is the protection of this information.

(technical director, p11)

The role of networks in the transmission of information is further underlined by the fact that many types of information that are easily available and formally distributed in most modern industrialized countries, such as credit registries, may be hard to obtain or totally lacking in Russia:

When you are closing a big contract, for example, it is important for you to know how capable your client is of paying. You want to talk with the firms or people who have been dealing with the client. This information is not public. If you have good relations with these people, they are willing to reveal this information as much as they wish, and this is very important. To get to know something about this client or theme.

(CEO, p16)

The specific feature of offshore companies compared to firms operating only in Russian markets was that the former rarely had to compete for the same customers due to the size of the global markets. Consequently, monitoring the actions of competitors in this regard was often not considered to be of primary importance. Instead, the firms competed fiercely on the local labor markets for employees, and the arrival of foreign competitors was important information for Russian firms:

> Q: Do you often exchange useful advice or recommendations through acquaintances
> P11: Yes, of course. (...) Usually this is news about technologies or labor markets. For example, when Intel arrived and recruited all the programmers. One had to know about this beforehand, so that one would not start a new project at the same time as they start their staff recruiting campaign
> Q: But how can you know this beforehand?
> P11: Usually some information exists (...) e.g. an office being set up. How would you get to know that Sun is opening a new office? Naturally only through some acquaintance.
>
> (technical director, p11)

One respondent referred to the exchange of information as 'gossip', which took place among acquaintances over informal lunches or dinners. If gossip is defined as 'the provision of information by one person (*ego*) to another person (*alter*) about an absent third person (*tertius*)' (Wittek and Wielers 1998), our interviews contain several examples of interviewees gossiping to the interviewer about competitors, enemies, or well-known figures in the St. Petersburg IT industry. The relatively small field of St. Petersburg's IT sector offered fertile ground for gossiping about third persons:

> There are different kinds of gossip. There is gossip that is related to the mobility of staff, the behavior of clients, the strategic plans of well-known Moscow firms in St. Petersburg markets, to the serious problems and failures of certain companies. Or if one has to start hunting for personnel. Well, some kind of new information about which they don't write in the news (...) but which it pays to know in order to understand the context of many official events.
>
> (general director, p3)

Services

Not only information is transmitted through networks, but also concrete services related to, for example, technical and legal problems. A universal 'benefit' for IT professionals is the requests for help

concerning the computing problems occurring in one's personal network of family, kin, and acquaintances. This feature was well known
and several concrete examples of it were given in the interviews:

> Here is a fresh example: Next to our office is hairdresser [field of the
> activity has been changed], where they continuously have problems
> with their computer. They stop by and I say, 'guys, whoever has time,
> go lend a hand.' And I myself regularly visit various friends precisely
> to fix computer problems. And my friends help me to solve some
> problems related to business administration. Someone works in state
> structures and I regularly turn to him for help in various problems.
> Q: What kind of problems? What was the latest case?
> P4: I was interested in the credit system in the Russian Federation.
> I phoned my friends who work in a bank, consulted them and under-
> stood that in Russia this is not favorable. (...) And then, when open-
> ing an office I turned to my friend who works in fire protection.
> Q: Why?
> P4: In order for an office to start working, it has to fulfill certain
> requirements concerning, among other things, fire protection. And if
> the landlord has not solved these problems, they fall upon the renter.
> I phoned, found out what I have to do in order not to have problems
> with fire inspection in the future.
>
> (general director, p4)

Nothing in the quote above implies that the employees of the hair
salon next to the IT company were charged money for the computer
maintenance services. Similarly, it is plausible to assume that, in the
case that one of the staff of the IT firm was in need of a haircut, this
was done for free.

The computing problems of the personal networks of an IT firm's
employees are thus dealt with in an informal manner:

> [The service department] is constantly dealing with these things –
> installing computers. All my acquaintances go there all the time in
> a spirit of neighborliness, and someone helps. My home computer
> was also fixed this way.
>
> (marketing manager, p15)

The interviews contained several examples of these kinds of exchanges
crisscrossing the personal and professional spheres of life. The father
of the boss-friend of Valentina (marketing manager, p15), for example,

was a lawyer who took care of checking the contracts of Valentina's company. In a similar manner, Anna (PR-manager, p2) asked the lawyer of her firm to help Anna's friend in a law case:

> A good example concerning the lawyers. Just a while ago my personal friends needed an attorney in a civil case. We have a lawyer in our firm who deals with contracts. I went to him and asked if he has some acquaintances at the [law] institute or in lawyer circles who have specialized in civil law. (...) Contacts were transmitted. Of course, this happens constantly. It is a constant practice.
>
> (PR-manager, p2)

In the recently established company of Nikita (technical director, p20) 'many acquaintances from various fields' had provided concrete help for the firm in terms of registration, finding an office, taxation, server installation, bookkeeping, juridical advice, and advertising. As a next step he was planning to use his acquaintances to establish a front-end office in the US to draw in American customers.

In sum, these examples illustrate the significance of personal networks in Russian managers' business activities. The non-market exchanges effectuated through their personal ties provided them with a wide variety of both tangible and intangible resources. The next chapter will analyze the social mechanisms governing these transactions.

7

Social Mechanisms Governing the Informal Transactions between Russian IT Managers

While the previous chapter dealt with the contents of Russian managers' informal transactions (e.g. information, advice, money), this chapter describes the social mechanisms regulating these transactions. Instead of trying to cover all such mechanisms, the chapter focuses on reciprocal obligations, brokerage, and mixing of professional and personal spheres of life, that is, mechanisms that are supposed to create continuity in relationships and enlarge personal networks by introducing new members.[1]

Reciprocal expectations in Russian managers' transactions

The norm of reciprocity vs. the importance of socializing

It seems natural to think that a given favor evokes an expectation of a counter favor, thus contributing to the maintenance of the network tie. In his article *The Norm of Reciprocity: A Preliminary Statement* (1960), sociologist Alvin Gouldner explains this expectation by the existence of a universal, generalized norm of reciprocity.[2] Gouldner considers reciprocity to be as universal and important in cultures as the incest taboo, though he admits that its 'concrete formulations' may vary according to time and place.[3] Moreover, the norm may also differ within one society according to the status of participants or certain other conditions. Gouldner also mentions how the norm may function differently to some degree in different cultures, and also leaves room for the lack of reciprocal obligations:

> Relations with little or no reciprocity may, for example, occur when power disparities allow one party to coerce the other. There may also be special mechanisms which compensate for or control the tensions

which arise in the event of a breakdown in reciprocity. Among such compensatory mechanisms there may be culturally shared prescriptions of one-sided or unconditional generosity, such as the Christian notion of 'turning the other cheek' or 'walking the second mile', the feudal notion of *'noblesse oblige'*, or the Roman notion of 'clemency'.

(Gouldner 1960: 164)

Edwina Uehara (1995) notes that the formulation of Gouldner's norm is very general. In actual interaction situations, people have to make concrete decisions about, among other things, how much, when, and how to reciprocate

> [O]ur expectations as to how and when we can 'legitimately' meet our reciprocity obligations are quite diverse, and some relationships afford more flexibility in this regard than others. For example, in relationships where indirect and/or delayed reciprocity is permitted, we are afforded a relatively wide degree of latitude in meeting reciprocity obligations.
>
> (Uehara 1995: 487)

We asked about the existence of reciprocal expectations and their actual realizations in concrete interaction situations among our Russian respondents with the help of two questions. The first question considered the possibility of a 'free lunch', and the other the possibility of an unreciprocated favor. The English expression 'there's no such thing as a free lunch' was translated into the Russian saying 'there is free cheese only in a mouse trap' (*besplatnyi syr tol'ko v myshelovke*).[4]

In general the respondents admitted that doing a favor for someone created a need for a counter favor:

> Q: There is a saying 'there is free cheese only in a mouse trap.' To what extent do you agree with this?
> P4: Basically, of course, I agree. If someone does you a favor, you suppose as a silent agreement that you are ready to do some kind of a reciprocal favor. If not now, then in the future. In my opinion these are normal human relations (*eto normal'nye chelovecheskie otnosheniia*)
>
> (general director, p4)

Some of the respondents, however, disputed the whole principle by criticizing the barter logic inherent in our question (and in Gouldner's norm). Instead, they related the giving of favors to a broader process of *obshchenie* – building and maintaining personal networks through communicating and socializing:

> Q: Generally when you do someone a favor or someone does you a favor, do you expect something in return?
> P6: No, I don't. If I do a favor, I don't do it on the basis of barter. But I have noticed that very often some contacts will overlap. They probably won't bring concrete results right away, but perhaps later. But this is similar to human communication (*srodni chelovecheskomu obshcheniiu*). I am not giving you an interview because I expect something in return. Absolutely not. I give you an interview because it won't take me much time. I can grant you half an hour. If this helps you, as I understand, why not?
>
> (marketing director, p6)

This quote echoes the words of Luc Boltanski in a recent interview (Basaure 2008). Boltanski noted how expecting no reciprocity might seem like an unreachable ideal but 'I think in daily life it happens very often, because it would become completely impossible, if anyone would constantly calculate what he is doing and what is being done for him, as equivalencies must permanently be evoked' (Basaure 2008: 7, translated by M. L.).

The quote may be interpreted as a criticism of the economic-rational perspective implied in the question, which considers the individual act of exchange as abstracted from its actual context. The reciprocal expectations do not, for this respondent, figure as a motive for action or relate to individual actions but rather to the nature of the ongoing 'human communication' (cf. Gronow 2008). In a similar manner, another of our respondents (general director, p4) justified his helping others out without reciprocation as 'normal human communication' (*normal'noe chelovecheskoe obshchenie*).

Alexey Yurchak (2006: 148–51) has paid attention to the importance of *obshchenie*, which has no adequate equivalent in English:

> It refers to 'communication' and 'conversation', but in addition involves nonverbal interaction and spending time together or being together. It is different from just 'hanging out' with friends, as used in the United States, because it always involves an intense and intimate commonality and intersubjectivity, not just spending time in the company of others. The noun *obshchenie* has the same root as *obshchii*

(common) and *obshchina* (commune), stressing in the process of inter-action not the exchange between individuals but the communal space where everyone's personhood is dialogized to produce a common intersubjective sociality. *Obshchenie*, therefore, is both a process and a sociality that emerges in that process, and both an exchange of ideas and information as well as a space of affect and togetherness.

(Yurchak 2006: 148)

Quoting Vail and Genis (1988: 69), Yurchak (2006: 148) notes how *obshchenie* as a cultural practice intensified and evolved into a dominant pastime during late socialism. Though he remarks that in present day Russia people are regretting the diminishing chances for *obshchenie*, our interviews testify to its continuous existence and importance.

Indications of the importance of this practice were the frequent cases of *obshchenie* that took place not only among the Russian IT profes-sionals, but also between our native Russian *interviewer* and the respond-ents. The interviewer was advised to record her observations about the respondent and the interview situation on tape after each interview session. As a result, our 'meta-level data' of the interviewer–interviewee encounters contain several instances of the following type:

[The respondent was a] very sociable (*obshchitel'nyi*) person. The con-versation took place in the office. The respondent offered me coffee and introduced me to his partner. After the interview we still talked about some topics that were of interest t0o both of us. For example, the respondent has a very wide circle of sociality (*krug obshcheniia*).

(interviewer's comment on the interview
with general director, p3)

This quote illustrates not only an encounter between two individual persons, but a *coupling* of two personal networks (*krug obshcheniia*) through the commonly shared practice of socializing and communicat-ing. Note that the interviewer uses the word 'conversation' (*beseda*) in addition to 'interview'. The conversation ended with the respondent's invitation to the interviewer to join his personal network on a social networking website. Despite the time constraints of our respondents, these kinds of instances of socializing took place frequently *after* the formal interview had ended:

During the conversation after the interview it became clear that the respondent is studying English and has been in English courses abroad. He regretted not being able to talk 'kitchen English' because of the lack of occasions to practice. During the informal conversation after the interview we moved to a first-name basis (*my pereshli na ty*), and talked about the respondent's relationship to the city.

(interviewer's comment on the interview
with development director, p5)

The importance of *obshchenie* was also key to understanding the interviews: our Western interview questions about the importance of reciprocating a given favor were often answered with examples emphasizing the importance of *obshchenie*. Metaphorically speaking, when asked if a person donating seeds to a gardener would expect a counter gift, many respondents suggested that it was more important to communicate and socialize with the gardener. The contact established might or might not bear fruit in the future:

> I presume that if I help someone, I can also turn to this person with some questions. But I do not think at all that there is some kind of unavoidable principle of equality, some kind of calculation like 'I helped you once, you will help me later'.
>
> (development director, p17)

Many respondents agreed with the norm of reciprocity in principle but nevertheless told several examples of favors they had done without expecting something in return. First, some examples of unreciprocated favors considered cases where resources had been distributed so unevenly between the participants of the exchange that both understood that reciprocity was not an option (cf. Ledeneva's 'regime of status', 1998: 150–2):

> Sometimes I can do a favor understanding that I will never get anything back. Because the person, for example, cannot give me anything.
>
> (PR manager, p19)

Second, the respondents analyzed various factors related to situational contexts affecting reciprocal expectations:

> I don't know why you should necessarily do others a favor in order to be able to ask for one. If I ask you to bring me a cup of coffee, what reasons do you have to refuse?
> Q: None
> P5: You can bring it. This is an example. If it is not difficult and does not require a lot of work. You just do it. Another variant is that you

have no reason to refuse but you feel lazy. And you will say that I do not feel like it. This will also be a variant of communication (*eto tozhe budet variantom obshcheniia*) (...) A wish is simply a wish and not a command. One cannot count on that what you want will be done. But one can hope for it.

(development director, p5)

Third, several respondents stressed the dependency of the reciprocal expectations on the nature of the relationship. According to them, friendship relations, for example, had different rules than business relations in terms of reciprocity (see the end of this chapter for a more detailed account on friendship):

> Q: They say that there is free cheese only in a mouse trap. If you do someone a favor, you will expect something in exchange, some kind of help or favor. Do you agree with this saying?
> P13: No I don't. It does not work in friendship relations (*v druzheskikh otnosheniiakh*). In them everything is different, otherwise they would not be friendship relations but something completely different.

(general director, p13)

In sum, although the majority of the respondents agreed with Gouldner's norm of reciprocity in principle, many told examples of situations where they themselves had given help without expecting to be reciprocated; some denied it altogether; and others refined the norm in several respects, pointing to, among other things, the importance of *obshchenie*. Even a professional encounter between the interviewer and the interviewee could be transformed into a coupling of their personal networks through *obshchenie*.

These denials and variations of the norm of reciprocity suggest that, in addition to reciprocal obligations, other social and *moral* mechanisms were at work in the personal networks of our respondents. In the next section the denials of reciprocity are discussed based on Alena Ledeneva's (1998) work on the 'Russian economy of favours' already addressed in the previous sections.

Denials of reciprocity as misrecognition

Ledeneva (1998: 141) analyzes reciprocal obligations in *blat* exchanges in a manner that is relevant to the current study. According to her, the particular nature of *blat* favors has an impact on reciprocal expectations since it can be located between gift and commodity exchanges. On the one hand, *blat* favors are different from commodity exchanges because they bear the personal stamp of the donor, but on the other hand *blat* favors may also be distinguished from gift exchanges because they happen upon request. Consequently, *blat* is protected from the 'compulsion of the gift' and imposed generosities.

To find a way to deal with the complexity of reciprocal obligations in *blat* exchanges, Ledeneva (1998: 142–4) refers to Luc Boltanski's distinction between the 'affective regime' and the 'regime of justice'. To summarize Ledeneva's presentation, which draws on Luc Boltanski's lecture at Princeton in 1992: in the 'regime of justice' parties search for equivalencies – or a common point of reference – to manage disputes whereas in the 'affective regime' people shove aside all calculations of equivalencies.[5]

Based on the theorizing of Boltanski and Thévenot, Ledeneva herself constructs three different 'regimes of reciprocity': the regime of equivalence, the regime of affection, and the regime of status, between which the exchange partners may switch depending on the situation. In the regime of equivalence, the reciprocal expectations are most explicit since the focus is on the potential utility of the exchange partner. In the regime of affection participants stress the relationship itself rather than counter favors, and are bound by personal ties irrespective of their involvement in *blat* transactions. Finally, unlike the two other regimes, the regime of status is asymmetrical and can follow the pattern of patron–client relationships. This regime is affected by the status, power, and authority of the participants in *blat* exchanges and shows how reciprocal expectations may be irrelevant since some favors cannot be paid back even in principle (Ledeneva 1998: 142–52).

While Ledeneva's trichotomy sheds light on various aspects of the reciprocity of *blat* exchanges, it also contains problems, since elsewhere in her book she analyzes *blat* transactions with the help of Pierre Bourdieu's notion of *misrecognition* (*méconnaissance*) in gift transactions. According to Bourdieu, the temporal delay between the gift and the counter-gift enables parties to create an illusion of the non-reciprocal nature of the gift. In reality, the reciprocal obligations do exist, and only the collective participation in the 'misrecognition game' makes it possible to conceal this objective fact.

In *blat* exchanges, however, the misrecognition game was incomplete, because people were able to recognize an exchange of favors as *blat* when it was conducted by others, but unable to do this when they were themselves involved in *blat* transactions:

> The complexity of the *blat* 'misrecognition game' cannot be fully grasped by Bourdieu's concept of misrecognition, where even being

outside of the gift exchange transaction, a member of a community would admit that it is a gift that has been given. As not all individuals accept the internal rhetoric of *blat* and recognise it indicates that this did not endanger the foundation of community – that is, there was no universally shared sense of 'honour' involved in *blat*.

(Ledeneva 1998: 59–60; see also Ledeneva 2008: 129–30)

The disclosing of the objective truth underneath the respondents' discourse in the misrecognition game seems to be at odds with the theory of Boltanski and Thévenot (2006), according to which '[t]he regime in which one makes calculations is no more true, no more real, than the regime in which people inhibit their calculation abilities'. However, according to Ledeneva – who illustrates this regime mainly with examples of friendship ties – in the regime of affection 'the feelings of affection disguise *blat* relations' and 'the rhetoric of friendship tends to conceal mutual obligations' (Ledeneva 1998: 148–9). If these mutual obligations are not obeyed, the real state of affairs is revealed:

But in fact, if the balance in the relationship is broken, if one takes offence and feels that the code of friendship has been violated, the relationships are likely to slip into the regime of equivalence.

(Ledeneva 1998: 149)

In other words, it looks as if in Ledeneva's trichotomy the regime of affection would be a somewhat unstable discursive layer, under which the 'objective reality' of reciprocal obligations is to be found – as in Bourdieu's misrecognition game.

Denials of reciprocity as references to shared moral principles

Instead of applying the notion of misrecognition to denials of reciprocity, this section follows the lead opened by Luc Boltanski and Laurent Thévenot (2006) in their book *On Justification. Economies of Worth* ([1991], 2006).[6] From this perspective, the respondents' reflections on reciprocity may be considered ways of justifying their actions by referring to shared moral principles.

Our respondents' appeal to moral principles in the interviews concerning their professional activities suggests that economic relations are far from being emptied of moral considerations. Moreover, it shows how economically relevant actions may be justified by referring to moral principles unrelated to the market logic of competition. Finally, respondents' replies reveal how reciprocal obligations may also be shoved aside completely in the name of non-instrumental friendship (Boltanski 1990; Kharkhordin 2005, 2009).

In the remaining text of this section, justification theory is first described in short and then, in the next section, applied to the Russian managers' interview data.

The basic idea of justification theory is that the normal, conventional course of action – for example, running a business – tends from time to time to drift into a dead end. Justification theory focuses on these 'critical moments' – crises, conflicts, and disputes – which force the disagreeing parties to argue and justify their actions by referring to 'a common good' recognized and accepted by both parties.[7]

In order to settle the dispute, the parties have to establish a principle of equivalence, against which the arguments presented in the dispute can be evaluated, and the 'worth' (*grandeur*) of the disputants can be measured.

Boltanski and Thévenot describe six different orders of worth, each of them referring to a different principle defining the 'worth', 'size', or 'greatness' (*grandeur*) of the disputing parties. They distinguish six common worlds based on these principles and on the beings (persons or things) that inhabit these worlds.[8]

First, in the *market* world, the greatness (*grandeur*) of an actor is defined by wealth and ultimately measured by markets. The greatness of a physician in this world, for example, could be measured by her commercial success in medical business. Second, in the *industrial* world, to continue the example, the same physician may be valued – irrespective of her commercial success – by her efficiency and measured in concrete terms, for example, by the number of patients handled per day. Third, in the *domestic* world, the greatness of the physician is evaluated by her position in the system of mutual dependency. Valued or 'worthy' in this world is one's trusted family doctor who has been treating all the members of the family for years and with whom one can always jump the queue to get an appointment. Fourth, in the *civic* world, a doctor is evaluated by her willingness to treat all patients equally as citizens. Fifth, in the world of *fame*, a great person would be a well-known media figure (such as Dr. Phil), whereas in the *inspired* world such a figure would be a genius surgeon who is the only one able to conduct certain operations because of her unique, God-given artistic capabilities.[9]

In this book the focus is mostly on the domestic and market orders of worth and the tensions between them. It is important to note that economic relations are not to be identified with market worth since a firm, for example, may be analyzed as a 'compromising device' between the market and industrial worth (Thévenot 2001).

The originality of justification theory is that none of these moral orders are tied to particular social groups or superior to the others. The argumentation which is valid in one world may be out of place in another. Moreover, justification depends on the *situation*. The same person may, in the course of one day (or one hour), refer to different orders of worth to justify his actions.[10]

Since the orders of worth are equal, there is no privileged position for a critical sociologist à la Bourdieu – or any other outside observer. From this perspective the misrecognition game turns out to be part of the project that tries to reveal a deeper truth lurking behind the backs of the actors. Justification theory, on the contrary, analyzes the interviews as examples of the competence of actors to justify their actions.

In the next section we turn to the analysis of the empirical data, trying to follow the methodological principle of justification theory as summarized by Nicholas Dodier (1993: 567):

[L]et us take peoples' justifications seriously and study them in their plurality; let us observe how explanations are displayed, and accumulate the accounts people give of their actions; and let us examine the sense of justice they thereby express.

Reciprocity and the domestic ethics of helping others out

Though it is plausible to think of reciprocal obligation as a universal phenomenon in line with Alvin Gouldner, it is similarly likely that the actual expectations and forms of reciprocity are likely to vary between cultures. Edwina Uehara's review of the North American studies of reciprocity helps to place the observations of the previous section into a comparative context.[11] Uehara's goal was to find out to what extent:

(1) [people] feel obliged to return support or assistance received from others and to act on this obligation; and (2) tend to resolve/give meaning to the reciprocity 'balance' in their relationships in a manner that avoids the interpretation that they are 'overbenefiting'.

(Uehara 1995: 488)

Uehara concludes that the studies reviewed support the idea of the existence of an obligation of reciprocity. But unlike it is postulated by the equity and utilitarian theories, in Western countries people seem in their reciprocal behavior rather to try to *overbenefit* a favor received – that is, to pay their debts with interest – than to strive for balance or to take advantage of their exchange partner. Uehara's results are indicative of a context where the principles of market worth such as self-reliance and competitiveness are particularly valued:

> All in all, the normative 'deck' [in Western countries] appears to be heavily stacked against the individual in need of assistance from others.

(Uehara 1995: 499)

Justification theory does not, however, confine various orders of worth to specific cultures, but sees them rather as universal points of reference whose weight may nevertheless differ depending both on cultural context and situation.

In Russian society, for example, reciprocal expectations exist in a context where – due to the Soviet heritage and probably the much longer domestic tradition of the Russian village community – people are bound to each other within a system of mutual dependency and thus accustomed to turning to each other for help in various daily life problems. Though this 'domestic' idea of helping others out is now being challenged by the introduction of market-based principles in post-Soviet Russia, it has not disappeared. More importantly, it can be referred to even in the context of an interview concerning business-related favors, as the following quote from a Russian owner of a successful IT company shows:

> T: How and why does this [system of mutual favors] work?
> P1: Because mother was reading us fairy tales in childhood. In the fairy tale Mashen'ka is running on a field, where there stands an oven. 'Take the pie out, it is burning,' the oven says. Mashen'ka takes the pie out of the oven. Then an apple tree asks: 'Shake me.' Mashen'ka shakes the tree. But the bad girl just runs ahead and does not help anyone. And she will end up badly. This is what we were taught in childhood, to share things with everyone, to cooperate, to help.

(general director, p1)

The respondent is referring to a Russian fairy tale where the good girl Mashen'ka is helpful and gets rewarded at the end while things end up badly for the girl who does not help out other creatures. Many of Ledeneva's (1998) respondents recognized the same 'obligation to help'. Like our respondent quoted above Ledeneva herself describes this phenomenon, referring to another Russian fairy tale with similar contents:

> As in the fairy tale about Ivan-the-Fool who, despite his grand mission to liberate Helen-the-Beauty, helped different creatures on his

way, sharing food with them and saving their homes or lives. He would have had no chance in his fight with the Deathless (in Russian folklore a bony, emaciated old man, rich and wicked, who knows the secret of eternal life), but because every creature returned his favour, in their small ways in particular moments, in the end with their assistance he managed to kill the Deathless and marry the girl.

(Ledeneva 1998: 164–5, footnote 9)

Though these quotes may be read as examples of the reciprocal returning of favors, as Ledeneva remarks, here they will be interpreted as *referrals to the importance of helping out others within a system of mutual dependency*. Without this principle things will turn ugly for everyone: the pie will get burned and Mashen'ka will suffer. It is because of this systemic importance of mutual dependence that the one helping others out will finally be rewarded.

One of Ledeneva's respondents describes this domestic principle from a comparative perspective, contrasting it to the 'Western' world plagued by competition and self-reliance.

Western people, in contrast to us, are very independent. They rely on themselves and do not fancy helping out or accepting help from others. Russians assume that they can always ask for help and will help themselves. I am sure that if I ask I will be helped. And the other way around. If I am asked, I drop everything and help the other person, because I can imagine myself in his place. Indifference or refusal is a psychological trauma. I try not to refuse, giving out everything I can.

(Ledeneva 1998: 163)

This interview quote could be read as a stereotypical Russian self-identification vis-à-vis a mythical and idealized Western business life. However, instead of this kind of interpretation or trying to find out whether the respondent above in actual fact helped others, in this text these kinds of expressions will be considered *moral justifications of action*.

In line with the evidence on the importance of mutual help drawn from our interviews, Vadim Radaev (1998: 15) describes 'the ethics of implicit contracts' based on the surveys conducted among Russian managers and entrepreneurs at the end of the 1990s. When asked if the entrepreneurs were willing to loan a considerable sum of money to a firm of their regular partner who was confronting financial difficulties, only one out five entrepreneurs responded negatively. Of the respondents, 27 percent would not require any interest, 25 percent would loan money on low interest, and only 3 percent on market interest (25 percent chose the option 'difficult to say').

Though the willingness to give discounts to trusted partners was probably partly related to the exceptional circumstances of the 1990s, by referring to the ethics of helping out some of our respondents still recognized the mutual dependence of people – and particularly the dependence between the members of one's own personal network. Recognizing and sharing this moral principle means, first, that in Russia it is easier to ask for help and favors than in a context emphasizing competition and self-reliance. Second, it means that a request for help is more difficult to turn down in Russia by saying that 'it is not my business'.

At the risk of exaggeration, one may claim that while *asking for help* is interpreted in 'Western' culture as a sign of weakness, in Russia *turning down a request for help from one's network member* is a sign of rude, uncivilized behavior. One of our respondents (development director, p5), for example, having criticized at length the barter logic implied in our question on reciprocity, summarized that the topic of discussion was related, rather than to the professional sphere, 'to the worldview' (*eto skoree vsego otnositsia k mirovospriiatiiu*).

If this hypothesis is valid, we can better understand the replies of our respondents about the variations and denials of reciprocity as indicative of a context in which 'owing favors' is common and allowed. Where problems are often solved 'with a little help from my friends,' the pressure to reciprocate may be less stringent than in a context stressing the individual's capacity to do it 'my way'.

If we think of the reciprocal expectations as a cohesive force in networks (as a kind of 'social glue'), the pressure on self-reliance and immediate reciprocating in fact tries to *dissolve* this glue by a quick and full return of favor.[12] The weaker pressure on reciprocation goes hand in hand with the tendency to help others out, the importance of *obshchenie*, and the maintenance of network ties.

Nevertheless, referring to the ethics of helping out does not mean that it is applied in practice automatically in all circumstances. Instead, its application is likely to depend on the specific situation and person. Rather then describing Russian IT professionals as altruistic actors always ready to sacrifice their own interest, the analysis of this section has tried to illustrate the tensions between the new market-based logic emphasizing independence, competitiveness, and self-reliance, and the traditional domestic logic of helping out others in a system of mutual dependency.

Brokerage

> Q: Have you sometimes exchanged useful contacts through your acquaintances? For example, have you recommended your acquaintance who can help you with a question you cannot?
> P6: Of course. It is an element of everyday communication (*eto kak element povsednevnogo obshcheniia*). It happens very often beginning with small details. It is difficult to tell examples, because it is so self-evident.
>
> (marketing director, p6)

This section considers middlemen or brokers as another important social mechanism regulating transactions in personal networks. Brokers may, among other things, create trust between network members, transmit and evaluate resources circulating in networks, and enlarge the networks through the introduction of new members. In addition to these connective and collaborative functions, brokers may also try to use their position as middlemen between unconnected network members to their own advantage.

According to our respondents, the inclination to use third persons in transmission or evaluation of resources is a conventional and routinized way of acting in the Russian business environment:[13]

> According to my personal experience I can here [in Russia] freely phone a quite distant acquaintance, that is, someone whom I know well enough to phone, and ask him a favor or propose something. In Germany [where the respondent had worked] this is not as usual.
>
> (general director, p4)

Recent research has emphasized that brokers do not only pass on resources but also participate actively in the process by adapting and refining them (Mustikkamäki 2008; Sverrisson 2001; Obstfeld 2005; Obstfeld and Borgatti 2008; see also Gould and Fernandez 1989).[14] This active involvement is particularly important in the field of information technology where the transmission of information is often accompanied by its sorting, filtering, and analysis.

The first part of this section discusses the dividing and connecting aspects of brokerage on the basis of Ronald Burt's and David Obstfeld's theorizing. The remaining part focuses on the connecting and collaborative aspects of brokerage, illustrating them on the basis of our empirical data.

The broker as divider and as connector

One of the central ideas concerning brokerage is the theory of structural holes by Ronald Burt (1992). According to David Obstfeld (2005) Burt's theory is based on a variant of Georg Simmel's idea of the *tertius gaudens* broker (third who gains), where the third person in a triad takes advantage of the missing contact between the two other actors:

> He [Burt] argued that social networks rich in structural holes present opportunities for using a *tertius gaudens* strategy, by which an actor positioned between two disconnected parties can manipulate or exploit those parties to the actor's benefit.
>
> (Obstfeld 2005: 103)

Though Obstfeld notes that Burt has also addressed a broader variation of triadic behaviors, structural hole theory concentrates on the *separation* of actors suggested in Simmel's original usage. Burt's theory is marked by competition, control, and conflicts, and his *tertius gaudens* broker attempts to profit from his position by keeping the triad's other parts separate.

Unlike Burt's, Obstfeld's approach to brokerage builds on the *tertius iungens* (third who joins)[15] – a non-competitive and non-adversarial 'behavioral orientation toward connecting people by either introducing disconnected individuals or facilitating new coordination between connected individuals' (Obstfeld 2005: 102; see also Obstfeld and Borgatti 2008).[16]

Obstfeld (2005) distinguishes four types of brokerage. The first type (*conduit*) refers to coordination of action or information between parties who have no immediate prospects for direct introduction or connection. The second type (*tertius gaudens*) contains Burt's theory of structural holes. The third type (*brief tertius iungens*) introduces or facilitates ties between parties where a continuing coordinative role is unnecessary, diminishes in importance, or simply is not offered. The fourth type (*sustained tertius iungens*) introduces or facilitates interaction between parties while maintaining an essential coordinative role.

Obstfeld's idea of *tertius iungens* does not, however, exclude the presence of structural holes – which would lead to completely closed networks – because the introduction of new members to the network by a cooperative broker may, together with closing old structural holes, also create new holes.

In brief, the viewpoints of Burt and Obstfeld shed light on the two sides of brokerage, competition and collaboration, both of which merit attention. In this section the focus is, in line with the main emphasis of this book, on the latter, particularly on the role of brokers in connecting, transmitting, and evaluating resources circulating in the personal networks.

The remaining two sections do not aim at a fine-grained conceptual analysis of different brokerage types or functions but rather try to illustrate the significance of middlemen in the Russian IT business through the examination of our empirical data. Particular focus is placed on the brokers' role in recruiting employees, since competent staff was the most valuable and scarce resource in the St. Petersburg IT industry at the time of our interviews.

Brokers as connectors

> I simply have a huge database [of connections] in my head. Probably not in details, but I know how to connect people who can help each other.
>
> (project leader, p26)

According to our respondents, brokerage chains and triads were common in IT business. The inclination to turn to middlemen for help was illustrated in the expressions used by our respondents, where the instances of brokerage were described as, for example, 'self-evident' or were considered part of 'human communication' (*chelovecheskoe obshchenie*), and contact information was actively transmitted within one's personal network:

> In my circle of communication (*v kruge moego obshcheniia*) we usually let each other know about useful contacts. All colleagues in this circle think like this: 'I got to know an interesting person and for you it would be useful to talk with him'.
>
> (general director, p7)

Through brokers the network ties transferred information about a wide variety of resources such as technologies, markets, and competition. Though contacts with customers were a heavily contested resource, even they were at times transmitted from one firm to another provided that the firms were not active in the same markets:

> Q: Have you sometimes exchanged useful contacts through acquaintances?
> P10: Of course. This is banal: two weeks ago I got a phone call from my acquaintance who is also working in the IT industry. His firm has a slightly different specialization. He was contacted concerning a project which is our specialty but not theirs. So he transmitted a contact with a potential customer.
>
> (director, p10)

In the basic 'brokerage triad' between the donor, broker, and receiver, three different but interrelated ties will be born, in which the broker may function either as the third person introducing the donor and the receiver, or the guarantor of their interrelation, or both. In some cases these brokerage chains could grow long and complex. One of the respondents (director, p39) told about a phone call he got on a Sunday from his colleague 'from a friendly company'. This colleague needed to find a programmer for his project that same day. Our respondent asked the colleague to describe the requirements of the job and turned then to his personal contact notebook which contained almost 200 names. The second broker in this transmission chain was our respondent's acquaintance working in another firm, whom our respondent phoned explaining the problem:

> He [the respondent's acquaintance] said: 'This is not my field. Phone N. N'. I phoned N. N. who said: 'Yes this person exists but he is now devil knows where. You cannot reach him by phone, but he can be found through a third person'. (...) Finally, the person was found on Sunday, after three hours of searching.
>
> (director, p39)

This quote is illustrative both of the dense networks between the managers of the St. Petersburg IT companies and of the speed and efficacy of personal networks, but most importantly, of the inclination and willingness of all links in the search chain – including at least four professionals – to work as middlemen. This inclination is related to the ethics of helping out described in the previous sections and forms an important aspect of the functioning of personal networks in Russia.

Brokers as evaluators

Brokers were central not only in transmitting and connecting, but also in evaluating various resources circulating in the networks. Among the most valuable and scarce resources were competent employees, whose assessment through networks will be at the center of this section.

The particular significance of personal evaluations and recommendations in Russia may be understood against the lack or distrust of formal means and institutions of evaluation. Overcoming this distrust with the help of personal network ties was underlined by a 40-year-old company director who had conducted a survey about how customers had found their company. He illustrates the significance of trusted third persons with the following example:

> If a person tells his friend that I've bought a TV set at this specific firm, his friend will go there automatically, without thinking, just trusting his friend. Even though this person may have bought his TV set there by chance, his friend will anyhow automatically also buy his TV set there. Provided, of course, that everything was OK with this firm. His friend will go there and the friend of his friend, and this chain will work on and on. [According to our customer survey] a significant percentage of our clients come here because of recommendation from somebody. Moreover, when there is a personnel change in a [customer] company, the new employee will first see with whom the company has worked before. And if they've been happy, they will continue to work with us.
>
> (director, p22)

The need for recommendations from a third person was even more acute in the field of IT services, where defining the quality of the services, products, or labor was a much more complex process than evaluating the quality of TV sets. Though international certification standards such as ISO9000 and CMM were referred to by some of our respondents,[17] only a minority of small- or medium-sized firms have been granted these certifications.

The remaining text of this section focuses on the use of brokers in recruiting personnel which, at the time when our interviews were conducted, was the main problem for St. Petersburg IT firms. Despite high-level theoretical knowledge, the graduates from the local universities lacked practical experience of, say, project management or language skills necessary for a successful career in the IT business, and the evaluation of their *de facto* capacities was crucial for the employers.

When assessing the potential candidates for recruitment all information available was used, including formal applications and written testimonials from previous workplaces. However, written testimonials could have strings attached. A good testimonial, for example, could turn out to be an attempt to save the face of an incompetent employee and avoid problems which would have resulted from his firing:

> [Y]ou have to fire a person. He says OK, gets up, leaves his resignation of his own free will and saves his face. You will save his face. He could say that I won't resign, fire me according to the laws. He takes the issue to court after which the real show begins. He will say that you are paying salaries under the counter. And you will say that I will send 13-year-old hooligans to your home to explain to him where to look for his salary (...) who needs this? You will write him a letter of recommendation (...) and he continues on the markets, shows the letter.
>
> (general director, p3)

Moreover, in a formal testimonial the image given of the evaluation target is positive and flawless. The possible failures, conflicts, and other shortcomings at work have been excluded, whereas in an informal recommendation both pros and cons of the target can be dealt with.

Because a testimonial as a rule is written to an anonymous reader, it implies a different kind of responsibility than an informal recommendation given in a brokerage chain to an old acquaintance or friend:

> If for example one of my former employees is looking for job in some firm and asks for a recommendation (...) if he does not ask anything supernatural, I'll write a recommendation regardless of how our work relationship ended. And I don't feel any responsibility for it to other people (...) If I recommend to a friend, good acquaintance or my partner a person whom I know personally, then I will bear a certain responsibility for it. And therefore I think ten times, I weigh everything before I will give a recommendation. These are completely obvious things.
>
> (general director, p4)

Therefore, when possible, an attempt was made to check the information of the formal testimonial against the evidence obtained from trusted third persons. In a typical case, the new employer would contact the former employer of the applicant to inquire about the background, trustworthiness, and competence of the employee:

> If I see from the application that the applicant has worked, e.g., with Volkov [a well-known St. Petersburg IT entrepreneur – name has been changed], and I am not hiring a cleaner but a programmer, I will certainly phone Volkov and ask: Gennady Viktorovich, you had so-and-so working for you. What can you tell me about him? 'Nutcase' (*pridurok*). Thanks a lot, Gennady Viktorovich.
>
> (general director, p3)

In this example the written testimonial was bypassed in favor of a personal recommendation which was not made public: unlike formal evaluations, informal ones are often made orally and the persons evaluated do not necessarily know about the contents of these assessments or even about their existence.

Checking the background of the applicant over the phone was a common way of inquiring about the applicant's character and competences. During one such conversation concerning an applicant, the advice given was 'to chase him out with a broom' (project leader, p24).

However, informal recommendations were also evaluated critically and were cross-checked with different sources:

> If I see from the applicant's CV that he worked in a particular firm, it is very important for me to be able to phone some acquaintance in this firm and ask how things are with this person. Why did he leave the firm, what he was unhappy with, what are his weak and strong points? It is of course very important to talk directly with the employee because the information received from a third party is not always objective. Thus one shouldn't blindly trust some recommendations but always communicate directly with the person in question.
>
> (technical director, p11)

Moreover, neither good informal recommendations nor testimonials will secure a job if the candidate does not pass the formal tests required, for example, to land a programming job.

In one company the applicants had to fill in a form where they were asked if they had acquaintances in the company. In the case of a positive reply, the recruiters turned to this acquaintance for additional information ranging from the applicant's professional competence to a detailed description of his personality: 'This person is psychologically unstable. I studied with him at school and he used to throw paper balls at the teacher' (PR-manager, p2).

In another company recruiting through networks was formalized in the form of a bonus paid to employees for bringing in a new worker. In this case the company's employee functioned as a broker responsible for the new candidate:

> If I recruit staff through my own employees the one who brings in a new person is personally responsible for him to me. The employee is still my subordinate and thereby bound to me 'by blood' (*po krovi poviazan*). If I recruit an employee through acquaintances and am unsatisfied with him, I am forced either to cut my relations with this acquaintance or carry that burden (*derzhat' kamen' za pazuhoi*) for the rest of my life.
>
> (general director, p7)

While employers tried to evaluate the competences of the potential employees, the employees themselves were simultaneously turning to third persons to evaluate the quality of the employers. Because of the mobility of the workforce and the relatively small size of St. Petersburg markets, the reputation of both employers and employees spread quickly through networks:

> Q: How important are social networks to the formation of a person's reputation?
> P11. Extremely important. Particularly important is the lack of negative information. Negative information about the company or the director may stain the project right away. It will be more difficult to find staff if it is commonly known that the company does not treat employees fairly. This information will quite soon become common knowledge.
> Q: And will be particularly damaging for recruiting?
> P11: Of course. Such negative information is spread primarily through acquaintances. It is not usually published and therefore you can find negative information only through acquaintances.
>
> (technical director, p11)

In sum, the role of brokers was central both in introducing new members to personal networks and evaluating the resources circulating in them. Inclination to turn to brokers and willingness to act as one were marked features of the Russian managers' activities. The role of brokers was further emphasized by the lack and distrust of formal systems of evaluation and was facilitated by the relatively small circles within the industry.

The mixing of personal and professional spheres of life

This section describes how the personal and professional spheres of life get intertwined in Russian managers' networks. This mixing was due to both the historical development of the Russian IT field discussed in previous chapters and more general cultural factors related to the Russian workplace. Once established, this intertwining affected the ways transactions were conducted.

The main focus of this section is on strong ties, particularly the ties of friendship, and their mixing with the economic activities of our respondents. The remaining text analyzes both the advantages and the problems and tensions caused by the efforts to combine friendship and business.

The role of strong ties in the Russian ICT business

As described in the previous chapter, for a Russian entrepreneur just starting out it was a natural choice to turn to personal network members such as kin, family, or friends in order to start up a firm, arrange starting capital, and recruit personnel (cf. Oleinik 2004: 88). Several of our respondents had indeed built their companies upon this kind of 'strong ties' (Granovetter 1973) which in itself had contributed to the dissolving of the boundary between personal and professional spheres of life.

The roots of this mixing can be traced back to the cultural aspects of the Soviet workplace, which regulated most aspects of the citizens' daily life, including those which in Western countries were considered 'private'. It is not coincidental that the Soviet workplace was sometimes dubbed 'second home' (*vtoroi dom*) by workers and the relations within the 'labor collective' (*trudovoi kollektiv*) in many ways mixed with other aspects of life.

Though in many ways different from the Soviet era, some of the cultural meanings and practices have been carried over to post-Soviet workplaces, and studies of the workplace as the nexus of social life in post-Soviet Russia have found a strong overlap between the personal and public spheres (Lonkila 1998, 2010; Lonkila and Salmi 2005).

Similar to these studies, our data illustrates how having people at work who were not only colleagues but also kin, friends, or good acquaintances extended work-connected favors to other areas of life.[18] In the company of one of our respondents, which belonged to the group of the most central software firms in St. Petersburg it was, for example, a customary practice to borrow discount cards for shopping from one's colleagues:

> I guess that every person has some kind of discount cards for various shops, furniture, home appliances and so on. There are a lot of these cards but everyone does not have a card for every shop. Before we had a quite common practice that an employee planning to buy a bed, for example, would turn to the management asking information about who in our firm would have a discount card for *Maksidom*. And often it happened that there was such a person: 'Yes, Boris, go to the office 402, your card is waiting for you'. At some point of time we understood that we had to organize this information because there were so many letters coming in. Thus we published information in our company intranet about all cards owned by the firm employees, naturally hoping that no single person would be too much bothered.

Another respondent (project leader, p26) whose girlfriend worked for the same company turned to his boss in order to find a loan to buy an apartment. Other examples of mutual help crossing the borders of the professional and personal spheres of life, such as borrowing a colleague's car or loaning money, abounded in the interviews and were likely to affect the nature of our respondents' economic activities.

The importance of friendship

In addition to showing up in the respondents' life stories recorded in the interviews, the mixing of close relationships, particularly friendship, with business ties also emerged in the online survey data (see section on data collection). Quite surprisingly, given the instrumental formulation of the survey questions,[19] the characterizations by Russian respondents contained a lot of morally and emotionally loaded descriptions, for example, 'friend and colleague, consults me on work matters', 'boss and a good friend', 'we are good family friends, we spend spare time together, play football', 'my boss and simply a good person', 'good and understanding friend, we are working on some projects together', and so forth. Particularly interesting was the share of characterizations describing the emotional closeness between the respondent and his network members or the moral qualities of the latter.

These characterizations suggest that friendship ties were strongly present also in the professional life of the Russian IT managers. This observation was supported by the fact that, of all social ties useful for business or career reported by the respondents, 22 percent were friendship relations. Moreover, 62 percent of all respondents recorded at least one friend in their personal network.[20]

In themselves, these figures seem to testify to the importance of friendship relations – and thus also to the mixing of professional and personal spheres of life. But we also conducted an analysis of all relationship descriptions that implied a crisscrossing of the borders of personal and public spheres of life. Because the survey question inquired about the help received in the context of *professional* activities, each instance of friendship or kin ('pleasant acquaintances' – *priiateli* and acquaintances were not included) was counted as an instance of this blurring of boundaries by definition. To them were added other kinds of descriptions in which boundary crossing was clearly indicated, such as 'work and personal relationship', 'more than just a director', 'we play football together', and so forth. Altogether 108 such descriptions (31 percent of all ties) were found, lending further credence to the mixing of the spheres.

Finally, when 40 network *structures* reported by the respondents were selected for closer inspection, the role of friendship in the support networks of the Russian managers turned out to be even more vital.[21] When the number of ties involving at least one friend at the other end (or both ends) was calculated relative to all ties in the network, the average indication of the *structural importance* of friends in the networks was on average around 60 percent, reaching 100 percent for nine networks.

This is not to say that all St. Petersburg firms are populated by kin and friends or that friendship ties in business are necessarily only a Russian particularity. On the contrary, several studies (e.g. Dulsrud and Grønhaug 2007; Halpern 1994; Ingram and Roberts 2000; Kadushin 1995) point to the importance of the role of friendship also in Western economic life.[22] The mere number of the relations, however, is not enough to make conclusions about the significance of these ties, since the meaning of friendship varies between cultures (Fischer 1982; Castrén and Lonkila 2004; Kharkhordin 2005). In other words, Russian friends may expect different kinds of behavior from each other than American or Finnish friends. For instance, helping out a friend seems to be constitutive of the Russian friendship relation to a different degree than in Finland.[23]

Having friends as colleagues, bosses, business partners, principals, or clients may be both a blessing and a curse. The remaining text of this chapter analyzes the pros and cons of combining business and friendship.

Combining friendship with business

When we asked about possible *conflicts* between friendship and business, managers' replies revealed the complex relation between these two kinds of social tie.[24]

First, some respondents distinguished strictly between friendship and business ('the best way to get rid of a friend is to lend him money'). In this case the worlds of friendship and business were clearly separated (Dulsrud and Grønhaug 2007).

Second, respondents emphasized the positive aspects of friendship for business. The trust inherent in friendship can, for example, help in work tasks which otherwise might require complicated arrangements. In cases of possible conflict, finding a compromise with a good friend might be easier because of a common past and shared worldview.

Third, respondents questioned – similar to the replies to the question on reciprocity – the generalization implied by the question. In this case respondents started reflecting upon the combination of friendship and business in relation to the situation and person in question. Thus, the reply to the question of whether it is possible to combine friendship and business would be 'that depends on the friend and the situation'. A good friend might be, because of his disorganized character or other features, completely unsuitable for business:

> P5: I find it is stereotypical to think that friendship and work fit poorly together. There are many practical considerations related to this. On the other hand we have live examples of how good friends run businesses together very successfully. I think this depends a lot on the people.
> Q: In which way?
> P5. Punctuality, organized character. A person could be your friend but not necessarily a well-organized and good business partner.
> (development director, p5)

Fourth, the success of the 'marriage' between business and friendship was considered to depend on the sequential order in which they were born. As described above, in many cases firms were established on the basis of an existing friendship relation or network:

> Q: Do you know if the owners of your firm are friends?
> P6: Yes.
> Q: Were they friends already before starting business?
> P6: Yes. This is not an individual example. For instance the firm of my husband was established originally by a small group of enthusiasts (...) they all know each other and are friends.
>
> (marketing director, p6)

Since friendship contains elements, such as trust, which are beneficial in running a company, building a firm upon a circle of friends, kin, and acquaintances was not an uncommon way to establish an IT business in St. Petersburg during the 1990s. But sometimes these two ties may come into conflict, as in a case where friends disagree upon an important decision:

> Q: How in your opinion do business and friendship fit together? Have you been in situations where there was a conflict between friendship and business?
> P1: I have been lucky not to be in such a situation. Though the present managing director and partner is our good friend. But I know several cases where friendship and business disturb each other.
> Q: Why?
> P1. Because often it is a question about a decision made by one person. (...) In business there are situations when one person has to be leader and sometimes this causes conflicts. In friendship it is difficult to be a leader.
>
> (general director, p1)

In the worst possible cases, the emerging disagreement may end with the destruction of the friendship tie or business, or both. It may, to take a concrete example, be a rational decision to fire an incompetent business partner-friend.

> Generally I think that one should not work with friends. If you, for example, get into a situation, and these situations occur often, when you will have to fire your best friend (...) I got into exactly such a situation.
>
> (technical director, p11)

One of our respondents referred to business as an ongoing 'test' (*ispytanie*) for friendship. In his opinion, friends doing business together have to be on guard all the time, because of the fragility of this combination:

> Q: How in general do friendship and business relate to each other? Have you been in a situation where they got into conflict?
> P10: (...) business is quite a test for friendship (*ispytanie dlia druzhby*). Many passed the test but many did not, and either friendship or business crashed. (...) it is a difficult test (*tiazheloe ispytanie*). I have at the moment no conflicts between friendship and business, but if you are conducting business with friends you have to be constantly ready that it will lead to conflict. The same with family relations. Some think that it is a bad idea to conduct business with your wife. But there are situations where it works well.
>
> (director, p10)

The respondent does not detail the nature of the test. But this could mean, for example, giving a customer-friend credit without guarantees, or not demanding written, formal contracts which could be interpreted as a lack of trust between friends.

Unlike in previous examples, friendships could also be built upon *already existing business relationships*. Some respondents considered this variation easier than the preceding one:

> In my opinion if a good business exists, a friendship will be born. The other way around is rarer and that's why I try to avoid building business with friends.
>
> (general director, p7)

Another respondent supported this reflection by warning against starting a business with someone only because he is a friend. It may be pleasant to drink beer with a friend, but besides this, he may turn out to be a useless business partner:

> But the other way around [turning business into friendship] – as much as you like. You can have a great time working together and in addition you may also spend free time together.
>
> (director, p39)

This difference may be due to asymmetric dynamics of transformation of the ties. Trying to turn a business relationship into friendship, the first type of tie is more or less conditioned by calculative rationality. Dissolving these conditions may happen by giving up the formal practices step by step ('I trust you as an old buddy so I won't ask for guarantees for this loan'). In this case a limited tie will be gradually transformed into a more diffuse one.

The reverse transformation will impose limits on the diffuse friendship tie (for example, the friends will be forced to formalize their relationship in a written contract). Sometimes this may lead to complete revaluation of the relationship and breaking up of the friendship.

Combining friendship and business ties may thus strengthen a relationship but may also create tensions. For our online survey respondents, these tensions are all the more serious considering both the long duration of the reported friendship ties in the web survey data – 19 years on average – and the particular role of friendship in Russian culture.[25]

In all, this chapter analyzed the functioning of social mechanisms and practices governing network exchanges in the Russian software industry. It showed how economically relevant resources are not only channeled and evaluated through middlemen, but that transactions also include a moral domestic element alternative to market-based logic. Combining this domestic logic, ties of friendship, and the new world of market competition is a potential source of conflicts between the two sometimes-contradictory worlds.

The chapter also illustrated the complex interplay of the Soviet past and the post-Soviet present addressed in previous chapters. The role of strong ties, for example, cannot be only conceived of as a Soviet legacy since it was also a solution to the problem of trust in the turbulent conditions in the 1990s in Russia.

In sum, the present-day Russian market economy seems to lean in many ways on the functioning of personal networks and the domestic logic of action. The next chapter will analyze if this could be a basis for generalizing the value of particular and trusted links to *any* potential new relationship as suggested by Luc Boltanski and Ève Chiapello in their account of the 'new spirit of capitalism'.

8
The Spirit of Russian IT Capitalism

This chapter connects the analysis of the actors and their micro-level networks to the macro-level question of the nature of emerging Russian capitalism by asking what makes individuals *commit themselves* to working in the new Russian economy. The chapter will investigate the Russian IT business by comparing its moral aspects with the 'new spirit' of Western contemporary capitalism found by Luc Boltanski and Ève Chiapello ([1999], 2005) in their study of modern French business life.[1]

The main idea of this chapter is to see to what extent this new spirit, based on continuous networking and searching for new contacts and projects, are detectable in the most modern part of the Russian economy. The chapter presents first the basic ideas of Boltanski and Chiapello concerning this new spirit and then analyzes our Russian online survey data in order to find out if those data contain traces of it.

The connexionist spirit of Western capitalism

Boltanski's and Thévenot's justification theory presented in the previous chapter was criticized for, among other things, its allegedly ahistoric nature. In their book *The New Spirit of Capitalism*, Boltanski and Chiapello (2005, 2001) try to address the issue by examining capitalism from a historical perspective as a system that is not only constantly transforming itself, but also needs to get employees committed to participating in the system.

Boltanski and Chiapello focus on the dynamic relationship between capitalism and its critique, showing how capitalism has historically been able transform itself by adapting to the critique addressed to it. For example, while during the 1960s employees were lamenting loss of autonomy and increasing control, in the 1990s employees were *required* to be autonomous, and the control of employees was transferred to the customers (Boltanski and Chiapello 2005: 81).

To get employees committed to capitalism, something more than mere profit motive is needed. Capitalism has to stimulate participants through generating enthusiasm, offer security for them and their families, and be coherent with people's sense of justice by explaining how it contributes to the common good. By 'the spirit of capitalism' the authors refer precisely to the ideology justifying this commitment and making it attractive.

Boltanski and Chiapello distinguish three different spirits of capitalism, each of which corresponded with a particular form of the capital accumulation process. The first spirit depended mainly on domestic and market orders of worth. It corresponded with the traditional bourgeois capitalism which blossomed until the end of nineteenth century and was characterized mainly by small firms. The second spirit leaned more on the industrial and civic orders of worth and corresponded with the mode of capitalism which reigned from 1940–70 and was marked by managerial firms, big industrial companies, mass production and state economic policy. The third form has been emerging since 1980 and is characterized by network firms, Internet and biotech, global finance and varying and differentiated production (Chiapello and Fairclough 2002: 186–8, 191). Chiapello and Fairclough summarize this 'new spirit' in the following manner:

> Life is conceived as a series of projects, the more they differ from one another, the more valuable they are. What is relevant is to be always pursuing some sort of activity, never to be without a project, without ideas, to be always looking forward to, and preparing for, something along with other persons, who are brought together by the drive for activity. When starting on a new project, all participants know that it will be short-lived. The perspective of an unavoidable and desirable end is built in the nature of the involvement, without curtailing the enthusiasm of the participants. Projects are well adapted to networking for the very reason that they are transitory forms: the succession of projects, by multiplying connections and increasing the number of ties, results in an expansion of networks.
>
> (Chiapello and Fairclough 2002: 193)

This new 'connexionist' order of worth (*cité*) – as the six original orders of worth described in *On Justification* – is 'a model of justice, not an empirical description of the state of the world' (Boltanski and Chiapello 2005: 356). As other orders of worth, it consists of conventions that enable the establishing of equivalences that transcend the particularities of persons and things. On the basis of a common axiom, each order of worth proposes an architecture which specifies the qualities of the things that it contains, whether human beings or objects, and thus defines the contours of a corresponding 'world' (*monde*) (Boltanski and Chiapello 2005: 527). This model (*cité connextionniste*) is translated into English in *The New Spirit of Capitalism* as a 'projective city' and the corresponding world as a 'connexionist' or 'network' world.[2]

Unlike their counterparts in the 1960s, the workers of the new connexionist world are expected to put everything they have into their work, including emotions, personal relations and creativity. Worthiness or 'greatness' in this world means avoiding life-long projects. An ideal employee has distaste for stability, rootedness, and commitments to people, things or institutions:

> [A]ccess to the condition of great man presupposes sacrificing anything that might impede availability – that is to say, the ability to engage in a new project. The great man renounces having a single project that lasts a lifetime (a vocation, a profession, a marriage, etc.). He is mobile. Nothing must hamper his movements. He is a 'nomad'.
>
> (Boltanski and Chiapello 2005: 122)

These visionary leaders, coaches and experts are thus 'light' and mobile, renouncing stability and rootedness. They are capable of establishing and maintaining numerous diverse and enriching connections, and of extending networks. A truly great man (*network extender*) cannot, however, only serve his own selfish interest as a mere *networker* would do but has to think of the common good by being willing to help share his contacts and extend the networks:

> The relations between great men and little people is just when, in exchange for the trust that the little people place in them and their zeal for engaging in projects, great men enhance the value of the more humble, in order to increase their employability – that is to say, their capacity, once one project is finished, to integrate themselves into another. Terminating a project without worrying about what becomes of those who have participated in it is unworthy of a great man.
>
> (Boltanski and Chiapello 2005: 121)

The crucial *tests* of greatness and network extending capabilities are the moments at the end of the project 'when people are in search of a new engagement, their ability to integrate themselves into a new project constituting one of the palpable signs of status. They have potential, know how to engage others, they are employable and also capable of employing others' (Boltanski and Chiapello 2005: 106, 112).

The *exploitation* in a network world is related to mobility differential: the great men are mobile, and exploit the local and stable nature of the small. At the same time, it is because of the local connections of the small that the great men can have success. The small men live in constant worry of being disconnected or abandoned by those who move around (Boltanski and Chiapello 2005: 364).

In the next section we turn to empirical analysis of our online survey data in search of the light and mobile network extenders in Russian IT business.

The domestic spirit of Russian IT capitalism

At first sight the IT industry would seem to be a perfect arena for the emerging new 'connexionist' spirit of Russian capitalism, since it is typically based on successive projects conducted by ambitious, well-educated managers and employees. Moreover, as has become clear in previous chapters, leaning on networks is an essential component of the new Russian economy. Could we thus find traces of the new network spirit in the Russian IT industry?

We searched for the answer through detailed examination of our online survey data on St. Petersburg IT professionals' personal networks.[3] These data contain information on 72 respondents and their 343 network members. In the survey, the respondents were asked to name a maximum of six network members, three of whom had helped them to accomplish a successful project in 2003, and three others who had supported their career in IT (for a more detailed description, see Chapter 2).

For each supportive network member (e.g. colleague, boss, subordinate, client), the respondents were encouraged to record different kinds of information in our online survey questionnaire, such as a free-form qualitative description of the nature of the tie between the respondent and the network members (e.g. 'partner and a good friend', 'client and good acquaintance'), and the content of the help received from the network member (e.g. 'helped in leading the negotiations', 'invited me to work in big and interesting projects').

Because our data comes directly from IT professionals and not from business management guides as for Boltanski and Chiapello (2005), our results are not directly comparable. The nature of our data has to be distinguished from the texts of 'how to behave' management guides. However, studying Russian management guides probably would not have been a reliable method since many Russian IT managers do not have formal training in business management and were forced to learn everything by themselves or through imitating their more experienced colleagues. In all, our online survey produces interesting information about the possibly emerging new order among Russian managers *in their own words* in one of the most modern sectors of the Russian economy.

Since the survey was not originally planned to map the emerging moral orders of worth, it had some limitations. For example, the replies were often either too laconic or too general to give a precise idea of the order of worth in question. Despite this limitation, it seems reasonable to argue that if a new, connexionist spirit is about to be born in Russia, traces of it should be found in the Russian IT managers' reports of their networking activities connected to their ongoing projects or in their characterizations of the persons having supported these activities or their professional careers in general. These data seemed a good test case to see if a world populated by flexible Russian network extenders continuously in search of new connections and with a distaste for stability and rootedness was to emerge.

We analyzed both the qualitative descriptions concerning the contents of help received from network members and the nature of the network ties to find indications of an emerging connexionist order of worth based on projects and visionary team leaders, coaches, or project heads (Boltanski and Chiapello 2005: 79).

We thus examined all the qualitative descriptions reported by our Russian respondents concerning the *contents of the help* received to see if the help was related to searching out and extending network connections. However, most descriptions (43 percent) concerned the organizing and implementing of various work tasks (e.g. 'help in programming', 'helped to solve several difficult problems'). Sometimes these descriptions also contained moral evaluations explicitly valuing hard work and efficiency, thereby referring to the industrial order of worth ('Worked 16 hours without a break. Showed exceptional organizational capabilities', 'energetic approach to work, professionalism, capability to solve problems').

In only 17 cases (5 percent) of 343 instances of help or support was explicit reference made to a 'connexionist' type of activity (e.g. 'he found the first indispensable contact for the project', 'he introduced me to several people in the beginning of my career'). But under closer examination six cases out of these 17 concerned contact with 'useful people' (*nuzhnye liudi*) – a Russian expression for the closed circles of personal acquaintances needed to get things done. These instances of the data ('he recommended that I turn to a "useful person"' [*porekomendoval obratit'sia k nuzhnomu cheloveku*]) were thus rather part of the domestic world of personal dependencies than of the emerging new connexionist world.

Neither did the image of a charismatic and visionary team leader emerge in the descriptions of the contents of help. Though the personal networks clearly had a training and education function for the new Russian entrepreneurs, this happened rather through the moral category of *mentoring*. In the language of justification theory, mentoring is a 'domestic' category since it mostly implies a position in a system of mutual dependence. Mentoring was referred to, for example, through the forms of direct teaching or learning through following the example of a mentor. Thus, descriptions such as 'collaboration with him was my first "school" of working in IT', 'I learned from him', 'he taught me' and so forth, were noted in the data.

Mentors were sometimes described as generating enthusiasm and new ideas ('together we came up with many creative ideas which were implemented in the project') and as open-minded people who helped to find new ways of looking at things ('He taught me a non-standard approach to solving problems'). These descriptions were written with the vocabulary of curiosity, openness, and creativity, referring rather to the inspired than to the connexionist world.

More often, however, mentoring relationships implied a type of social tie similar to the relationship between master and apprentice (e.g. between the employer and employee, professor and student, or a newcomer in the field of IT and a more experienced colleague). The descriptions of mentors were often characterized as 'help' and expressed respect and filial liking extending far beyond the professional sphere of life.

The impression of the importance of moral evaluations in economic activities was further supported by the analysis of *the nature of the relationships* between our respondents and their network members. First, the respondents used a colorful, refined, and emotionally loaded vocabulary when assessing their professionally relevant ties. In addition to *drug* (friend), network members were also characterized as *priiatel* (pleasant acquaintance), *tovarishch* (buddy) or *znakomyi* (acquaintance), often preceded by an attribute detailing the emotional closeness between *ego* and *alter* (Lonkila 2006).

Second, though 41 percent of all network members were character-ized solely in terms of their professional role ('colleague', 'client', 'sub-ordinate'), 35 percent of the descriptions contained a mixture of the role-based and relation-based aspects of the tie, often combined with a moral assessment of the network member ('client and good friend', 'trustworthy subordinate, an open and frank workmate'). Moreover, 24 percent of the depictions characterized the tie only in terms of 'infor-mal' aspects of the relationship, without any reference to the formal role ('good friend', 'good acquaintance', 'pleasant acquaintance').

Finally, strong ties, mainly friendship, accounted for 24 percent of all tie descriptions. This proportion of friendship relations, along with the long average duration of these ties, also lend credence to the conclusion that the 'distaste for stability and rootedness' of the connexionist world was very alien to our Russian respondents.

In general these results reinforce the image of the importance of moral evaluations in economic activities. Moreover, concluding from the analysis of the content and nature of the ties it is fair to suggest that the world populated by light and mobile nomads and governed by the new, connexionist spirit was not visible in our Russian data. Rather than placing general value on linking to others *per se*, Russian IT managers appreciated trusted links with *specific* individuals they knew personally or through someone.

More than anything, our results suggest that Russian IT capitalism seems rather to be animated by a 'domestic' spirit valuing the tradi-tional and trusted ties of one's personal network. In the turmoil of the Russian transition, these ties create stability and a fixed reference point in an otherwise constantly changing society.

9
Conclusions

This book began with a reference to Anders Åslund's (1995) claim that 'Russia has become a market economy'. With the wisdom of hindsight, it can be said that this was a hasty statement considering the share of barter in the Russian economy in the 1990s. Later Åslund specified his claim by noting that Russia fulfils the five criteria of a functioning market economy: economic actors are independent from the state and are able to act freely, private ownership of enterprises is prevalent and property rights reasonably secured, prices and trade are predominantly free, state subsidies are limited and transactions are largely monetized (Åslund 2007: 2–3).

These criteria implicitly assume that economically relevant transactions take place through market exchange where the price mechanism is the sole or main criterion regulating these transactions. This book has contested these assumptions and argued that an understanding of the functioning of the Russian markets requires a micro-level examination of the cultural, political, and moral foundations of the actual transactions.

Åslund's statement implies that the problems and peculiarities observed during transition were due to the Soviet legacy and would disappear in due time. However, the anthropological students of transformation were quick to point out how the lack of knowledge of the actual economic processes on a grassroots level led to interpretation of even the problems which were actually created by the reformers themselves as Soviet legacies. The spread of barter, for example, followed from the monetization of the economy as an unintended result of the reforms and differed qualitatively from its Soviet-era counterpart. It was thus 'a product of shock therapy rather than the legacy of a paternalistic Soviet state' (Burawoy and Verdery 1999b: 9; Woodruff 1999, 2000).

This book has similarly proposed that the formation and significance of personal networks in post-Soviet Russia is not only a legacy of connections dating from the Soviet era but also an unintended result of the very process of transformation of the Russian society and economy: the turmoil of the post-Soviet transition forced the newly emerging Russian entrepreneurs to turn to their trusted social ties such as family, kin, friends, and acquaintances.

The tendency of turning to one's own personal network members went hand in hand with the mixing of the personal and public spheres of life, the overlap of instrumental and sociability aspects of mutual favors – such as the importance of *obshchenie* – and the use of the domestic principle in justifying transactions. At the same time, this principle is constantly being challenged by the newly introduced logic of market competition, resulting in frictions and tensions in the networks.

Andrei Shleifer and Daniel Treisman (2005) raised recently a heated debate on the nature of the Russian economy and politics by claiming that Russia was a 'normal' case when compared to the countries in the same middle-income range. They sought to prove, among other things, that the scale of the collapse of the Russian economy and the decline in output in the 1990s have been exaggerated. In their opinion, when compared to other eastern European nations and the former Soviet Union, Russia's economy performed by and large as might have been expected (see Shleifer and Treisman 2005).

Nevertheless, it is somewhat unfruitful to argue whether Russia is a 'normal', 'real' or 'distorted' market economy. All market economies are different and a more urgent and interesting research task is to investigate the specificity of the Russian case (Rautava and Sutela 2000: 242; Sutela 2003).

This specificity is in many ways rooted in the developmental path of the Russian transition. Introducing a capitalist system in Russia was a conscious, foreign-led modernizing project whose critics were identified with the old Communist regime and thereby sidelined. Post-Soviet Russian capitalism was constructed with the help of foreign advisors in an extremely short time in the hope that market competition and capitalist relations would dissolve the old Soviet patterns and networks. In fact, the opposite seems to have happened: the combined result of the imported capitalism and the existing networks produced a socioeconomic and political system very different from the original intentions of the reformers.

In Western countries, on the contrary, capitalism developed during a long period of time, in which it was constantly exposed to various forms of criticism. Probably partly because of this differing evolutionary path, this study found no support for the existence of a 'new spirit' of Russian network capitalism similar to the one proposed by Luc Boltanski and Ève Chiapello (2005) in the French context. This kind of spirit would stress the importance of continuous networking and constant mobility and would have an aversion to stable and strong ties. As has become apparent in this book the Russian IT industry seems, on the contrary, to lean in many ways on trusted and established personal ties.

As noted in the introduction to this book, the development of information and communications technology has also, in addition to its functions in the economy, an important *political* role in the post-Soviet Russia. President Medvedev himself brought up the link between technological progress and political freedoms in his 'Go, Russia!' – speech in 2009:

> The growth of modern information technologies, something we will do our best to facilitate, gives us unprecedented opportunities for the realization of fundamental political freedoms, such as freedom of speech and assembly. It allows us to identify and eliminate hotbeds of corruption. It gives us direct access to the site of almost any event. It facilitates the direct exchange of views and knowledge between people all around the world. Society is becoming more open and transparent than ever – even if the ruling class does not necessarily like this.
>
> (Medvedev 2009b)

The president's faith in the democratizing effects of technological development contrasts starkly with the avalanche of worrying news about the state of the Russian democracy. These include, among others, harassment of opposition demonstrations, killings of journalists, biased broadcasting by the main national TV channels, selective punishment of citizens or democratic institutions under various pretexts, and arbitrary practices of the Russian police. The president also neglects the possibility that new technology may be used to monitor, control, and repress citizens. Moreover, his statement is internally inconsistent since 'the Russian ruling class' is simultaneously supposed to facilitate democratization through the means of modern information technologies and not to like this development.

The president returned to the modernization theme and the relation between information technology and politics in his speech at the St. Petersburg International Economic Forum plenary session in

June 2010, citing several recent policy reforms aimed at building 'a modern, strong and prosperous Russia'. This new Russia would, according to him, be among the co-founders of the new global economic order and political leadership (Medvedev 2010).

The new Russian economy would not be built 'from above', but through the efforts of private business in a competitive environment where the job of the state is 'to ensure a good business climate for Russian and foreign entrepreneurs, and a fair and honest competitive environment'. The most ambitious of the new reforms are the plans to make Moscow a global financial center and to create a Russian version of the Silicon Valley near the capital. The reforms also include, among other things, incentives to innovation companies, a law limiting possibilities of arresting businesspeople in connection with investigations into economic crimes, simplifying immigration rules for highly qualified foreign specialists, and cutting the list of strategic enterprises.

This kind of new Russian economy would go hand in hand with the development of democracy in a process where information technology has a specific role:

> Information technology is one of the key elements in developing democracy in general. The speed and quality of feedback between the authorities and society, greater technological possibilities for guaranteeing freedom of speech, and internet technology in operation of political and electoral systems are all important for developing our political structures and institutions.
>
> (Medvedev 2010)

Even though both the intrinsic connection between capitalism and democracy in general and the blessings of information technology in particular may well be questioned, the emergence of a more diversified economic structure in Russia with a great number of small- and medium-sized enterprises is more likely to be conducive to democratization than an economy dominated by a few big companies owned or controlled by the state. Similarly, the role of the Internet and new technology for political and opposition activism in Russia is likely to grow in importance in parallel with the decrease of the Russian traditional media's ability to fulfill its watchdog function (cf. Lonkila 2008).

However, as with the efforts to weed out corruption from the Russian economy and society, the question is, who is going to implement these macro-level reforms and how? The answer has to do with the functioning of personal networks, which has been the focus of this book.

Because of its qualitative nature, this book has not attempted to answer the question of whether or not the Russian economy and networks are dominated by immoral and illegal practices. Rather, it suggests, along the lines proposed by Oleg Kharkhordin (2005, 2009), that personal networks may be one of the main resources that the Russian society and economy have at their disposal and therefore merit special attention.

Appendix: List of Respondents

Respondent	Pseudonym	Year	Sex	Age	Position
1	Andrey	2005	male	55–60	general director
2	Anna	2005	female	25–30	PR-manager
3	Boris	2005	male	35–40	general director
4	Dmitry	2005	male	30–35	general director
5	Vladislav	2005	male	30–35	development director
6	Svetlana	2005	female	25–30	marketing director
7	Nikolay	2005	male	44–50	general director
8	Mikhail	2005	male	35–40	COO, director
9	Evgeny	2005	male	25–30	director
10	Leonid	2005	male	20–25	director
11	Sergey	2005	male	25–30	technical director
12	Vasily	2005	male	25–30	CEO
13	Anton	2005	male	25–30	general director
14	Denis	2005	male	44–50	business development manager
15	Valentina	2005	female	20–25	marketing manager
16	Konstantin	2005	male	44–50	CEO
17	Viktor	2005	male	30–35	development manager
18	Galina	2005	female	20–25	marketing manager
19	Petr	2006	male	35–40	PR-manager
20	Nikita	2006	male	20–25	technical director
21	Vadim	2003	male	20–25	programmer
22	Pavel	2004	male	35–40	director
23	Jury	2004	male	35–40	project leader
24	Anatoly	2002	male	25–30	project leader
25	Grigory	2004	male	25–30	journalist
26	Oleg	2004	male	25–30	project leader
27	Fedor	2004	male	25–30	team leader
28	Eduard	2004	male	40–45	director
29	Filipp	2004	male	35–40	director
30	Taras	2004	male	30–35	programmer
31	Roman	2004	male	30–35	company director
32	Ivan	2004	male	20–25	system administrator
33	Aleksandr	2004	male	30–35	department head
34	Artem	2004	male	20–25	IT service expert
35	Valery	2004	male	30–35	director
36	Larisa	2004	female	25–30	programmer
37	Nina	2004	female	35–40	team leader

(continued)

Continued

38	Kirill	2004	male	45–50	technical director
39	Lev	2004	male	30–35	director
40	German	2004	male	35–40	programmer
41	Alina	2004	female	45–50	director
42	Egor	2004	male	30–35	company director
43	Gleb	2004	male	25–30	director
44	Maksim	2004	male	25–30	journalist
45	Ruslan	2004	male	40–45	company director
46	Vyacheslav	2004	male	missing	company director
47	Matvey	2004	male	25–30	company director
48	Stanislav	2004	male	30–35	general director
49	Vladimir	2004	male	35–40	technical director
50	Vera	2004	female	25–30	operator

Notes

1 Introduction

1. The software industry or software sector comprises businesses involved in the development, maintenance and publication of computer software and software services such as training, documentation and consulting (Software Industry, Wikipedia 2010). Together with the hardware industry it makes up the IT (information technology) sector and IT and telecommunications together make up the ICT (information and communications technology) sector. Giving exact definitions of ICT or drawing strict boundaries between its subsectors is problematic because of the dynamic nature of the field. Official statistical categories, for example, often lag behind the development of technology and cannot grasp its rapid evolution. The main focus of the analysis of this book is on the software sector, but it will be contextualized by a review of the Russian ICT sector. Later in this book the terms IT and ICT will often be used interchangeably.

2. Their realizing the necessity of diversification is likely to have been affected by the worldwide financial crisis in 2008. Anders Åslund considered Russia 'as one of the countries likely to be worst hit by the international financial crisis, although it entered the crisis with huge budget and current accounts surpluses since 2000 and the third-largest currency reserves in the world' (Åslund 2008). Until the crisis Russia's annual growth in the 2000s had been among the world's fastest and in the beginning of 2008 Russia rose to join the world's top ten largest economies (Sutela 2008a; Gaddy and Ickes 2009).

3. In Anders Åslund's (2008) opinion, except for the fiscal policy, almost everything else in Russia's economic policy has gone wrong after the arrest of Khodorkovsky in 2003. Among other errors (such as failure to develop the banking sector and a nationalistic energy policy after 2003) Putin's main project to develop 'huge state-owned mastodons' financed by foreign loans rather than equity has stalemated large parts of the economy because of their inertia and corruption and has also prevented diversification of the economy.

4. See also: Lomnitz (1988); Srubar (1991).

5. While accepting the general conclusion on the significance of networks in the Soviet Union, Anna-Maria Salmi (2006, 2009) presents three critical notes on the discussion of Soviet-era networks. First, focusing *solely* on connections may run the risk of overemphasizing their role and underestimating that of money which, despite the significance of networks, still had an important role in Soviet society. Second, there is a lack of reliable empirical data on the actual use of connections in Soviet society since conducting field research on the topic in the Soviet Union was impossible. Finally, the discussion of Soviet era networks has not addressed the inequality of citizens' access to these networks in terms of, say, gender, place of residence and class position.

Salmi suggests that the debate on networks should not get stuck on the irresolvable question of whether or not the networks are more important than they used to be. Rather, more empirical research is needed to examine the use of networks in various, specific contexts: *to whom and in which ways do the networks matter in present-day Russia?* Finally, she notes how a surprisingly small percentage of the claims about networks is based on the application of conceptual tools and methods developed in the social network analysis tradition (Salmi 2006, 2009).

6. See, for example, Castrén (2000); Castrén and Lonkila (2004); Lonkila (1999a, b, 2010); Lonkila and Salmi (2005); Rose (1998); Ledeneva (1998, 2006).

7. *Sotsial'noe neravenstvo v sotsiologicheskom izmerenii*, 2006.

8. Though Simon Clarke's (2002) study of the subsistence of Russian households in the 1990s warns against overestimating the role of networks at the expense of formal monetary sources of income such as salaries and pensions, he also found that social networks were an important resource for Russians. Nevertheless the most significant exchange of help took place between close kin, and there was no evidence of private transfers constituting an important component of a household's survival strategy (Clarke 2002: 206).

9. See also: Radaev (2003); Dolgopyatova (2000); Kosonen (2002); Lonkila (2006); Ledeneva (2006); MacMylor et al. (2000); Salmi and Bäckman (1999); Salmi (1995).

10. In Western sociology of economic life, the role of social networks in the economy has been at the center of attention since Mark Granovetter's seminal article *Economic Action and Social Structure: The Problem of Embeddedness* (1985). In the article Granovetter emphasizes how economic action is not carried out by atomized actors and cannot be explained only by individual motives, but is embedded in ongoing networks of personal relations (Granovetter 1985, 1992, 2002; Swedberg and Granovetter 2001; Swedberg 2004: 318).

Granovetter borrowed the notion of embeddedness from Karl Polanyi – though the notion actually derives from the book *Die menschliche Gesellschaft* published in 1932 by the German anthropologist Richard Thurnwald (Beckert 2006: 37) – who used it to refer to the intertwining of the economy and other fields of life in premodern societies. According to Granovetter, Polanyi not only overestimated the embeddedness of the premodern societies, but also underestimated it in modern societies where economic action is also 'embedded' in social life through networks of actors.

There is neither the possibility nor the need to summarize here the findings of the vast literature about networks in economic life inspired by Granovetter and other students of social networks. This literature covers a wide variety of themes, from job seeking, leadership, organizational power, information diffusion, board interlocks, joint ventures and inter-firm alliances to knowledge management, innovation and entrepreneurship. Many of these studies employ the notion of embeddedness though Granovetter himself has later considered the term rather as a general approach than a variable to be measured empirically (Rahman 1998: 88, 92–3; see also Krippner et al. 2004; for critical views, see Swedberg 2004; Krippner 2001; Krippner and Alvarez 2007; Beckert 2006). For a general review of the network research in economic life, see Smith-Doerr and Powell (2005), for a review of network research in organizational research, see Borgatti and Foster (2003) and in entrepreneurship, see Hoang and Antoncic (2003).

11. Examples of this lack of confidence in most institutions of the Russian economy and society abound both in surveys and research literature, on Russian Internet forums and in discussions with Russians. Prior to sending their children to a kindergarten or school, going to the hospital, seeing an unknown doctor or dentist or turning to a travel agency or a car mechanic, Russian citizens are first likely to consult their personal network members.

The Russian traffic police are particularly notorious for their bad reputation of arbitrarily fining car drivers and driving schools for refusing driving licenses to the candidates not giving bribes (Lonkila forthcoming). Moreover, because of the hazing and bullying that takes place in the Russian army, educated young Russian men try to avoid obligatory military service either through bribing, using social relations or through other informal means (Lonkila 2008).

The lack of trust also has concrete implications for economic activities. One of the IT professionals whom we interviewed, for instance, expressed a fear that an application filed at the patent registration office would be sold to outsiders.

12. The quotation marks around 'Western countries' indicate the problematic nature of this expression, often used in constructing the 'otherness' of Russian society. It is clear that 'Western' countries do not constitute a homogeneous category. Nor are they, if used to refer to modern industrialized countries, located westwards from Russia. On the other hand, as will be evident from the next note, the Russians themselves are keen to use 'West' in their own identity construction, which has long roots in Russian history.

13. One of the Russian IT directors we interviewed described his experience and difficulties in conducting business in Russia vis-à-vis Western countries 'as having to walk five meters under water'. An example of this 'inertia of daily life' is the fact that up to and at the present time, there has been no phone directory published in St. Petersburg, and getting a lost number through a number inquiry service is extremely difficult. Therefore losing one's phone book – a database and an embodiment of one's personal network – is a small-scale social and economic catastrophe.

14. The functioning of these favors overlaps with the notion of informal economy: as in the informal economy, favors are neither regulated by states nor by market forces, but governed by social and cultural conventions. However, grasping the use of networks in terms of the 'informal' (Portes and Haller 2005), 'shadow' or 'underground' *economy* or even 'non-market economic practices' (Smith and Stenning 2006) is difficult since the term 'economy' tends to miss the intertwining sociability aspect of the favors. Rather, we are dealing not only with strictly speaking economic but also economically relevant social practices, which are often impossible to conceptualize in terms of livelihood or income formation. It is also important to note that the *sites* of the use of networks 'engage the full range of social and economic sites of everyday life – homes, workplaces, schools, hospitals, shops, bars, restaurants and local government offices, among others' (Smith and Stenning 2006: 202).

2 Using Networks to Find Out about Networks

1. Social network studies should be distinguished from the Actor-Network Theory, by Bruno Latour and his colleagues (see, e.g. Latour 1996, 2005), which extends the nodes of the network to non-human actors.
2. In this text, when there is no danger of confusion, I will use both the terms 'network' and 'social network' when referring to personal networks.
3. In addition to the direct relations between the respondent and his network members ('first order star'), a researcher may also study the relations between the network members themselves ('first order zone'), or widen the reach of the network, also considering the relations mediated by the network members themselves ('second order star'). This book deals mostly with the first order star, with some consideration to the first order zone and the second order star.
4. These notions are in quotation marks to warn against uncritical application of binary dichotomies to Russian society. Rather, network research helps to deconstruct such dichotomies as official/unofficial or public/private in Russia (Yurchak 2006). As the text below will show, network research in Russia shows a continuous overlapping of 'personal' and 'professional' ties as well as the crisscrossing of traditional social cleavages.
5. These terms are more neutral than instrumental expressions referring to strategic use of personal relations, such as *svoi liudi, poleznye/nuzhnye liudi* (useful people). The Russian language also makes fine-grained distinctions concerning the proximity of personal network members that are difficult to grasp in many other languages. For instance, there is an intermediate category of *priiatel'/priiatel'nitsa* (meaning literally 'a pleasant acquaintance') located between friend (*drug/podruga*) and acquaintance (*znakomyi*), which does not have an exact English translation (though it could be translated as 'buddy' or 'mate' depending on the context, see Kharkhordin 2002, 2005).
6. The approach utilizing the notion of personal networks as a consciously chosen theoretical and methodological tool has been used in a series of comparative studies based on the structured daily diaries that Russian and Finnish secondary school teachers kept of their social relations. These studies, led by Professor Risto Alapuro at the University of Helsinki, have supported the hypotheses of the centrality of personal networks in Russian culture and the mixing of professional and personal spheres of life in these networks.

   Lonkila (1998), for example, in his comparative study of the 'social meaning of work' for the Russian and Finnish teachers found that, contrary to expectations, Russian networks contained clearly more social ties related to the workplace than the networks of the supposedly more work-centered Finns.

   An explanation for this puzzling discovery was only found through a detailed micro-level study of the formation of the teachers' personal networks. This examination revealed how the difficulty of getting an apartment but ease of finding work in the Soviet era led many teachers to change their workplace in order to teach at a school next to their home. This not only saved time in commuting to work in the crowded public transportation of the city, but also allowed teachers to put their own children in the same school and thereby to ensure the quality of their education.

Ultimately this led to a geographically dense formation of teachers' personal networks around the school, and the mixing of professional and personal spheres of life. The colleague of a Russian teacher could, for example, simultaneously also be her child's teacher, living in the vicinity, and be engaged in the informal exchanges effectuated through the workplace (Lonkila 1998).

7. Multiplexity refers to a social tie combining two or more different kinds of relations. One may, for instance, be a friend or a neighbor of one's colleague.

8. Noteworthy also are the numerous studies conducted by Simon Clarke's group, see: http://www.warwick.ac.uk/russia/, accessed September 4, 2010.

9. The qualitative analysis of the interview data on the Russian directors and managers is a dialogue on at least three levels. First, the respondents are often arguing with themselves: it is not uncommon to note that at the end of the interview the respondent is contradicting his earlier statements. Second, the respondents often detail, contradict, or confirm information obtained from other respondents. Third, respondents engage in discussion with the interviewer by answering the questions and, in the best cases, reinterpreting, denouncing, and criticizing the researcher's formulations, as will become evident later in this book.

This polyphonic and polymorphic network of interrelations cannot be represented 'as is'. The researcher has to construct the most reliable and plausible image of the study topic from varied and sometimes contradictory material. In doing this, one has to make selections, emphasize some connections and cut others and, finally, present one's own interpretation. We have, however, tried to give voices to multiple opinions as much as possible, including those deviating from the majority of the respondents.

10. The growing popularity of qualitative and mixed method studies has been visible in, for example, the panels on qualitative network analysis at the yearly conferences of the International Network of Social Network Analysis (INSNA). See also Hollstein and Straus (2006), Dominguez and Hollstein (forthcoming).

11. Later in this book the interviewees are referred to as 'respondents' or 'managers' and each interviewee is identified by work assignment and code (e.g. technical director, p20) and at times also by an invented first name. The first 20 codes (p1–p20) refer to the interviews of the second round and the next 30 (p21–p50) to the interviews of the first round. A complete list of all respondents is found in the appendix. The data were collected in the research project 'Russia, Finland and globalization from a micro perspective', led by Markku Lonkila. The Russian interviews were conducted by Tatyana Kozlova.

12. Because of the prevalence of male respondents both in the interviews and the industry, this book uses 'he' instead of 'she' where gender-neutral language use is not possible.

13. The Russian licentiate degree (*kandidat*) corresponds roughly to the US doctoral degree.

14. In the first round of interviews (30 respondents) the task was to inquire more generally as to the structure, evolution, and practices of the IT sector in St. Petersburg. In order to get a diverse image of the field, the firms were

selected from different areas of the IT industry, such as software design, telecommunications, hardware, computer magazines, consulting companies, and so forth, and the respondents from different positions in the company hierarchy, including programmers. In the second round of interviews (20 respondents) the focus was on software developers' networks, and the respondents were selected from among the top- and mid-level directors, managers, and company owners.

The book is mainly built on the systematic analysis of the second round of interviews, but the first round of interviews is also utilized to complement and contextualize the analysis. Combined, the data corpus of 50 interviews gives a rich and versatile view of the different parts of the St. Petersburg IT industry, with the detailed and systematic analysis of the software sector during the second round of interviews.

15. According to one of the respondents (general director, p3), this modest lifestyle was, however, dictated by the relatively small profits made in the software development sector in St. Petersburg: 'They [the company directors] drive used cars, nobody wears an expensive Swiss watch. All wear suits made in St. Petersburg and shoes that cost less than 400 USD (...) there is no money'.

16. The interviews were recorded and transcribed in Russian with MS Word and coded with ATLAS/ti text analysis software. In actual fact this meant that the interviews were first read through once. After the first reading, my native Russian research assistant coded the interviews according to the themes appearing in the interview protocol and the new ones which had emerged during the first reading. The coded parts of the text were then printed out and read through while starting to write the manuscript.

During the process of writing, new themes, which were similarly coded in ATLAS/ti, emerged. In like manner, some old themes were observed to be futile and were abandoned. During the last round of research, the data were still read through once to test the interpretations from previous rounds.

17. The first results of the research are published in Lonkila (2006). This volume re-analyzes the web survey data for the purposes of this study.

18. These data were stored in a MS Access database located in a Finnish server. The free-form descriptions concerning the nature of the *ego–alter* relationship and the content of the support that *ego* had received from *alter* were coded by the author for analysis. Finally the personal network graphs were drawn with the help of UCINET 6 (Borgatti et al. 2002) and used in the analysis of the friendship ties (see Chapter 7).

19. This is not to say that networks would automatically be less important for big companies but that their contents and functions may differ: a big company may, for example, have crucial networks connected to other major economic or political actors or both.

3 The Evolution of Russia's IT Sector

1. I am obliged to Gordon Cook for his kind permission to use the interview. The interview quotes from the Cook report are indicated in parentheses after the quotes; all others are from the author's interviews.

2. The first L in the abbreviation refers to the small city of Lomonosov, located 40 km west of Leningrad on the Baltic Sea. The whole name of the firm was *Lomonosovskoe spetsializirovannoe montazhno-naladochnoe upravlenie 'Spetsavtomatika'*, which can be roughly translated as 'The Lomonosov city agency "Specialautomation"'.

3. The rise and fall of the joint venture Dialogue would merit a separate study not attempted here.

4. 'A Bulletin Board System, or BBS, is a computer system running software that allows users to connect and log in to the system using a terminal program. Once logged in, a user can perform functions such as uploading and downloading software and data, reading news and bulletins, and exchanging messages with other users, either through electronic mail or in public message boards. (...) Bulletin Board Systems were in many ways a precursor to the modern form of the World Wide Web and other aspects of the Internet' (http://en.wikipedia.org/wiki/Bulletin_board_system, accessed November 17, 2009). The Moscow BBS built by Dialogue was the second and the St. Petersburg BBS the ninth Russian node in FidoNet, a global network named after its developer's dog Fido. FidoNet enabled communication between the bulletin board systems and was most popular in the early 1990s, before easy and cheap access to the Internet became available (http://en.wikipedia.org/wiki/FidoNet, accessed November 17, 2009).

5. For other founding fathers of Soviet computing, see Trogemann et al. (2001a: 1). For a more detailed account of Soviet computing, see, for example, Trogemann et al. (2001b).

6. See also: Khetagurov (2001: 189); Fitzpatrick et al. (2006).

7. *Strela* was developed in the special design bureau SDB-245 in Moscow. This bureau created the Scientific Research Center for Computer Technology in 1969, which was to become known as the leading center for copying the IBM 360 models (Klimenko 1999: 19). For a recent detailed account of the development of *Strela*, see Ichikawa (2006).

8. The naming of M-20 referred to its capacity of conducting 20,000 operations per second (vis-à-vis the 50 of the first BESM).

9. Lebedev was also supervising the construction of BESM-6, the first Soviet supercomputer. The great number of different kinds of mainframe computers at the beginning of the 1970s complicated the development of the Soviet computer industry. To solve this problem, a series of 'Unified System of Computers' (*ES-riad*), computers with a modular structure corresponding to the architecture of the IBM 360/370 families, was designed to enable a large volume of production (Prokhorov 1999: 8–10).

10. Opinions on this point seem to differ to some extent. According to Crowe and Goodman (1994), for example, the first models of IBM 709 delivered in early 1958 were faster than the M-20, the most advanced Soviet computer at the time. Because of this failure, the makers of M-20 failed to be awarded the Lenin prize. Similarly, Klimenko (1999: 25) claims that by the early 1980s, the Soviet computer industry was lagging 20–25 years behind the Western one in comparison with five years in 1967 and one year in 1959. According to Igor Apokin on the other hand (2001: 79), 'By the end of the 1950s, when one of the best pioneer computers M-20 was

already in operation, Soviet computers had already reached, and in some sense even surpassed, the level of American computers'. See also Susiluoto (2006: 144).

11. For more detail, see Nitussov and Malinovskiy (2001: 163–7).
12. The report was written during the last years of the existence of the Soviet Union leaning on both Western and Russian sources as well as on unidentified 'knowledgeable Soviets'. The part of the report concerning the Soviet Union and CMEA countries is clearly worried about the possibility of Gorbachev reviving Soviet economic and military might with the help of technology transfer from the West.
13. Though Academician Dorodnitsyn, the long-time director of the center, related to the first PCs 'indifferently', considering them as toys, he allowed the establishment of a group focusing on PC use already around 1982. The group worked with IBM XTs writing Russian applications (such as the word processing software LEKSIKON) for it and publishing Russian-language literature on the PCs. Due to the fall of the Soviet Union the center lost its financing and custom base and had to give up the project of installing a supercomputer built on Russian technology. (Evtushenko et al. 2001)
14. This section follows mainly Castells' interpretation. For other views on the development of Soviet computing, see Adirim 1991; Crowe and Goodman 1994; Klimenko 1999; Prokhorov 1999; Trogemann et al. (2001b).
15. According to Castells, *statism* is a system in which the surplus value is appropriated by the powerholders of the state apparatus, whereas in *capitalism* the surplus is appropriated by those in control of the economic system. Castells defines *industrialism* as a mode of development in which productivity is based on the quantitative growth of factors of production (work, capital, and natural resources), whereas in *informationalism* 'the main source of productivity is the qualitative capacity to optimize the combination and use of factors of production on the basis of knowledge and information'. A social structure that would correspond to an informationalist mode of development is dubbed a 'network society' by Castells. In his theory the economy's shift from industrialism to informationalism went hand in hand with the shift from an industrial to a network society (Castells 2000: 8).
16. This section describes Russian IT as a part of the ICT sector.
17. *Elektronnaia Rossiia* website (http://www.e-rus.ru/site.shtml?id=11&n_id=4677, accessed December 15, 2006). See also RUSSOFT's annual report from 2008, in which the ICT sector's share of the GDP was estimated at 4.8 percent in 2007 (*RUSSOFT Annual Survey*, 2008).
18. The data concerning the ICT sector should be read with care since acquiring exact and reliable figures of its current size is problematic. The area's young and dynamic nature complicate its description with the help of traditional statistics. Also, publicly available accounts are often based on market research conducted by private companies or industry associations, which have marked financial interests. The telecommunications sector is also one of the Russian state's strategic lines of business, in which the activities of foreign companies are subject to license (Vahtra 2007).
19. Lanit-Tercom merged with Artezio software company in 2008 to form AT software.

20. Levada Center (2010). The data is based on representative surveys of the Russian population over 16 years of age. The questions asked about cellphones and personal computers were: 'Do you personally have a cellphone?' and 'Is there a computer at home in your family?' The question asked about Internet use was: 'Do you personally use Internet (except e-mail) at home, at work, or at any other place? If yes, how often?' The answering options were 'daily', 'a few times a week', 'about once a week', '2–3 times a month', 'about once a month', 'less than once a month', and 'never'. The Figure 3.1 summarizes the first five options. These figures are clearly smaller than those concerning the six months audience (see FOM estimate below).

21. In 2007 Vladimir Putin decreed the formation of the *Rosokhrankul'tura*, an organization supervising media and culture, with the federal body *Rossviaz'nadzor* controlling telecommunications and IT, thereby creating fears about tightening Internet control in Russia. These fears were also increased by the arrest and conviction of a Russian blogger, who wrote in his LiveJournal blog that the Russian police were 'scum' and called for officers to be tossed on a bonfire ('Putin decrees creation of a media and Internet regulator', *New York Times*, March 15, 2007).

22. No attempt is made here to deal with either all possible relations between the Russian state and the ICT industry or the amount of control the Russian state has over the economy. Suffice it to say that in general Vladimir Putin's term as president has been marked by an increase in state involvement in the economy, especially in strategically important sectors. According to Yakovlev (2006), state–business interaction under Putin swung from the control of the federal and regional authorities by the 'oligarchic capital' – also called 'state capture' – in 1998–99 to the dominance of the state over big business by 2003–4. The state managed to gain control over the economy and dissenters, such as Mikhail Khodorkovsky, were removed from power.

However, the notion of the state's control of the economy is a complicated matter. Though the privatization of the Russian economy had cut the number of state-owned firms to 9 percent in 2007 (in addition 2 percent had mixed ownership according to the estimates from Troika Dialog 2008, cited in Sprenger 2008: 2), federal and regional authorities controlled about 40 percent of the market capitalization of the Russian stock market at the end of 2007, compared to 24 percent in 2004. The largest companies controlled by the state in 2008 were in the energy, banking, and communications sectors (Sprenger 2008: 2, 13).

In terms of ICT, the Russian state also has both financial and strategic interests, which are particularly visible in the telecommunications sector, consisting of the state-owned *Sviaz'invest* and three major mobile operators. As described in previous sections, telecommunications has been the locomotive of the Russian ICT industry with the lion's share of the turnover. An intensive struggle for the ownership of Megafon, one of the biggest Russian operators, has been ongoing for years along with the debate regarding the allegedly close ties between the Russian political elite and mobile teleoperators. According to the decision of a Swiss court in 2006, Leonid Reiman secretly owned a large part of the country's telecom industry through an offshore fund (Amsterdam 2007). Reiman denied the allegation.

23. See also interview with Economy Minister German Gref (Part 1), RIA Novosti, May 1, 2007, available at: https://www.usrbc.org/goverment/russian_government/executivebranchrus/event/170, accessed August 7, 2009.
24. Of the companies that participated in the poll, 66 percent considered the situation not to have changed, and 2 percent considered it to have worsened.
25. See *ACM-ICPC Programming contest*, 2009. However, one of our respondents (development director, p5) considered the idea of Russian education being better than Western to be a 'stereotype', and another (department head, p33) regarded the level of Russian IT education as 'insufficient'.
26. International Intellectual Property Alliance placed Russia on its 'priority watchlist' with Argentina, Chile, India, Israel, Pakistan, People's Republic of China, and Thailand in 2006–7, when estimating trade losses due to business software copyright piracy. See www.iipa.com.
27. For a recent comparative account of Russian ICT, see Dutta and Mia (2010). See also Bardhan and Kroll (2006).
28. At the time of writing, the first signs of the worldwide recession, which began from the US, could also be seen in the growth of supply in the job market.

4   The Soviet Legacy and Its Transformation in the Russian IT Field

1. It also pays to remember the role of *material legacy* – probably the most visible form of Soviet legacy for Western visitors of Russia. Buildings, roads, communication infrastructure, trains, airplanes, tramways, trolleybuses, and cars and many other material objects from daily life still remind one of the Soviet era and will continue to do so for many years to come.
2. Michael Burawoy and Katherine Verdery (1999b) suggest that the emphasis laid on the legacy aspect of post-Soviet transformation is a combination of the development path advocated (revolution vs. evolution) and one's point of orientation (past vs. present). Institutional economists, for example, orient to the future and consider the transformation in evolutional terms whereas the similarly future-oriented neoliberalists stress the revolutionary nature of the change and try to get rid of the reminders of the past as quickly as possible in order to give life to the new market order. The defenders of totalitarian theories likewise stress the revolutionary changes but are more interested in the extinction of Communism than genesis of the new system. Finally, sociologists have suggested various notions to grasp the legacy aspect of the systemic transformation, such as path dependency, cultural persistence, circulation of elites, or recombinant forms of property (Stark 1996).
3. Oksana Shmulyar Grèen (2009: 270–84) considers Komsomol entrepreneurs as a part of a 'co-operative movement'. She also distinguishes an additional three economic areas in which entrepreneurial activities were developed in the Soviet Union: the Soviet second economy, state-run institutions and ministries, and the independent private business sector. The last category, which in her mind is 'probably one of the least studied groups' among

Russian entrepreneurs, can be further divided into groups of young entrepreneurs with credentials in education who started as junior managers in small private firms or Western companies; 'mass entrepreneurs' such as commuter traders; and members of the younger generation of the Soviet intelligentsia coming from academic backgrounds.

4. Presently AT Software.

5. Though navigating in the interstices of the Soviet system is likely to have taught entrepreneurial skills to part of the population, one also has to keep in mind that private entrepreneurial activity was illegal in the Soviet Union until the end of the 1980s, and some of this official hostility was carried over to the transition period (Aidis et al. 2008: 658). In addition, during transition the emergence of entrepreneurs involved in criminal or semi-legal activities created considerable amount of envy, annoyance, and fear among the population. This hindered the formation of a positive image and social status for the new social strata of Russian entrepreneurs. On the other hand, the collapse of the publicly funded research institutes (military research among others) freed up an educated workforce, which supplied the pioneering builders of the ICT sector, for the work market (see Yurchak 2002; Rogers 2006; and Shmulyar Gréen 2009 for closer accounts of the evolution of entrepreneurship and the related legislation in Russia).

6. Analyzing the transformation of Soviet *blat* networks requires many caveats already referred to in the Introduction. First, the lack of systematic data on *blat* practices in the Soviet Union makes comparisons difficult. Second, discussing Soviet networks solely in terms of *blat* runs the risk of neglecting the role of non-instrumental ties. Finally, as remarked by Michael Burawoy and Katherine Verdery (1999b), phenomena which at first glance appear to be remnants from the Soviet era may have not only taken on new and different meanings and functions in post-Soviet society, but may also have new causes.

7. I am obliged to Tiina Saajasto from the Bank of Finland Institute for Economies in Transition for compiling Figure 4.1.

8. Belchenko (2008) also quotes the annual survey conducted by the Institute of Transition Economics (*Institut ekonomiki perekhodnogo perioda*, IEPP) in October 2008, according to which the payments in arrears had doubled in a short time: in October 22 percent of the survey respondents had had experience of arrears, whereas the same figure in a spring/summer survey in 2008 had been 10–12 percent.

9. Kosals and Ryvkina (2001) define the notion in the following way: 'Otkat – a "kick-back" – is the charge demanded by an official for granting an order (usually, a state order), credit (often with interest below market rates), subsidy, or grant. It is measured as a percentage of the amount provided and it can reach more than half the total sum. *Otkat* is thus a specific form of corruption. Basically, *otkat* operates within the state sector or between the state and private sectors of the economy, but it is sometimes even found in relations between private companies. It reflects the privatization by an official (or a manager of a private company) of his or her position, which is used as a resource for carrying out private entrepreneurship. Often, *otkat* appears as a stable partnership between officials of different

ranks (in the case of misuse of budgetary funds), or between officials and businesspeople. *Otkat* became the norm for the system of state allocations and state orders'.

10. Integrum is the largest collection of Russian and CIS databases, containing roughly 400 million documents, among them a great number of Russian national and regional newspapers. The search was conducted in December 2008 among the issues of 1992–2007 of the following newspapers: *Izvestiia, Kommersant, Kuranty, Literaturnaia gazeta, Moskovskii komsomolets, Nezavisimaia gazeta, Pravda, Rossiiskaia gazeta, Sem'ia, Sovetskaia Rossiia*. The search takes into account also the conjugation of the search words. I am obliged to Sylvi Nikitenkov for conducting the search.
11. http://www.transparency.org/, accessed September 5, 2010.
12. Another respondent told about tax evasion practices and a third one admitted to having bribed officials.

5 Social Milieus and Personal Network Growth in the St. Petersburg IT Industry

1. Another mechanism for network growth is through a third person introducing separate parties. In Chapter 7 the central role of brokers is described in detail.
2. The relative importance of various milieus and types of brokers varies depending on context and culture. Anna-Maija Castrén (2000) showed how the role of spouses in Helsinki teachers' networks was more important than in St. Petersburg teachers' networks; Lonkila (1998; see also Lonkila and Salmi 2005) suggests that the work milieu was more central in transmitting ties in St. Petersburg than in Helsinki.
3. Perelman refused both the Fields Medal and the monetary prize attached. He left his academic career in a top US university and is currently living near St. Petersburg with his mother.
4. Certainly not all or even the majority of the IT managers in St. Petersburg have studied in the specialized schools, nor did all the graduates of these schools go into the IT business. The tradition of keeping in touch with one's old classmates is common to all kinds of schools in Russia, though probably more so in schools with a special reputation.
5. According to RUSSOFT, software companies particularly value graduates from St. Petersburg State University, St. Petersburg State University of Information Technologies, Mechanics and Optics, St. Petersburg State Polytechnical University, St. Petersburg State Electrotechnical University, Bonch-Bruevich Telecom University, Transport University, and Aerospace Instrument Engineering University (*RUSSOFT Annual Survey*, 2008: 33).
6. See http://vkontakte.ru/club336, accessed August 12, 2009.
7. It is considered common knowledge that during both the Soviet and post-Soviet eras, a study place at a university could be either bought or obtained through relations. Though in mathematic-technical fields the share of these practices is probably smaller, since the studies require certain competences, one of our respondents (IT service expert, p34) told of having entered a technical university 'through recommendation'. In

practice this meant an agreement where the candidate prepared for the entrance examination under the guidance of a specified teacher accepted by the university, which was enough to guarantee passing the entrance exams. In the case of the interview quote mentioned above one has to remember that the student in question had already shown special mathematic talent.

8. Source: http://www.sergey.com/cgi-bin/list-239.cgi, accessed August 19, 2009. The period 1985–95 was chosen because of the relatively large number of graduates reported yearly (on average 69 graduates). The list is based on the voluntary reports by the graduates and thus certainly only forms a small and possibly biased sample. Though the list was updated in January 2008, the last reported graduate is from 2005, and the yearly number of graduates in the 2000s is negligible.

   The overall number of highly skilled migrants is, however, much smaller than the total migration flow. Moreover, Russians accounted for only 1.4 percent of the high-tech professionals working with special visas in the US in the early 2000s whereas Indians accounted for one third (Gapova 2006). For a closer account of the brain drain of the early 1990s from the former Soviet Union, see Moody (1996). Moody examines the issue mainly from the viewpoint of international security. He considers that the most serious brain drain has taken place internally in terms of scientists, engineers, and technicians leaving science and defense-related fields for other professions such as business.

9. The Russian Internet also contains specific forums for job searches, such as www.job.ru, www.rentacoder.com, and www.freelancer.ru.

10. www.vkontakte.ru, accessed May 24, 2009.

11. These figures are overlapping since many people are registered on both sites.

12. http://www.tns-global.ru/rus/projects/media/asmi/inet/descrip/, accessed May 24, 2009.

13. http://my.mail.ru/cgi-bin/login?page=http%3A%2F%2Fmy.mail.ru%2F, accessed May 24, 2009. Specific cases are discussion forums and user groups on technical matters such as Java or database programming or Russian Linux users, which occasionally also offer meetings in pubs in St. Petersburg.

14. http://www.russoft.org/russoft/?makarov, accessed May 22, 2009.

15. When discussing Makarov, one of our respondents remarked that 'He is now in civil duty, but the [officer] stars shine through'.

16. http://www.russoft.org/russoft/?benefits, accessed May 22, 2009.

17. Mikhail Piotrovsky, the director of the Hermitage museum, was congratulated on his sixty-fourth birthday on December 9, 2008 by Valentin Rodionov, the director of Tretyakov Gallery with the following words: 'Deeply honored Mikhail Borisovich! Allow me to congratulate you on your birthday. For many museum directors you are a model for museum professionals. Under your leadership the Hermitage was transformed into a museum which maintains its traditions and is simultaneously developing according to international standards. We thank you for many years of cooperation with Tretyakov gallery and for your work for our common effort' (http://www.idelo.ru/535/17.html, accessed June 15, 2009).

18. *Kommersant*, May 14, 2010. Available at: http://www.kommersant.ru/doc. aspx?DocsID=1368383, accessed June 16, 2010.

6 The Types of Economic Resources Transmitted through the Networks of St. Petersburg IT Professionals

1. Ledeneva relies on 40 interviews provided for her by Nonna Barkhatova. The data was collected in Novosibirsk regarding small enterprises (cooperatives) including service, production of consumer goods, and educational and organizational services (Ledeneva 1996: 184, footnote 4).
2. Many US success stories in the field of IT were originally based on study mates' circles. However, as will become evident, the institutional environment of post-Soviet transformation makes the cases very different.
3. As with the banking sector, venture investment activity is still in a rudimentary state in Russia. Polynskaya et al. (2008) remark on the establishment of the Russian foundation for venture investment (*Rossiiskii fond venchurnykh investitsii*) in 2007 in the IT field. We do not, however, have information on its functioning.
4. This evaluation is supported by Anders Åslund's critical estimate of Russia's financial markets dominated by inept state banks (2008).
5. The interviews were conducted prior to the worldwide economic crisis of 2008.

7 Social Mechanisms Governing the Informal Transactions between Russian IT Managers

1. There is thus no intention of developing a general theory of network cohesion. The social milieus discussed in Chapter 5, for example, also support the maintenance of the networks.
2. Gouldner divides the norm into two parts, of which only the first will be dealt with in the text below: '(1) people should help those who have helped them, and (2) people should not injure those who have helped them' (Gouldner 1960: 171).
   Reciprocity is naturally also the subject of a vast anthropological literature starting from the classic work by Marcel Mauss (2000), the review of which is beyond the purposes of this study (see, e.g. Boltanski 1990). In the sociological debates on reciprocity, balanced and generalized reciprocity are generally distinguished from each other. Balanced reciprocity refers to a 'tit for tat' kind of exchange between A and B, where A gives an object to B who returns another object corresponding to the original one in a short time. In generalized reciprocity – one variant of which is often discussed as 'social capital' – A gives a gift or favor to B and gets it back from a third, unknown person.
3. See Parry (1986) about criticism concerning the universalism of reciprocity.
4. The exact formulations were: (1) There is a saying 'there is free cheese only in a mouse trap', meaning that if you do someone a favor, you expect the favor to be returned. Do you agree with this saying? (2) Have you yourself

ever given or received favors in business without any wish or chance that the favor would be returned? Examples?

5. It is evident that Ledeneva's discussion of the 'affective regime' is based on Luc Boltanski's (1990) work, whereas the 'regime of justice' draws from Boltanski's and Thévenot's work on justification (1991, see the next section) – even though the latter is not among the list of references mentioned:

> Boltanski (1992) suggested the distinction of 'affective regime' and 'regime of justice' which the same relationship may undergo. In the regime of justice the stress is laid on the equivalencies, explicated to manage disputes. On the contrary, in the ordinary course of common actions equivalencies are not subjected to deliberate reflection. In the affective regime, persons actively cooperate in the process of shoving the equivalencies aside in order to make the cumulation and calculation operations which are required to blame and criticise difficult. This regime is described with the stress on the present moment, and on a form of forgiveness which borders on forgetting. The person who goes on shifting from one regime to another looks back over past events in a disillusioned way: 'how was it possible to be such a fool; so naive of me. For the last twenty years I have been doing [all these favours] ... Now, I realize'. But this experience of the moment of truth is not more real than the other. The regime in which one makes calculations is no more true, no more real, than the regime in which people inhibit their calculation abilities, he argues. It is the [change] in the perception of the world stemming from a quick shift from one regime to another which gives the illusion of a glaring truth.
>
> (Boltanski 1992, cited in Ledeneva 1998: 143–4)

6. The book was published in French already in 1991 under the name *De la justification. Les économies de la grandeur* (Boltanski and Thévenot 1991). It is considered to be a cornerstone work both for the French 'pragmatic sociology' as well as for the 'Convention School' of French economic sociology. For English introductions and reviews, see Dodier (1993), Boltanski and Thévenot (1999), Wagner (1999), Eulriet (2008), Naccache and Leca (2008). For critical views, see Amable and Palonbarini (2005). Justification theory has also been applied to comparative studies (e.g. Lamont and Thévenot 2000, Luhtakallio 2010). The main ideas of justification theory will be presented here on the basis of the authors' summarizing article (Boltanski and Thévenot 1999).

7. See Buck (2006) for the application of justification theory to postsocialist forms of patronage and Stark (1996) for an early application of justification theory to eastern European forms of recombinant property.

8. The number of the orders is not fixed. Boltanski and Chiapello (2005), for example, have proposed a hypothesis of the emergence of an order of worth based on networks (*cité connexionniste*) related to the 'third spirit of capitalism' (see also Chapter 8), and Michèle Lamont and Laurent Thévenot (2000) have investigated the emergence of 'green worth'.

9. Justification theory is built upon an unorthodox connection between the contemporary how-to-behave management guides and the classical texts of political philosophy including *City of God* (St. Augustine – the inspired order

of worth); *La politique tirée des propres paroles de l'Écriture sainte* (Bossuet – the domestic order); *Leviathan* (Hobbes – the order of renown); *Contrat social* (Rousseau – the civic order); *Wealth of Nations* (Adam Smith – the market order); *Le Système Industriel* (Saint Simon – the industrial order). These orders define the worth of the persons present in the dispute. Though the principles of equivalence differ, all orders share the same common structure or model (*modèle de la cité*), which explains how actors may easily switch from one order to another depending on the situation.

To solve an emerging dispute, the parties have to agree upon a test (*épreuve*) which, if successful, will bring the dispute to an end. The other party may disagree on two grounds. In *internal* criticism he may argue that the test itself is 'impure', and contains beings from another world. A more radical, *external* criticism does not aim to improve the test to be fairer, but instead wants to replace the test altogether with another one relevant in another world.

Finally, it is also possible to end the dispute by constructing a *compromise* between two orders of worth where 'people maintain an intentional proclivity towards the common good by cooperating to keep present beings relevant in different worlds, without trying to clarify the principle upon which their agreement is grounded' (Boltanski and Thévenot 1999: 374). These compromises tend to be fragile because they maintain the inherent tension and, instead of solving it, temporarily 'sweep it under the rug'.

10. In addition to the regimes of *justification* in which the participants look for a common principle of equivalence to settle the dispute, there are other possibilities for ending a dispute. One of them is giving up arguing altogether and shoving aside all calculations of reciprocity in a regime of affection (*regime d'agapè*). More generally the settling of disputes contains two dimensions: the presence or absence of dispute on the one hand, and the presence or absence of a principle of equivalence on the other. These two dimensions produce a four by four matrix where the regime of justification combines dispute with the search for the equivalence principle, whereas the regime of affection combines the peaceful solution (absence of dispute) with the absence (or bracketing) of the equivalence principle (for the remaining variants, see Boltanski 1990; Basaure 2008).

11. Uehara (1995: 492) is conscious of the limits of his mainly North-American data and warns against generalization to the US ethnic groups or other cultures.

12. According to Sahlins (1969: 178), balanced exchange is not an effective glue in social ties, because it will dissolve the motive to maintain the relationship. Contrary to Sahlins, Leithart (2006) has proposed that one's interest in maintaining a relationship with one's trusted car mechanic does not disappear even though one pays for his services.

13. Ledeneva (1998) also describes the Soviet practice of referring to a third person in arranging *blat* services (*ia ot Ivana Ivanovicha*).

14. Obstfeld and Borgatti (2008) suggest that brokerage should be defined as a process which has a *structural condition* (three or more network nodes). Separating the analysis of the brokerage process from the social network structure would help to uncover processes which are otherwise easily neglected.

15. *Iungens* is based on the Latin verb *iungo* meaning to join, unite, or connect. According to Obstfeld, this view is related to a variant of Simmel's thinking where the *tertius* serves as a means to the ends of the group. However, Obstfeld remarks that the examples by Simmel refer mostly to the adversial tensions within a group.

16. According to Obstfeld, Burt's structural holes create new ideas but contain an 'action problem', for the weakly or not at all connected people that make up the 'holey' network are difficult to mobilize. People connected by dense networks are for their part easy to mobilize, but they have the 'idea problem' already noted by Granovetter (1973): the information circulating in the network is known to all and thus redundant.

17. See Thévenot (2009) and Feakins (2007) for the role of standards as governing mechanisms.

18. At least six of our respondents worked in the same firm with their family members.

19. The survey questions asked the respondents to name people who had helped them to accomplish a successful project or supported them in their professional career.

20. The respondents were encouraged to describe both the character of the relationship between themselves and their network members and the type of help received in their own words. Analyzing the qualitative descriptions revealed a fine-grained and complex image of the relations in business life in general, and friendship in business in particular. Of all characterizations of the network members in the web-survey, 41 percent were role-based descriptions ('colleague', 'client', 'subordinate'), 24 percent relationship based ('friend', 'pleasant acquaintance' (*priiatel'*)) and 35 percent were mixing role and relationship based characterizations ('partner and good friend') (Lonkila 2006). Sometimes respondents themselves wanted to clarify the nature of ties by calling them formal (*formal'nye*), matter-of-fact (*delovye*), or work relationships (*rabochie otnosheniia*).

21. Only the networks containing five or six network members were included in the analysis. The network graphs were drawn with the help of UCINET 6 software for network analysis (see Borgatti et al. 2002).

22. An online survey among Finnish ICT professionals also yielded an important number of friendship ties. Due to the small number of replies, however, the results are only indicative. Various aspects of friendship have been addressed by a great number of studies (e.g. Shlapentokh 1984; Paine 1969; Silver 1990; Pahl 2000; Eve 2002; Doyle and Smith 2002).

23. In a comparative case study of the personal networks of female secondary school teachers in St. Petersburg and Helsinki during the 1990s, Castrén and Lonkila (2004) noted, among other things, differences between the friendship ties and practices of the Russian and Finnish teachers. Though trust, common values, and sharing were important in both cities, for Russian teachers, unlike for Finns, all kinds of helping were an indistinguishable part of their friendship relations. The Russian teachers exchanged more favors of a more varied nature than the Finns.

24. The interview questions were: 'How do business and friendship fit together? Have you been in a situation where you felt that business and friendship were in conflict?'

25. In their work on the 'third spirit of capitalism', Luc Boltanski and Ève Chiapello (2005) have also analyzed the tension between friendship and business relations in the emerging new world based on continuous networking and searching for new projects and connections. In this kind of new capitalism, there is an anxiety about the instrumentalization and commodification of friendship relations.

The anxiety of French businessmen about the possible instrumental motivations behind a dinner invitation by a friend seems to be, however, very different from the cases from the Russian data we have described above. Probably because helping out friends in any possible way is a constitutive part of the Russian friendship, our respondents were not afraid of corruption of friendship by business but rather of either the incompatibility of these worlds or of practical questions of how to organize this connection.

8 The Spirit of Russian IT Capitalism

1. For English reviews of the study, see, for example, Budgen 2000. For accounts in German, see Boltanski and Chiapello 2001; Potthast 2001. Later in this text references are made to the English translation.
2. English translations of the French original differ depending on the source used. The French term *cité* (Boltanski and Thévenot 1991) was translated as 'order of worth' in *On Justification* (Boltanski and Thévenot 2006) but as 'city' in the *New Spirit of Capitalism* (Boltanski and Chiapello 2005). In order not to confuse the reader, the former translation is used in the remaining text of this section. It is illustrative of the difficulties of translation that in German *cité* is translated as *polis* (Basaure 2008).
3. This section is partly based on Lonkila (2006), but contains reanalysis of those data for the purposes of this book.

References

ACM-ICPC Programming Contest (2009) International collegiate programming contest. Available at: http://cm.baylor.edu/welcome.icpc, accessed May 9, 2009.

Adirim, I. (1991) 'Current Development and Dissemination of Computer Technology in the Soviet Economy'. *Soviet Studies* 43 (4): 651–67.

Aidis, R., Estrin, S., and Mickiewicz, T. (2008) 'Institutions and entrepreneurship development in Russia: A comparative perspective'. *Journal of Business Venturing* 23 (6): 656–72.

Akhlaq, A. (2005) *Getting a Job in Finland: The Social Networks of Immigrants from the Indian Subcontinent in the Helsinki Metropolitan Labour Market*. Doctoral dissertation, Department of Sociology. University of Helsinki.

Alapuro, R. (2001) 'Reflections on Social Networks and Collective Action in Russia'. In S. Webber and I. Liikanen (eds), *Education and Civic Culture in Post-Communist Countries*. Basingstoke: Palgrave Macmillan, 13–27.

Alapuro, R. and Lonkila, M. (2000) 'Networks, identity, and (in)action. A comparison between Russian and Finnish teachers'. *European Societies* 2 (1): 65–90.

Alexander, M. (2004) 'Internet and Democratization: The Development of Russian Internet Policy'. *Demokratizatsiia* 12 (4): 607–27.

Amable, B. and Palombarini, S. (2005) *L'économie politique n'est pas une science morale*. Paris: Éditions Raisons d'Agir.

Amsterdam (2007) Russia's Offshore Telecom Corruption Case. Available at: http://www.robertamsterdam.com/2007/11/russias_offshore_telecom_corru.htm, accessed February 28, 2010.

Apokin, I. (2001) 'The Development of Electronic Computers in the USSR'. In G. Trogemann, A. Nitussov, and E. Wolfgang (eds), *Computing in Russia: The History of Computer Devices and Information Technology Revealed*. Braunschweig/Wiesbaden: Fried. Vieweg & Sohn Verlagsgesellschaft, 76–107.

Ashwin, S. (1999) *Russian Workers: The Anatomy of Patience*. Manchester: Manchester University Press.

Averin, A. and Dudarev, G. (2003) *Busy Lines, Hectic Programming*. Helsinki: ETLA.

Bardhan, A. D. and Kroll, C. A. (2006) 'Competitiveness and an Emerging Sector: The Russian Software Industry and its Global Linkages'. *Industry and Innovation* 13 (1): 69–95.

Basaure, M. (2008) 'Die pragmatistische Soziologie der Kritik heute. Luc Boltanski im Gespräch mit Mauro Basare'. *Berliner Journal für Soziologie* 18 (4): 1–24.

Batjargal, B. (2003) 'Social Capital and Entrepreneurial Performance in Russia: A Longitudinal Study'. *Organization Studies* 24 (4): 535–56.

Batjargal, B. (2005a) 'Software Entrepreneurship: Knowledge Networks and Performance of Software Ventures in China and Russia'. *William Davidson Institute Working Paper* 751, February 2005. Available at: http://wdi.umich.edu/files/publications/workingpapers/wp751.pdf, accessed May 10, 2010.

Batjargal, B. (2005b) 'Entrepreneurial Versatility, Resources and Firm Performance in Russia: A Panel Study'. *International Journal of Entrepreneurship and Innovation Management* 5 (3–4): 284–97.

Batjargal, B. (2006) 'The Dynamics of Entrepreneurs' Networks in a Transition Economy: the Case of Russia'. *Entrepreneurship and Regional Development* 18 (4): 305–20.

Batjargal, B. (2007) 'Comparative Social Capital: Networks of Entrepreneurs and Venture Capitalists in China and Russia'. *Management and Organization Review* 3 (3): 397–419.

Beckert, J. (2006) 'Jens Beckert Answers Ten Questions about Economic Sociology'. *Economic Sociology: The European Electronic Newsletter* 7 (3): 34–9.

Belchenko, V. (2008) 'Zdravstvui, barter!' *Ogonek* 51.

Boltanski, L. (1990) *L'amour et la Justice comme competences: Trois essais de sociologie de l'action*. Paris: Métailié.

Boltanski, L. (1992) 'The Sociology of Critical Capacity'. Lecture at IAS, Princeton, March.

Boltanski, L. and Chiapello E. (1999) *Le Nouvel Esprit du Capitalisme*. Paris: Gallimard.

Boltanski, L. and Chiapello E. (2001) 'Die Rolle der Kritik in der Dynamik des Kapitalismus und der normative Wandel'. *Berliner Journal für Soziologie* 11 (4): 459–77.

Boltanski, L. and Chiapello E. (2005) *The New Spirit of Capitalism*. London: Verso.

Boltanski, L. and Thévenot, L. (1991) *De la justification: Les économies de la grandeur*. Paris: Gallimard.

Boltanski, L. and Thévenot, L. (1999) 'The Sociology of Critical Capacity'. *European Journal of Social Theory* 2 (3): 359–77.

Boltanski, L. and Thévenot, L. (2006) *On Justification: Economies of Worth*. Princeton: Princeton University Press.

Borgatti, S. P., Everett, M. G., and Freeman, L. C. (2002) *Ucinet 6 for Windows: Software for Social Network Analysis*. Harvard, Analytic Technologies.

Borgatti, S. and Foster, P. (2003) 'The Network Paradigm in Organizational Research: A Review and Typology'. *Journal of Management* 29 (6): 991–1013.

Brygalina, J. and Temkina, A. (2004) 'The Development of Feminist Organisations in St.Petersburg 1985–2003'. In A-M. Castren, M. Lonkila, and M. Peltonen (eds), *Between Sociology and History: Essays on Microhistory, Collective Action, and Nation-Building*. Helsinki: Kikimora Publications, 207–26.

Buck, A. D. (2006). 'Postsocialist Patronage: Expressions of Resistance and Loyalty'. *Studies in Comparative International Development* 41 (3): 3–24.

Budgen, S. (2000) 'A New "Spirit of Capitalism"'. *New Left Review* 1: 149–56.

Burawoy, M. and Verdery, K. (eds) (1999a) *Uncertain Transition: Ethnographies of Change in the Postsocialist World*. Lanham (Md.): Rowman & Littlefield.

Burawoy, M. and Verdery, K. (1999b) 'Introduction'. In M. Burawoy and K. Verdery (eds), *Uncertain Transition: Ethnographies of Change in the Postsocialist World*. Lanham (Md.): Rowman and Littlefield, 1–17.

Burt, R. (1992) *Structural Holes: The Social Structure of Competition*. Cambridge: Harvard University Press.

Butrin, D. and Granik, I. (2009) 'President svoiu komissiiu vypolnil'. *Kommersant* 86 (4141), May 16. Available at: http://www.kommersant.ru/doc.aspx?DocsID=1171306&print=true, accessed January 17, 2010.

Castells, M. (2000) *End of Millennium*. 2nd edn. Oxford, Malden, MA: Blackwell.

Castells, M. and Himanen, P. (2001) *Suomen tietoyhteiskuntamalli*. Helsinki: WSOY.

Castrén, A-M. (2000) *Perhe ja työ Helsingissä ja Pietarissa. Elämänpiirit ja yhteiskunta opettajien sosiaalisissa verkostoissa*. Helsinki: SKS.

Castrén, A-M. and Lonkila, M. (2004) 'Friendship in Finland and Russia from a Microperspective'. In A-M. Castrén, M. Lonkila, and M. Peltonen (eds), *Between Sociology and History: Essays on Microhistory, Collective Action and Nation-Building*. Helsinki: SKS / Finnish Literature Society, 162–74.

Chachin, P. (2008) 'Vklad ICT-otrasli v VVP rastet'. *PC Week/RE* 5 (611).

Chiapello, E. and Fairclough, N. (2002) 'Understanding the New Management Ideology: A Transdisciplinary Contribution from Critical Discourse Analysis and New Sociology of Capitalism'. *Discourse and Society* 13 (2): 185–208.

Clarke, S. (2000) 'The Household in a Non-Monetary Market Economy'. In P. Seabright (ed.), *The Vanishing Rouble: Barter Networks and Non-Monetary Transactions in Post-Soviet Societies*. Cambridge: Cambridge University Press, 176–206.

Clarke, S. (2002) *Making Ends Meet in Contemporary Russia: Secondary Employment, Subsidiary Agriculture and Social Networks*. Cheltenham: Edward Elgar.

Clarke, S. and Kabalina, V. (2000) 'The New Private Sector in the Russian Labour Market'. *Europe-Asia Studies* 52 (1): 7–32.

CNews Analytics (2007) Obzor 'IT v Sankt-Peterburge 2007'. Available at: http://www.cnews.ru/reviews/free/spb2007/articles/topCNA_spb.shtml, accessed August 7, 2009.

CNews Analytics (2010) CNews Analytics Agency. Available at: http://www.cnews.ru/reviews/rating/, accessed June 17, 2010.

Cooper, J. M. (2006) 'The Internet as an Agent of Socio-Economic Modernisation in the Russian Federation'. In M. Kangaspuro and J. R. Smith (eds), *Modernisation in Russia since 1900*. Helsinki: Finnish Literature Society, 285–304.

Crowe, G. D. and Goodman, S. E. (1994) 'S. A. Lebedev and the Birth of Soviet Computing'. *IEEE Annals of the History of Computing* 16 (1): 4–24.

Cook, G. (2009) 'Arcadia: A Case Study in Navigating the Turbulence of Post Soviet Russia. The Strategic Evolution of a Firm that Is not a Body Shop but People and Internet Centric'. *The COOK Report on Internet Protocol: Technology, Economics, and Policy* 18 (6). Available at: http://www.cookreport.com/, accessed May 10, 2010.

Cusumano, M. A. (2006) 'Where Does Russia Fit into the Global Software Industry: Exploring How Russia's Nascent Software Industry Measures Up to Other Countries'. *Communications of the ACM* 49 (2): 31–4.

Denisov, D. (2005) 'Territoriia "otkata"'. *Biznes-Zhurnal Online*, 6.6.2005. Available at: http://www.ippnou.ru/article.php?idarticle=001467, accessed January 24, 2010.

Dinello, N. (1999) 'The Russian F-Connection: Finance, Firms, Friends, Families, and Favorites'. *Problems of Post-Communism* 46 (1): 24–33.

Dodier, N. (1993) 'Review article: Action as a combination of 'common worlds'. *Sociological Review* 41(3): 556–71.

Dolgopyatova, T. (2000) 'The Evolution of New Institutions in the Small Business Sector'. In S. Harter and G. Easter (eds), *Shaping the Economic Space in Russia*. Aldershot: Ashgate, 163–88.

Dominguez, S. and Hollstein, B. (eds) (forthcoming) *Combining Mixed Methods: Social Network Studies*. A book manuscript under review.

Doyle, M. E. and Smith, M. K. (2002) 'Friendship: Theory and Experience'. *The Encyclopaedia of Informal Education*. Available at: http://www.infed.org./biblio/ friendship.htm, accessed May 10, 2010.

Dulsrud, A. and Grønhaug, K. (2007) 'Is Friendship Consistent with Competitive Market Exchange? A Microsociological Analysis of the Fish Export-Import Business'. *Acta Sociologica* 50 (1): 7–19.

Dutta, S. and Mia, I. (eds) (2009) *The Global Information Technology Report 2008–2009*. World Economic Forum. http://www.insead.edu/v1/gitr/wef/main/ fullreport/index.html, accessed September 10, 2010.

Elfring, T. and Hulsink, W. (2003) 'Networks in Entrepreneurship: The Case of High-Technology Firms'. *Small Business Economics* 21 (4): 409–22.

Emirbayer, M. and Goodwin, J. (1994) 'Network Analysis, Culture, and the Problem of Agency'. *The American Journal of Sociology* 99 (6): 1411–54.

Eulriet, I. (2008) 'Analysing political ideas and political action'. *Economy and Society* 37 (1): 135–50.

European Social Survey (2008) European Social Survey Round 4 Data. Data file edition 1.0. Norwegian Social Science Data Services, Norway – Data Archive and distributor of ESS data. Available at: http://ess.nsd.uib.no/ess/round4/, accessed June 17, 2010.

Eve, M. (1998) 'Qui se ressemble s'assemble? Les sources d'homogénéité à Turin'. In M. Gribaudi (ed.), *Espaces, temporalites, stratifications: Exercices sur les réseaux sociaux*. Paris: Éditions de l'École des Hautes Études en Sciences Sociales, 43–69.

Eve, M. (2002) 'Is Friendship a Sociological Topic?' *Archives européennes de sociologie* 43 (3): 386–409.

Evtushenko, Yu., Mikhailov, G., and Kopytov, M. (2001) 'Istoriia otechestvennoi vychislitel'noi tekhniki i akademik A. A. Dorodnitsyn (k 90-letiiu so dnia rozhdeniia)'. *Informatsionnye Tekhnologii i Vychislitel'nye Sistemy* 1: 3–12.

Feakins, M. (2007) 'Off and Out: the Spaces for Certification – Offshore Outsourcing in St. Petersburg, Russia'. *Environment and Planning* 39 (8): 1889–907.

Feld, S. (1981) 'The Focused Organization of Social Ties'. *American Journal of Sociology* 86 (5): 1015–35.

Fischer, C. S. (1982) 'What Do We Mean by Friend? An Inductive Study'. *Social Networks* 3 (4): 287–306.

Fitzpatrick, A., Kazakova, T. and Berkovich, S. (2006) 'MESM and the Beginning of the Computer Era in the Soviet Union'. *IEEE Annals of the History of Computing* 28 (3): 4–16.

Fligstein, N. (2001) *The Architecture of Markets: an Economic Sociology of Twenty-First-Century Capitalist Societies*. Princeton: Princeton University Press.

Fuhse, J. (2009) 'The Meaning Structure of Social Networks'. *Sociological Theory* 27 (1): 51–73.

Fungáĉová, Z. and Solanko, L. (2008) 'Risk-Taking by Russian Banks: Do Location, Ownership and Size Matter?' *BOFIT Discussion Papers* 21. Available at: http:// www.bof.fi/en/julkaisut/index.htm, accessed May 10, 2010.

Gaddy, C. G. and Ickes, B. (2009) 'Putin's Third Way'. *The National Interest Online*, 01.06.2009. Available at: http://www.nationalinterest.org/Article.aspx?id= 20496, accessed May 10, 2010.

Gapova, E. (2006) 'The Migration of Information Technology Professionals from the Post-Soviet Region: Migration Prespectives'. In R. Rodrigues Rios (ed.), *Migration Perspectives. Eastern Europe and Central Asia*. Available at: http://iom. ramdisk.net/iom/images/uploads/Migration%20Perspectives%20eng%20FINAL %20protected_1168947543.pdf#page=14, accessed May 10, 2010.

Gaslikova, I. and Gokhberg, L. (2001) *Information Technology in Russia*. Moscow: Center for Science Research and Statistics.

Gerovitch, S. (2001) '"Mathematical Machines" of the Cold War: Soviet Computing, American Cybernetics and Ideological Disputes in the Early 1950s'. *Social Studies of Science* 31 (2): 253–87.

Gianella, C. and Tompson, W. (2007) *Stimulating Innovation in Russia: The Role of Institutions and Policies*. London: Birkbeck ePrints. Available at: http://eprints. bbk.ac.uk/506/, September 10, 2010.

Gibson, J. (2001) 'Social Networks, Civil Society, and the Prospects for Consolidating Russia's Democratic Transition'. *American Journal of Political Science* 45 (1): 51–68.

Gladarev, B. and Lonkila, M. (2008) 'Social Networks and Mobile Phone Use in Russia: Local Consequences of Global Communication Technology'. *New Media & Society* 10 (2): 273–93.

Global Trends in Computer Technology and Their Impact on Export Control (1988) Committee to Study International Developments in Computer Science and Technology, Computer Science and Technology Board, National Research Council, Washington, DC: National Academy Press.

Goodman, S. (2003) 'The Origins of Digital Computing in Europe'. *Communications of the ACM* 46 (9): 21–5.

Gorbachev, M. (2007) 'Ot rassveta do otkata'. *Den'gi* 34 (640), 03.09.2007. Available at http://www.kommersant.ru/doc-rss.aspx?DocsID=800363, accessed January 24, 2010.

Gould, R. V. and Fernandez, R. M. (1989) 'Structures of Mediation: A Formal Approach to Brokerage in Transaction Networks'. *Sociological Methodology* 19: 89–126.

Gouldner, A. W. (1960) 'The Norm of Reciprocity: A Preliminary Statement'. *American Sociological Review* 25 (2): 161–78.

Granovetter, M. (1973) 'The Strength of Weak Ties'. *American Journal of Sociology* 78 (6): 1360–80.

Granovetter, M. (1974) *Getting a Job: A Study of Contacts and Careers*. Cambridge, MA: Harvard University Press.

Granovetter, M. (1985) 'Economic Action and Social Structure: The Problem of Embeddedness'. *American Journal of Sociology* 91 (3): 481–510.

Granovetter, M. (1992) 'Economic Institutions as Social Constructions: A Framework for Analysis'. *Acta Sociologica* 35 (1): 3–11.

Granovetter, M. (1995) *Getting a Job: A Study of Contacts and Careers*. 2nd edn. Chicago: The University of Chicago Press.

Granovetter, M. (2002) 'A Theoretical Agenda for Economic Sociology'. In M. F. Guillén, R. Collins, P. England and M. Meyer (eds), *The New Economic Sociology: Developments in an Emerging Field*. New York: Russell Sage Foundation, 35–60.

Gribaudi, M. (1998). 'Avant-propos'. In M. Gribaudi (ed.), *Espaces, temporalités, stratifications. Exercises sur les réseaux sociaux*. Paris: Éditions de l'École des Hautes Études en Sciences Sociales, 5–40.

Gronow, A. (2008) 'Not by Rule or Choice Alone: A Pragmatist Critique of Institution Theories in Economics and Sociology'. *Journal of Institutional Economics*, 4 (3): 351–73.

Guseva, A. and Rona-Tas, A. (2001) 'Uncertainty, Risk, and Trust: Russian and American Credit Card Markets Compared'. *American Sociological Review* 66 (5): 623–46.

Halpern, J. (1994) 'The Effect of Friendship on Personal Business Transactions'. *Journal of Conflict Resolution* 38 (4): 647–64.

Harford, J. (1997) *Korolev: How One Man Masterminded the Soviet Drive to Beat America to the Moon*. New York: John Wiley & Sons.

Hawk, S. and McHenry, W. (2005) 'The Maturation of the Russian Offshore Software Industry'. *Journal of Information Technology for Development* 11 (1): 31–57.

Hoang, H. and Antoncic, B. (2003) 'Network-based research in entrepreneurship. A critical review'. *Journal of business Venturing* 18 (2): 165–87.

Hollstein, B. and Straus, F. (eds) (2006) *Qualitative Netzwerkanalyse: Konzepte, Methoden, Anwendungen*. Wiesbaden: VS Verlag für Sozialwissenschaften.

Humphrey, C. (2000a) 'An anthropological view of barter in Russia'. In P. Seabright (ed.), *The Vanishing Rouble: Barter Networks and Non-Monetary Transactions in Post-Soviet Societies*. Cambridge: Cambridge University Press, 71–90.

Humphrey, C. (2000b) 'How is barter done? The social relations of barter in provincial Russia'. In P. Seabright (ed.), *The Vanishing Rouble: Barter Networks and Non-Monetary Transactions in Post-Soviet Societies*. Cambridge: Cambridge University Press, 259–97.

Humphrey, C. (2002) *The Unmaking of Soviet Life: Everyday Economies After Socialism*. Ithaca: Cornell University Press.

Ichikawa, H. (2006) 'Strela-1, the First Soviet Computer: Political Success and Technological Failure'. *IEEE Annals of the History of Computing* 28 (3): 18–31.

Ingram, P. and Roberts, P. (2000) 'Friendships among Competitors in the Sydney Hotel Industry'. *American Journal of Sociology* 106 (2): 387–423.

Ivanenko, V. and Mikheyev, D. (2002) 'The Role of Non-Monetary Trade in Russian Transition'. *Post-Communist Economies* 14 (4): 405–19.

Kadushin, C. (1995) 'Friendship among the French Financial Elite'. *American Sociological Review* 60 (2): 202–21.

Kadik, L. and Pyanykh, G. (2001) 'Rossiiskaia pressa okazalas' prodazhnoi'. *Kommersant* 34 (2164), 24.2.2001. Available at: http://www.kommersant.ru/daily/, accessed May 10, 2010.

Kalacheva, O. (2003) 'Formirovanie individual'noi i kollektivnoi identichnosti v kontekste neofitsial'nogo prazdnika (na primere prazdnovaniia Dnia rozhdeniia v Rossii sovetskogo i postsovetskogo perioda). [Formation of individual and collective identity in the context of unofficial celebration (example of celebrating birthday in Soviet and post-Soviet Russia)] Moscow: State University, Higher School of Economics.

Kharkhordin, O. (2002) 'The Politics of Friendship: Classic and Contemporary Concerns'. In Y. Elkana, I. Kraster, E. Macamo and S. Randeria (eds), *Unraveling Ties – From Social Cohesion to New Practices of Connectedness*. Frankfurt am Main: Campus Fachbuch, 75–98.

Kharkhordin, O. (2005) *Main Concepts of Russian Politics*. Lanham, MD: University Press of America.

Kharkhordin, O. (2009) 'Druzhba: klassicheskaia teoriia i sovremennye zaboty'. In O. Kharkhordin (ed.), *Druzhba: ocherki po teorii praktik*. Sankt-Peterburg: Evropeiskii universitet v Sankt-Peterburge, 290–423.

Khetagurov, Y. A. (2001) 'The Development of Special Computers in the USSR'. In G. Trogemann, A. Nitussov, and E. Wolfgang (eds), *Computing in Russia: The History of Computer Devices and Information Technology Revealed*. Braunschweig/ Wiesbaden: Fried. Vieweg & Sohn Verlagsgesellschaft, 189–204.

Klimenko, S. (1999) 'Computer Science in Russia: A Personal View'. *IEEE Annals of the History of Computing* 21 (3): 16–30.

Kolesnikov, A. (2009) *Taustalla ja tulilinjalla: Venäjän yksityistäjä Anatoli Tšubais*. Helsinki: WSOY.

Kosals, L. and Ryvkina, R. (2001) 'The Institutionalization of the Shadow Economy: Rules and Roles'. In K. Segbers (ed.), *Explaining Post-Soviet Patchworks, Volume 2: Pathways from the Past to the Global*. Aldershot: Ashgate, 227–50.

Kosonen, R., (2002) *Governance, the Local Regulation Process, and Enterprise Adaptation in Post-Socialism: The Case of Vyborg*. Helsinki: Helsinki School of Economics, A–199.

Krippner, G. (2001) 'The Elusive Market: Embeddedness and the Paradigm of Economic Sociology'. *Theory & Society* 30 (6): 775–810.

Krippner, G., Granovetter, M., Block, F., Biggart, N., Beamish, T., Hsing, Y., Hart, G., Arrighi, G., Mendell, M., Hall, J., Burawoy, M., Vogel, S. and O'Riain, S. (2004) 'Polanyi Symposium: A Conversation on Embeddedness'. *Socio-Economic Review* 2 (1): 109–35.

Krippner, G. and Alvarez, A. (2007) 'Embeddedness and the Intellectual Projects of Economic Sociology'. *Annual Review of Sociology* 33: 219–40.

Kupila, P. (2007) 'Nyt kelpaa olla Venäjällä'. *Talouselämä*, 5.3.2007. Available at: http://www.talouselama.fi/tyoelama/article156658.ece, accessed May 11, 2010.

Kärkkäinen, R. (2008) *Clustering and International Competitiveness of Information Technology Industry in Saint Petersburg Area*. Lappeenranta: Lappeenranta University of Technology, Faculty of Technology Management, Industrial Engineering and Management, Industrial Marketing and International Business. Report 199.

Lamont, M. and Thévenot, L. (eds) (2000) *Rethinking Comparative Cultural Sociology: Repertoires of Evaluation in France and the United States*. Cambridge, UK: Cambridge University Press.

Latour, B. (1996) 'On Actor-Network Theory: A Few Clarifications'. *Soziale Welt* 47 (4): 369–81.

Latour, B. (2005) *Reassembling the Social: An Introduction to Actor-Network-Theory*. Oxford: Oxford University Press.

Ledeneva, A. (1998) *Russia's Economy of Favours: Blat, Networking and Informal Exchange*. Cambridge: Cambridge University Press.

Ledeneva, A. (2000) 'Shadow Barter: Economic Necessity or Economic Crime?' In P. Seabright (ed.), *The Vanishing Rouble: Barter Networks and Non-Monetary Transactions in Post-Soviet Societies*. Cambridge: Cambridge University Press, 298–317.

Ledeneva, A. (2004) 'Ambiguity of Social Networks in Post-Communist Contexts'. *Working Paper* 48, Centre for the Study of Economic & Social Change in Europe, School of Slavonic and East European Studies, University College London.

Ledeneva, A. (2006) *How Russia Really Works: The Informal Practices That Shaped Post-Soviet Politics and Business*. Ithaca and London: Cornell University Press.

Ledeneva A. (2008) '*Blat* and *Guanxi*: Informal Practices in Russia and China'. *Comparative Studies in Society and History* 50 (1): 118–44.

Ledeneva, A. (2009) 'From Russia with *Blat*: Can Informal Networks Help Modernize Russia?' *Social Research* 76 (1): 257–88.

Leithart, P. (2006) 'Notes on Georg Simmel, "Faithfulness and Gratitude"', printed in Kurt H. Wolff, The Sociology of Georg Simmel (Free Press, 1950). Available at: http://www.leithart.com/archives/002056.php, accessed June 17, 2010.

Levada Center (2010) *Internet v Rossii*. Available at: http://www.levada.ru/press/2008022602.html, accessed November 13, 2009.

Lomnitz, L. (1988) 'Informal Exchange Networks in Formal Systems: A Theoretical Model'. *American Anthropologist* 90 (1): 42–55.

Lonkila, M. (1997) 'Informal Exchange Relations in Post-Soviet Russia: A Comparative Perspective'. *Sociological Research Online* 2 (2), Available at: http://www.socresonline.org.uk/index_by_issue.html, accessed May 11, 2010.

Lonkila, M. (1998) 'Social Meaning of Work: Aspects of Teacher's Profession in Post-Soviet Russia'. *Europe-Asia Studies* 50 (4): 699–712.

Lonkila, M. (1999a) *Social Networks in Post-Soviet Russia: Continuity and Change in the Everyday Life of St. Petersburg Teachers*. Helsinki: Kikimora Publications.

Lonkila, M. (1999b) 'Post-Soviet Russia: A Society of Networks'. In M. Kangaspuro (ed.), *Russia: More Different than Most*. Helsinki: Kikimora Publications, 99–112.

Lonkila, M. (2006) 'Social Networks among Russian Information and Communication Technology Professionals'. *Post-Communist Economies* 18 (1): 13–31.

Lonkila, M. (2008) 'The Internet and Anti-military Activism in Russia'. *Europe-Asia Studies* 60 (7): 1125–49.

Lonkila, M. (2010) 'The Importance of Work-Related Social Ties in Post-Soviet Russia: The Role of Co-Workers in the Personal Support Networks in St. Petersburg and Helsinki', *Connections* 30 (1): 46–56.

Lonkila, M. (forthcoming) 'Driving at Democracy in Russia: Protest Activities of St. Petersburg Car Drivers' Associations'. *Europe-Asia Studies*.

Lonkila, M. and Salmi, A.-M. (2005) 'The Russian Work Collective and Migration'. *Europe-Asia Studies* 57(5): 681–703.

Lovell, S., Rogachevskii, A. B., and Ledeneva A. (eds) (2001) *Bribery and* Blat *in Russia: Negotiating Reciprocity from the Middle Ages to the 1990s*. London: Macmillan.

Luhtakallio, E. (2010) *Local Politicizations – a Comparison of Finns and French Practicing Democracy*. Doctoral dissertation, University of Helsinki, Department of Social Research, Sociology Research Reports 265.

MacMylor, P., Mellor, R., and Barkhatova, N. (2000) 'Familialism, Friendship and the Small Firm in the New Russia'. *International Review of Sociology*, 10 (1): 125–46.

Mauss, M. (2000) *The Gift: The Form and Reason for Exchange in Archaic Societies*. New York: W. W. Norton & Company.

Medvedev, D. (2009a) *Opening Address at Meeting of Commission for Modernisation and Technological Development of Russia's Economy*. President of Russia's

Website, published June 18. Available at: http://eng.kremlin.ru/text/
speeches/2009/06/18/2019_type82913_218096.shtml, accessed January 17,
2010.

Medvedev, D. (2009b) *Go, Russia!* President of Russia's Website, published
September 10. Available at: http://eng.kremlin.ru/text/speeches/2009/09/10/
1534_type104017_221527.shtml, accessed January 17, 2010.

Medvedev, D. (2009c) *Presidential Address to the Federal Assembly of the Russian
Federation.* President of Russia's Website, published November 12. Available
at: http://eng.kremlin.ru/speeches/2009/11/12/1321_type70029type82912_
222702.shtml, accessed January 17, 2010.

Medvedev, D. (2010) Speech at St. Petersburg International Economic Forum
Plenary Session. Available at: http://eng.news.kremlin.ru/transcripts/456/
print, accessed June 18, 2010.

Minkomsviaz' (2009) Ministerstvo sviazi i massovykh kommunikatsii Rossiiskoi
Federatsii. Available at: http://minkomsvjaz.ru/industry/1193/, accessed
October 30, 2009.

Mitchell, J. C. (ed.) (1969) *Social Networks in Urban Situations: Analyses of Personal
Relationships in Central African Towns.* Manchester: Manchester University
Press.

Moody, R. A. (1996) 'Reexamining Brain Drain from the Former Soviet Union'.
The Nonproliferation Review 2 (3): 92–7.

Mustikkamäki, N. (2008) 'Välittäjät bioteknologia-alalla – Tiedon välityksestä
sosiaalisiin rooleihin'. In N. Mustikkamäki and M. Sotarauta (eds),
Innovaatioympäristön monet kasvot. Tampere: Tampere University Press, 264–94.

Naccache, P. and Leca, B. (2008) 'On Justification: Economies of Worth'.
Administrative Science Quarterly 53 (4): 762–4.

Nitussov, A. and Malinovskiy, B. (2001) 'Economic Changes in the Sixties and
Internationalisation of the Soviet Computing'. In G. Trogemann, A. Nitussov,
and W. Ernst (eds), *Computing in Russia: The History of Computer Devices and
Information Technology Revealed.* Braunschweig/Wiesbaden: Fried. Vieweg &
Sohn Verlagsgesellschaft, 163–7.

Obstfeld, D. (2005) 'Social Networks, the *Tertius Iungens* Orientation, and
Involvement in Innovation'. *Administrative Science Quarterly* 50 (1): 100–30.

Obstfeld, D. and Borgatti, S. (2008) 'Brokerage is a Process, *Not* a Structure:
A Clarification of Social Networks Language and Theory'. *Presentation at the
International Sunbelt Social Network Conference,* Florida, January 25.

Oleinik, A. (2004) 'A Model of Network Capitalism: Basic Ideas and Post-Soviet
Evidence'. *Journal of Economic Issues* 38 (1): 85–111.

Pahl, R. (2000) *On Friendship.* Cambridge: Polity Press & Blackwell Publishers
Ltd.

Paine, R. (1969) 'In Search of Friendship: An Exploratory Analysis in "Middle-
Class" Culture'. *Man* 4 (4): 505–24.

Parry, J. (1986) 'The Gift, the Indian Gift, and the "Indian Gift"'. *Man* 21 (3):
453–73.

Podolny, J. and Baron, J. (1997) 'Resources and Relationships: Social Networks
and Mobility in the Workplace'. *American Sociological Review* 62 (5): 673–93.

Polynskaya, G., Kazak, M., and Karacharovsky, V. (2008) 'IT-rynok v Rossii.
Glavnye tsifry goda'. *Marketing journal 4r Online* 15.08.2008. Available at:
http://www.4p.ru/main/research/111641/, accessed January 19, 2009.

Portes, A. (1998) 'Social Capital: Its Origins and Applications in Modern Sociology'. *Annual Review of Sociology* 24 (1): 1–24.

Portes, A. and Haller, W. (2005) 'The Informal Economy'. In N. Smelser and R. Swedberg (eds), *Handbook of Economic Sociology*. 2nd edn. Princeton, NJ: Princeton University Press, 403–25.

Potthast, J. (2001) 'Der Kapitalismus ist kritisierbar. *Le nouvel esprit du capitalisme* und das Forschungsprogramm der "Soziologie der Kritik"'. *Berliner Journal Für Soziologie* 11 (4): 551–62.

Prokhorov, S. (1999) 'Computer in Russia: Science, Education, and Industry'. *IEEE Annals of the History of Computing* 21 (3): 4–15.

Putnam, R. (1993) *Making Democracy Work: Civic Traditions in Modern Italy*. Princeton: Princeton University Press.

Radaev, V. (1998) 'Formation of New Markets in Russia: Transaction Costs and Business Ethics'. *Paper presented at the XIV World Congress of Sociology, Roundtable Session 'Entrepreneurship, Markets, and Self-Employment,' Research Committee 02,* Montreal, July 26–August 1.

Radaev, V. (2003) 'How Trust is Established in Economic Relationships When Institutions and Individuals are Not Trustworthy (The Case of Russia)'. *Paper prepared for the CEPR/WDI Annual International Conference on Transition Economies*. Collegium, Budapest, July 3–5.

Rahman, M. (1998) 'Mark Granovetter on Network, Embeddedness and Trust: Et intervju med Mark Granovetter av Masudur Rahman'. *Sosiologi i dag* 28 (4): 87–113.

Rantanen T. (2001) 'The Old and the New: Communications Technology and Globalization in Russia'. *New Media & Society* 3 (1): 85–105.

Rautava, J. and Sutela, P. (2000) *Venäläinen markkinatalous*. Helsinki: WSOY.

Rehn, A. and Taalas, S. (2004) '"Znakomstva i svyazi" (Acquaintances and connections) – *Blat*, the Soviet Union and Mundane Entrepreneurship'. *Entrepreneurship and Regional Development* 16 (3): 235–50.

Rivkin-Fish, M. (1997) *Reproducing Russia: Women's Health and Moral Education in the Construction of a Post-Soviet Society*. Doctoral dissertation. Princeton: Princeton University.

Rivkin-Fish, M. (2005) *Women's Health in Post-Soviet Russia: The Politics of Intervention*. Bloomington, IN: Indiana University Press.

Rogers, N. (2006) 'Social Networks and the Emergence of the New Entrepreneurial Ventures in Russia: 1987–2000'. *American Journal of Economics and Sociology* 65 (2): 295–312.

Rohozinski, R. (1999) 'Mapping Russian Cyberspace: Perspectives on Democracy and the Net'. *UNRISD Discussion Paper* 115.

ROMIR (2008) Tsifry i fakty. ROMIR Survey of 1300 Russian Internet Users Older than 18 Years, June 17, 2008. Available at: http://www.romir.ru/news/res_results/468.html, accessed November 13, 2009.

Rose, R. (1998) 'Getting Things Done in an Anti-Modern Society: Social Capital Networks in Russia'. Glasgow, *Studies in Public Policy* 304, Centre for the Studies of Public Policy, University of Strathclyde.

The Russian Economic Barometer. Russian Academy of Sciences, Institute of World Economy and International Relations (http://www.imemo.ru/en/period/barom/, September 10, 2010).

RUSSOFT Annual Survey (2007) Russian Software Developing Industry and Software Exports. 4th annual survey. RUSSOFT Association 2008.

RUSSOFT Annual Survey (2008) Russian Software Developing Industry and Software Exports. 5th annual survey. RUSSOFT Association 2008.

Sahlins, M. (1969) 'Economic Anthropology and Anthropological Economics'. *Social Science Information* 8 (5): 13–33.

Salmenniemi, S. (2008) *Democratisation and Gender in Contemporary Russia*. New York: Routledge.

Salmi, A. (1995) *Institutionally Changing Business Networks: An Analysis of a Finnish Company's Operations in Exporting to the Soviet Union, Russia and the Baltic States*. Helsinki School of Economics and Business Administration. Acta Universitatis Oeconomicae Helsingiensis, A-106.

Salmi, A-M. (2000) 'Bonds, Bottles, *Blat* and Banquets. Birthdays and Networks in Russia'. *Ethnologia Europaea* 30 (1): 31–44.

Salmi, A-M. (2003) 'Health in Exchange: Teachers, Doctors, and the Strength of Informal Practices in Russia'. *Culture, Medicine and Psychiatry* 27 (2): 109–30.

Salmi, A-M. (2006) *Social Networks as Everyday Practices in Russia*. Doctoral dissertation, Department of Sociology. Helsinki: Department of Sociology, University of Helsinki.

Salmi, A-M. (2009) 'Venäjä – verkostojen valtakunta? Sosiaalisten verkostojen merkitys Neuvostoliitossa ja Venäjällä. [Russia – a dominion of networks? The significance of social networks in the Soviet Union and Russia. A lecture at the Finnish Centre for Russian and Eastern European Studies, September 21–27, in Finnish].

Salmi, A. and Bäckman J. (1999) 'Personal Relations in Russian Business: Two Circles'. In R. Kosonen and A. Salmi (eds), *Institutions and Post-Socialist Transition*. Helsinki: Helsinki School of Economics and Business Administration, B–22, 139–68.

Schmidt, H., Teubener, K., and Konradova N. (eds) (2006) *Control + Shift: Public and Private Usages of the Russian Internet*. Norderstedt: Books on Demand. Available at: http://www.ruhr-unibochum.de/russcyb/library/texts/en/control_shift/control_shift.htm, accessed January 9, 2009.

Seabright, P. (ed.) (2000a) *The Vanishing Rouble: Barter Networks and Non-Monetary Transactions in Post-Soviet Societies*. Cambridge: Cambridge University Press.

Seabright, P. (2000b) Introduction. In P. Seabright (ed.), *The Vanishing Rouble: Barter Networks and Non-Monetary Transactions in Post-Soviet Societies*. Cambridge: Cambridge University Press, 1–11.

Shaw, T. J. (1967) *The Transliteration of Modern Russian for English-Language Publications*. Madison, Milwaukee, and London: University of Wisconsin Press.

Shlapentokh, V. (1984) *Love, Marriage, and Friendship in the Soviet Union: Ideals and Practices*. New York: Praeger.

Shleifer, A. and Treisman, D. (2005) 'A Normal Country: Russia after Communism'. *Journal of Economic Perspectives* 19 (1): 151–74.

Shmulyar Gréen, O. (2009) *Entrepreneurship in Russia: Western Idea in Russian Translation*. Gothenburg Studies in Sociology 40, University of Gothenburg.

Silver, A. (1990) 'Friendship in Commercial Society: Eighteenth-Century Social Theory and Modern Sociology'. *American Journal of Sociology* 95 (6): 1474–504.

Smith, A. and Stenning, A. (2006) 'Beyond Household Economies: Articulations and Spaces of Economic Practice in Postsocialism'. *Progress in Human Geography* 30 (2): 190–213.

Smith-Doerr, L. and Powell, W. (2005) 'Networks and Economic Life'. In N. Smelser and R. Swedberg (eds), *Handbook of Economic Sociology*. 2nd edn. Princeton, NJ: Princeton University Press, 379–401.

Software Industry – Wikipedia (2010) Available at: http://en.wikipedia.org/wiki/Software_industry, accessed February 2, 2010.

Sokolov, N. (1992) 'Telecommunications in Russia', *IEEE Communications Magazine* 30 (7): 66–70.

Sotsial'noe neravenstvo v sotsiologicheskom izmerenii (2006) Institut sotsiologii RAN. Available at http://www.isras.ru/analytical_report_Social_inequality_7_0.html, accessed January 19, 2010.

Sprenger, C. (2008) 'The Role of State-Owned Enterprises in the Russian Economy'. *Paper written for the OECD Roundtable on Corporate Governance of SOEs*. Moscow, October 27–28 .

Srubar, I. (1991) 'War der reale Sozialismus modern?' *Kölner Zeitschrift für Soziologie und Sozialpsychologie* 43 (3): 415–32.

Stark, D. (1996) 'Recombinant Property in East European Capitalism'. *American Journal of Sociology* 101(4): 993–1027.

Stewart, C. (2008) 'Russia signs Russian Technologies decree'. *The Sydney Morning Herald*, July 15. Available at: http://news.smh.com.au/technology/russia-signs-russian-technologies-decree-20080715-3f6u.html, accessed August 6, 2009.

Susiluoto, I. (2006) *Suuruuden laskuoppi. Venäläisen tietoyhteiskunnan synty ja kehitys*. Helsinki: WSOY.

Sutela, P. (2003) *The Russian Market Economy*. Helsinki: Kikimora Publications, series B:31.

Sutela, P. (2008a) 'The legacy of the Putin era'. In I. Korhonen, S. Lainela, H. Simola, L. Solanko and P. Sutela. *The Challenges of the Medvedev Era. BOFIT Online* 6: 4–11. Available at: http://www.bof.fi/bofit_en/tutkimus/tutkimusjulkaisut/online/2008/bon0608.htm, accessed May 25, 2010.

Sutela, P. (2008b) 'Medvedev's Economic Policy Guidelines'. In I. Korhonen, S. Lainela, H. Simola, L. Solanko and P. Sutela. *The Challenges of the Medvedev Era. BOFIT Online* 6: 36–40. Available at: http://www.bof.fi/bofit_en/tutkimus/tutkimusjulkaisut/online/2008/bon0608.htm, accessed May 25, 2010.

Sverrisson, Á. (2001) 'Translation Networks, Knowledge Brokers and Novelty Construction: Pragmatic Environmentalism in Sweden'. *Acta Sociologica* 44 (4): 313–27.

Swedberg, R. (2004) 'What has been Accomplished in New Economic Sociology and Where is it Heading?' *Archives Européennes de Sociologie* 45 (3): 317–30.

Swedberg, R. and Granovetter, M. (2001) 'Introduction to the Second Edition'. In M. Granovetter and R. Swedberg (eds), *The Sociology of Economic Life*. 2nd edn. Boulder (CO): Westview Press, 1–28.

Terekhov, A. (2003) 'An Overview of the Russian IT Industry'. *Baltic IT&T Review* 3: 22–6.

Thévenot, L. (2001) 'Organized Complexity. Conventions of Coordination and the Composition of Economic Arrangements'. *European Journal of Social Theory* 4 (4): 405–25.

Thévenot, L. (2009) 'Governing Life by Standards: A View from Engagements'. *Social Studies of Science* 39 (5): 793–813.

Trogemann, G., Nitussov, A., and Ernst, W. (2001a) 'ARIFMOMETR: An Archaeology of Computing in Russia'. In G. Trogemann, A. Nitussov, and W. Ernst (eds), *Computing in Russia: The History of Computer Devices and Information Technology Revealed.* Braunschweig/Wiesbaden: Fried. Vieweg & Sohn Verlagsgesellschaft, 1–19.

Trogemann, G., Nitussov, A., and Ernst, W. (eds) (2001b) *Computing in Russia: The History of Computer Devices and Information Technology Revealed.* Braunschweig/Wiesbaden: Fried. Vieweg & Sohn Verlagsgesellschaft.

Uehara, E. (1995) 'Reciprocity Reconsidered: Gouldner's "Moral Norm of Reciprocity" and Social Support'. *Journal of Social and Personal Relationships* 12 (4): 483–502.

Uzzi, B. (1996) 'The Sources and Consequences of Embeddedness for the Economic Performance of Organizations: The Network Effect'. *American Sociological Review* 61 (4): 674–98.

Uzzi, B. (1999) 'Embeddedness in the Making of Financial Capital: How Social Relations and Networks Benefit Firms Seeking Financing'. *American Sociological Review* 64 (4): 481–505.

Vahtra, P. (2007) Venäjän talouselämän toimialat strategisen merkityksen mukaan ja potentiaalisimmat toimialat ICT-näkökulmasta. PowerPoint presentation, TEKES, 26.4.2007.

Vail, P. and Genis, A. (1988) *60-e: Mir sovetskogo cheloveka.* [The 60s: The World of the Soviet Person]. Ann Arbor: Ardis.

Ves' Komputernyi Mir (2003) *St. Petersburg.*

Visson, L. (2003) *Russkie problemy v angliiskoi rechi.* Moscow: P. Valent.

Volkov, V. (2002) *Violent Entrepreneurs: The Use of Force in the Making of Russian Capitalism.* Ithaca: Cornell University Press.

Wagner, P. (1999) 'After Justification: Repertoires of Evaluation and the Sociology of Modernity'. *European Journal of Social Theory* 2 (3): 341–57.

Wellman, B. and Berkowitz, S. D. (eds) (1988) *Social Structures: A Network Approach.* Cambridge: Cambridge University Press.

Williams, C. C. and Round, J. (2007) 'Beyond Market Hegemony: Re-Thinking the Relationship between Market and Non-Market Economic Practices'. *International Journal of Economic Perspectives* 1 (3): 148–62.

Wilson, A. (2007) 'Computer Gap: The Soviet Union's Missed Revolution and Its Implications for Russian Technology Policy'. *Problems of Post-Communism* 6 (4): 41–51.

Wittek R. and Wielers R. (1998) 'Gossip in Organizations'. *Computational & Mathematical Organization Theory* 4 (2): 189–204.

Woodruff, D. M. (1999) 'Barter of the Bankrupt: the Politics of Demonetization in Russia's Federal State'. In M. Burawoy and K. Verdery (eds), *Uncertain Transition: Ethnographies of Change in the Postsocialist World.* Lanham (Md.): Rowman & Littlefield Publishers, 83–124.

Woodruff, D. (2000) *Money Unmade: Barter and the Fate of Russian Capitalism.* Ithaca (NY): Cornell University Press.

Yakovlev, A. (2006) 'The Evolution of Business – State Interaction in Russia: From State Capture to Business Capture?' *Europe-Asia Studies* 58 (7): 1033–56.

Yakubovich, V. and Kozina, I. (2000) 'The Changing Significance of Ties: An Exploration of the Hiring Channels in the Russian Transitional Labor Market'. *International Sociology* 15 (3): 479–501.

Yakubovich,V. (2005) 'Weak Ties, Information, and Influence: How Workers Find Jobs in a Local Russian Labor Market'. *American Sociological Review* 70 (3): 408–21.

Yurchak, A. (2002) 'Entrepreneurial Governmentality in Post-Socialist Russia: A Cultural Investigation of Business Practices'. In V. Bonell and T. Gold (eds), *The New Entrepreneurs of Europe and Asia*. Armonk, NY: M. E. Sharpe, 278–325.

Yurchak, A. (2006) *Everything Was Forever, Until It Was No More: The Last Soviet Generation*. Princeton, NJ: Princeton University Press.

Åslund, A. (1995) *How Russia Became a Market Economy*. Washington, DC: Brookings Institution.

Åslund, A. (2007) *Russia's Capitalist Revolution: Why Market Reform Succeeded and Democracy Failed*. Washington, DC: Peterson Institute for International Economics.

Åslund, A. (2008) 'Crisis Puts Putinomics to the Test'. *Moscow Times Online* published December 24. Available at: http://www.iie.com/publications/opeds/oped.cfm?ResearchID=1086, accessed March 1, 2010.

Index

GPSR Compliance
The European Union's (EU) General Product Safety Regulation (GPSR) is a set
of rules that requires consumer products to be safe and our obligations to
ensure this.

If you have any concerns about our products, you can contact us on

ProductSafety@springernature.com

In case Publisher is established outside the EU, the EU authorized
representative is:

Springer Nature Customer Service Center GmbH
Europaplatz 3
69115 Heidelberg, Germany